Caste, Class and Power

CASTE, CLASS AND POWER

R. Rajan

CENTRUM PRESS
NEW DELHI-110002 (INDIA)

CENTRUM PRESS
H.O.: 4360/4, Ansari Road, Daryaganj,
New Delhi-110002 (India)
Tel: 23278000, 23261597, 23255577, 23286875

B.O.: No. 1015, Ist Main Road, BSK IIIrd Stage,
IIIrd Phase, IIIrd Block, Bengaluru-560085 (INDIA)
Tel: 080-41723429

Email: centrumpress@gmail.com
Visit us at: www.centrumpress.com

Caste, Class and Power

First Edition, 2011

ISBN 978-93-81293-54-6

PRINTED IN INDIA

Printed at Suman Printers, Jagatpuri Extn., Delhi

Contents

Preface

Inspite of the great advances in education and knowledge, the majority of Hindu society follows the system of caste based marriages which are witnessed in thousands of advertisements in the newspaper. Again, political exploitation of caste has resulted in serious division among people of various communities with economic implications evident in the policy of job reservation for such groups as schedule caste, schedule tribes, Other Backward Classes (OBC) and so on. To enable the sociologist, the social scientist, the research scholar and the interested reader acquire a comprehensive view of the caste system as it has existed in India for all these centuries and the shape it has taken in modern times, the present book provides a holistic view that will prove of immense value in any social analysis of this phenomenon.

Social classes are economic or cultural arrangements of groups in society. Class is an essential object of analysis for sociologists, political scientists, economists, anthropologists and social historians. In the social sciences, social class is often discussed in terms of 'social stratification'. In the modern Western context, stratification typically comprises three layers: upper class, middle class, and lower class. Each class may be further subdivided into smaller classes (e.g. occupational).

How caste and class are interrelated and inhered into one another? How social mobility is realised and perceived as an asset? Who are the power elite? How can one identify them? What is the role of education in effecting changes in the caste system? What is the nature of social mobility among the weaker sections of Indian society such as the scheduled castes and the scheduled tribes? These and several other questions have been discussed in the book.

Although the Hindu scriptures contain some passages that can be interpreted to sanction the caste system, they also contain indications that the caste system is not an essential part of the Hindu religion, and both sides in the debate are able to find sections in scriptures that support their views. The most ancient scriptures-the Shruti texts, or Vedas, place very little importance on the caste system, mentioning caste only rarely and in a cursory manner.

This book Caste, Class and Power is a serious attempt towards realising the goal of distinguishing the fact from fiction. It highlights various aspects, factors, efforts and remedies of caste. This book elaborately discusses all relevant issues in comprehensive way. The books studies the changing patterns of stratification in Indian Caste System. It recounts the gradual transformation of a social system that, till the end of the nineteenth century, was structured primarily on distinctions of caste—between the Brahmins, the middle-level non-Brahmins and the Sudra.

—*Editor*

1

Indian Caste System and Structure

The caste structure in Goa was somewhat like pre-eminence in the social hierarchy based on the nobility of blood, very much resembling the idea of family nobility in the rest of India. All the castes or rather sub-castes or jatis like Saraswats, Karades, Chitpavans, Padhyes etc. among the various segments of the population of Goa, particularly the goldsmiths and some merchants probably, as seen from the surnames of members of communes purportedly all-Brahmin, were lumped into the Christian caste of Bamonn or Brahmin. The various groups among the Kshatriyas or locally known as Chaddho were mainly the noble and warrior class. Some of them engaged in the trading profession, known as Chatim, which was an occupational appellation common to Brahmins also. The caste appellation of Chaddho gradually fell into disuse. Later among the Hindus of this caste in Goa who did not embrace Christianity began preferring the appellation of Maratha. The Marathas and Vanis were incorporated into the Christian caste of Chaddho.

Those of the Vaishya-Vani caste men who could not get themselves merged as Christian Bamonn or Chaddho, appear as Gauddo in place in Bardez Taluka of Goa, among Christians and those among the Hindu remnants of this caste in the present Canacona taluka etc. Gauddo caste among Christians is treated as one of the three high castes. It is believed that large number of Vaishya-Vanis emigrated to the adjoining district of Sindhudurg in Maharashtra. Their descendants trace their origin to Goa and the flight of their ancestors at the time of the conversion fever. The Christian counterpart of the Hindu Vani is the Gauddo Christian caste. The goldsmiths call themselves 'Daivednya Brahmins' and are known in Goa as 'Shetti', they were put into the Christian caste of Sudir or Sudras, which is a lower caste. They did not get into the caste deemed superior because they were known as 'Panchal' or the artisan group of castes. The aboriginal stock in Goa is known as the 'Gavddi', is a higher caste. The Christian convert of the Gavdi aboriginal was termed as Kunbi. The Kunbis are found in large number in the Salcete taluka than in any other taluka of Goa.

At the time of the conversions carried out by the Portuguese missionaries, there were untouchables like the 'Mahara' and Chambars, who were converted to Christianity. They are found in Chandor village. Chambars have later merged with the Sudras among Christians. Bamonn and Chaddho are the two advanced castes among the Hindus in Goa. They continued to attach their caste to the Christian names and surnames even after conversion. The first mass baptisms or conversions to Christianity were effected in the two prominent villages in the vicinity of the then city of Goa, Divar Island and Carambolim villages, the first of the Bamonn and the second of the Chaddho. The majority of the total number of village communes converted to Christianity belonged to the two high castes. The priests in the Goan community should be recruited from the Bamonn and Chaddho. At some places the Christian name, is mentioned along with the old Hindu name while at others the Christian name is mentioned with the person's father name in the Hindu original or in case of the father being a Hindu. The surnames of Poi, Kamat or Vamotim, Desai Kudav, Naik, Prabhu or Porbu etc. are common to both the high castes of Bamonn and Chaddho. Christian Bahmonns and Chaddhos are the two leading rival classes among the Goan's.

The continued maintenance of the caste system among the Christians in Goa is attributed to the mass conversions of entire villages, as a result of which the religious complexion of the whole village was given a new coat of Christianity without affecting its age-old social structure which was rooted in caste foundations. The old usages and customs and age-old traditions, including superstitions of a varied order, especially the caste-system were transferred. The Portuguese, fearing the relapses of their coverts to Hinduism, destroyed all available material reminiscent of the old religion including literary works which are stated by historians to have been in Konkani, mainly religious or socio-religious in nature.

HISTORY OF CASTE SYSTEM

Some researchers believe that the caste system began with the Indo-Aryan migration to India. The early Indo-Aryans organized among themselves in groups that later led to the caste system. A 2001 study, led by Michael Bamshad of the University of Utah, revealed that Indians belonging to higher castes are genetically closer to Europeans than are individuals from lower castes, whose genetic profiles are closer to those of Asians. The researchers believe their results support the theory that Europeans who migrated into India may have merged with or imposed their social structure on the native northern Indians and placed themselves into the highest castes. However, the theory of Indo-Aryan migration itself is a highly disputed topic. The critics claim that it was formulated to undermine the historical significance of India, and was exploited by the British to show that they had the right to invade India, as the Indians supposedly themselves were invaders. A 2006 genetic study by India's National Institute of Biologicals supported the idea that Indians have acquired few genes from Europeans, thus disputing the Aryan Invasion Theory. Megasthenes, the Greek ambassador to Chandragupta Maurya's court in India classified people of India into seven classes: philosophers, peasants, herdsmen, craftsmen and traders, soldiers, government officials and councillors.

Although the Hindu scriptures contain some passages that can be interpreted to sanction the caste system, they also contain indications that the caste system is not an essential part of the Hindu religion, and both sides in the debate are able to find sections in scriptures that support their views. The most ancient scriptures-the Shruti texts, or Vedas, place very little importance on the caste system, mentioning caste only rarely and in a cursory manner. A hymn from the Rig Veda seems to indicate that one's caste is not necessarily determined by that of one's family: I am a bard, my father is a physician, my mother's job is to grind the corn. Rig Veda 9.112.3 In the Vedic period, there also seems to no discrimination against the Shudras (which later became an ensemble of the so-called low-castes) on the issue of hearing the sacred words of the Vedas and fully participating in all religious rights, something which became totally banned in the later times.

Later scriptures such as Bhagavad Gita and Manusmriti state that the four varnas are created by God. However, at the same time, the Gita says that one's varna is to be understood from one's personal qualities and one's karma (work), not one's birth. Some scholars believe that, in its initial period, the caste system was flexible and it was merit and job based. One could migrate from one caste to other caste by changing one's profession. This view is supported by records of sages who became Brahmans. For example, the sage Vishvamitra belonged to a Kshatriya caste, and only later became recognized as a great Brahmin sage, indicating that his caste was not determined by birth. Similarly, Valmiki, once a low-caste robber, became a great sage. Veda Vyasa, another sage, was the son of a fisherwoman. Vashishtha was a shudra and he became sage later. Manusmriti, dated between 200 BC and 100 AD, contains some laws that codified the caste system. Varna is mentioned as caste equivalent in Manusmriti. However, the Puranas use the term in the context of skin colour too. Manusmriti and some other shastras mention four varnas: The Brahmins (teachers, scholars and priests), the Kshatriyas (kings and warriors), the Vaishyas (traders, landowners and some artisan groups), and Shudras (agriculturists, service providers, and some artisan groups). Another group of untouchables excluded from the main society was called Parjanya or Antyaja. A varna can be viewed as a group of castes or a social division that consists of various sub-castes called jatis.

Passages in Manusmriti and other scriptures suggest that the Indian caste system was originally non-hereditary: As the son of Shudra can attain the rank of a Brahman, the son of Brahman can attain rank of a Shudra. Even so with him who is born of a Vaishya or a Kshatriya Manu Smriti X:65

The various smritis, like the Yagnavalkyasmriti and the Manusmriti strongly disapprove of marrying outside one's caste. The smritis also argue that new, despicable castes are formed out of such cases. According to these smritis, the chamars were born out of the union of a vaideha and a nishada, the chandals were born out of the sexual relations between a Brahmin and a Shudra.

HISTORICAL ADVANTAGES OF THE CASTE SYSTEM

Historically, the caste system offered several advantages to the population of the Indian subcontinent:

1. Preservation of order in society through the use of institutional stratification of social groups.
2. Integration of foreigners and invading forces into Indian culture by assigning a caste to them (a process that historian Jawaharlal Nehru referred to as "Indianization"): India has faced repeated invasions from outside the region, dating back to the Macedoniaan invasion by Alexander the Great. Most invaders were swiftly assimilated into ancient Indian society by assigning them specific castes. Examples include the Kambojas, believed to be of Indo-Scythian descent, who were retroactively assigned a social position in the Manusmriti.
3. The Varna system, with its normative interpretation as a division of labour, had and continues to have a heavy bias towards spiritual evolution. The deep religious proclivities and the urge for spiritual uplift had induced the people to search for simpler and effective ways to achieve the spiritual goal which led to innovations like the Bhakti movement which had a powerful impact on the socio-cultural-spiritual life of the people even at mass level without distinctions of caste or class or other social differences. It is these deeply run cultural roots which caused an abiding following for Hinduism even in the face of unrelenting assaults by other religions and had in fact continued to influence the lives of people even after their conversion to other faiths. Thus, the caste system can be said to have preserved ancient cultural values in Indian society.
4. The caste system played an influential role in shaping economic activities. The caste system functioned much like medieval European guilds, ensuring the division of

labour, providing for the training of apprentices and, in some cases, allowing manufacturers to achieve narrow specialisation. For instance, in certain regions, producing each variety of cloth was the speciality of a particular sub-caste.

5. Philosophers argue that the majority of people would be comfortable in stratified endogamous groups and have been in ancient times. Membership in a particular caste, with its associated narrative, history and genealogy would instill in its members a sense of group accomplishment and cultural pride. Such sentiments are routinely expressed by the Marathas, for instance.

Emergence of Rigid Caste Structures

In its later stages, the caste system is said to have become rigid, and caste began to be inherited rather than acquired by merit. In the past, members of different castes would not partake in various activities, such as dining and religious gatherings, together. In addition, the performance of religious rites and rituals were restricted to Brahmins, who were the designated priesthood. In recent years, more egalitarian reforms have enabled lower castes and even outcastes such as the Dalits to become religious clerics. The "Pandaram" priests are an example of an order of Dalit priests, based in Nepal and South India. The Pandaram maintain the same tradition as the Brahmin priests, including the use of the Sanskrit language (traditionally reserved for the Brahmins) for the rituals. While they are not generally as well trained as the Brahmin priests, they are highly respected within their community and are addressed with reverence. According to the Manusmriti, every caste belongs to one of the four varnas (Brahmin, Kshatriya, Vaishya, and Shudra).

However, there have been many disputes about the varna of many castes, such as castes being considered Kshatriya by some scholars, while described as Shudra by others. While texts such as the Manusmriti attempted to rationalize ambiguous castes by placing them in varna-sankaras (i.e. mixed varna), the fact remains that Indian society was, and is, composed of numerous geographically diversified but endogamous groups. With many occupational groups practicing endogamy within a particular region, as well as numerous sub-divisions within the four main castes, a more complex system of sub-castes and jatis is evident. The jatis have broken up into clans like Agarwal, Iyer, etc.

Mobility Across the Castes

The view of the caste system as "static and unchanging" has been disputed by many scholars. For instance, sociolgists such as Bernard Buber and Marriott McKim describe how the perception of the caste system as a static and textual stratification has given way to the perception of the caste system as a more processual, emprical and contextual stratification. Other sociologists such as Y.B Damle have applied theoretical models to explain mobility and flexibility in the caste system in India.. According to these scholars, groups of lower-caste individuals could seek to elevate the status of their caste by attempting to emulate the practices of higher castes. Flexibility in caste laws permitted very low-caste religious clerics such as Valmiki (of the Naga tribal caste) to compose the Ramayana, which became a central work of Hindu scripture. According to some economists, mobility across broad caste lines may have been "minimal", though sub-castes (jatis) may change their social status over the generations by fission, re-location, and adoption of new rituals..

Sociologist M. N. Srinivas has also debated the question of rigidity in Caste. In an ethnographic study of the Coorgs of Karnataka, he observed considerable flexibility and mobility in their caste hierarchies. He asserts that the caste system is far from a rigid system in which the position of each component caste is fixed for all time. Movement has always been possible, and especially in the middle regions of the hierarchy. It was always possible for groups born into a lower caste to "rise to a higher position by adopting vegetarianism and teetotalism" i.e. adopt the customs of the higher castes. While theoretically "forbidden", the process was not uncommon in practice. The concept of sanskritization, or the adoption of upper-caste norms by the lower castes, addressed the actual complexity and fluidity of caste relations.

Historical examples of mobility in the Indian Caste System among Hindus have been researched. The "Noniya" Caste of salt makers have claimed to the higher status of the "Chauhan Rajput". They have risen well above the untouchable line and their leaders have, in the past, mobilized upwards along the caste hierarchy. There is also precedent of certain Shudra families within the temples of the Shrivaishava sect in South India elevating their caste.

The caste system was first exposed to the modern Western world during the Portuguese occupation and rule of sections of India. The word 'caste' in this context is derived from the Portuguese, 'casta'. Later, other European empires, including the British, occupied parts of the subcontinent. British anthropologist Herbert Risley's The Tribes and Castes of Bengal, published in 1892, was one of the first works on the caste system in India written by a Western scholar. Some scholars state that the caste system was broken up greatly during British Raj in India. However, some other historians suggest that the impact of British reforms has been greatly exaggerated.

Initially, the British strengthened the caste system. They gave the Brahmins back special privileges the Muslim rulers had taken away. During the initial days of British East India Company's rules, caste privileges and customs were encouraged in the Bengal Army. But, British law courts disagreed with the discrimination against the lower castes. Many believe that the lack of British respect for sepoys' caste traditions was one of the reasons behind the Indian Rebellion of 1857. During British rule, the reservation of seats for the "Depressed Classes" was incorporated into the Government of India Act 1935, which went into force in 1937. The Act brought the term "Scheduled castes" into use, which was later clarified in The Government of India (Scheduled Castes) Order, 1936 which contained a list of scheduled castes.

British Census Officers determined caste hierarchy based on the principle, e.g. someone who accepts food and water from another person but the other person does not reciprocate the same way, then the other person is superior to the former. It was contested at many places (a notable example is that the Koris of UP who said they won't accept water from Brahmins, and so should be placed higher than them). Because it was met with rampant controversies, arbitration was very common during those days. The most notable arbitration stories are:

1. Caste status of Bhumihar
2. Caste status of Kayastha
3. Caste status of Kurmi
4. Caste status of Yadav.

It raised more questions than it answered and subsequent census records varied radically, making it free for all, after some time.

RELIGIOUS FORM OF CASTE SYSTEM

In Hinduism there exists four castes arranged in a hierarchy. Anyone who does not belong to one of these castes is an outcast. The religious word for caste is 'Varna'. Each Varna has certain duties and rights. Each Varna members have to work in certain occupation which only that Varna members are allowed. Each Varna has certain type of diet. The highest Varna is of the Brahman. Members of this class are priests and the educated people of the society. The Varna after them in hierarchy is Kshatriya. The members of this class are the rulers and aristocrats of the society. After them are the Vaishya. Members of this class are the landlords and businessmen of the society. After them in hierarchy are the Sudra. Members of this class are the peasants and working class of the society who work in non-polluting jobs. The caste hierarchy ends here. Below these castes are the outcasts who are untouchable to the four castes. These Untouchables worked in degrading jobs like cleaning, sewage etc.

The first three castes had social and economical rights which the Sudra and the untouchables did not have. The first three castes are also seen as 'twice born'. The intention in these two births is to the natural birth and to the ceremonial entrance to the society at a much later age. Each Varna and also the untouchables are divided into many communities. These communities are called Jat or Jati (The caste is also used instead of Jat). For example the Brahmans have Jats called Gaur, Kokanastha, Sarasvat, Iyer and others. The outcasts have Jats like Mahar, Dhed, Mala, Madiga and others. The Sudra is the largest Varna and it has the largest number of communities. Each Jat is limited to professions worthy of their Varna. Each Jat is limited to the Varna diet. Each Jat members are allowed to marry only with their Jat members. People are born into their Jat and it cannot be changed. This is the how the caste system is supposed to be in its religious form. But in reality it is much more complicated and different from its religious form.

BEGINNING OF THE CASTE SYSTEM

There are different theories about the establishment of the caste system. There are religious-mystical theories. There are biological theories. And there are socio-historical theories. The religious theories explain how the four Varnas were founded, but they do not explain how the Jats in each Varna or the untouchables were founded. According the Rig Veda, the ancient Hindu book, the primal man-Purush-destroyed himself to create a human society. The different Varnas were created from different parts of his body. The Brahmans were created from his head; the Kshatriyas from his hands; the Vaishyas from his thighs and the Sudras from his feet. The Varna hierarchy is determined by the descending order of the different organs from which the Varnas were created. Other religious theory claims that the Varnas were created from the body organs of Brahma, who is the creator of the world.

The biological theory claims that all existing things, animated and inanimated, inherent three qualities in different apportionment. Sattva qualities include wisdom, intelligence, honesty, goodness and other positive qualities. Rajas include qualities like passion, pride, valour and other passionate qualities. Tamas qualities include dullness, stupidity, lack of creativity and other negative qualities. People with different doses of these inherent qualities adopted different types of occupation. According to this theory the Brahmans inherent Sattva qualities. Kshatriyas and Vaishyas inherent Rajas qualities. And the Sudras inherent Tamas qualities.

Like human beings, food also inherents different dosage of these qualities and it affects its eater's intelligence. The Brahmans and the Vaishyas have Sattvic diet which includes fruits, milk, honey, roots and vegetables. Most of the meats are considered to have Tamasic qualities. Many Sudra communities eat different kinds of meat (but not beef) and other Tamasic food. But the Kshatriyas who had Rajasic diet eat some kinds of meat like deer meat which is considered to have Rajasic qualities. Many Marathas who claim to be Kshatriyas eat mutton. The drawback of this theory is that in different parts of India the same food was sometimes qualified to have different dosage of inherent qualities. For example there were Brahmans who eat meat which is considered Tamasic food.

The social historical theory explains the creation of the Varnas, Jats and of the untouchables. According to this theory, the caste system began with the arrival of the Aryans in India. The Aryans arrived in India around 1500 BC. The fair skinned Aryans arrived in India from south Europe and north Asia. Before the Aryans there were other communities in India of other origins. Among them Negrito, Mongoloid, Austroloid and Dravidian. The Negrito have physical features similar to people of Africa. The Mongoloid have Chinese features. The Austroloids have features similar the aboriginals of Australia. The Dravidians originate from the Mediterranean and they were the largest community in India. When the Aryans arrived in India their main contact was with the Dravidians and the Austroloids. The Aryans disregarded the local cultures. They began conquering and taking control over regions in north India and at the same time pushed the local people southwards or towards the jungles and mountains in north India.

The Aryans organized among themselves in three groups. The first group was of the warriors and they were called Rajayana, later they changed their name Rajayana to Kshatriya. The second group was of the priests and they were called Brahmans. These two groups struggled politically for leadership among the Aryans. In this struggle the Brahmans got to be the leaders of the Aryan society. The third group was of the farmers and craftsmen and they were called Vaishya. The Aryans who conquered and took control over parts of north India subdued the locals and made them their servants. In this process the Vaishyas who were the farmers and the craftsmen became the landlords and the businessmen of the society and the locals became the peasants and the craftsmen of the society.

In order to secure their status the Aryans resolved some social and religious rules which, allowed only them to be the priests, warriors and the businessmen of the society. For example take Maharashtra. Maharashtra is in west India. This region is known by this name for hundreds of years. Many think that the meaning of the name Maharashtra is in its name, Great Land. But there are some who claim that the name, Maharashtra, is derived from the Jat called Mahar who are considered to be the original people of this region. In the caste hierarchy the dark skinned Mahars were outcasts. The skin colour was an important factor in the caste system. The meaning of the word "Varna" is not class or status but skin colour.

Between the outcasts and the three Aryan Varnas there is the Sudra Varna who are the simple workers of the society. The Sudras consisted of two communities. One community was of the locals who were subdued by the Aryans and the other were the descendants of Aryans with locals. In Hindu religious stories there are many wars between the good Aryans and the dark skinned demons and devils. The different Gods also have dark skinned slaves. There are stories of demon women trying to seduce good Aryan men in deceptive ways. There were also marriages between Aryan heroes and demon women. Many believe that these incidences really occurred in which, the gods and the positive heroes were people of Aryan origin. And the demons, the devils and the dark skinned slaves were in fact the original residence of India whom the Aryans coined as monsters, devil, demons and slaves.

As in most of the societies of the world, so in India, the son inherited his father's profession. And so in India there developed families, who professed the same family profession for generation in which, the son continued his father's profession. Later on as these families became larger, they were seen as communities or as they are called in Indian languages, Jat. Different families who professed the same profession developed social relations between them and organized as a common community, meaning Jat.

Later on the Aryans who created the caste system, added to their system non-Aryans. Different Jats who professed different professions were integrated in different Varnas according to their profession. Other foreign invaders of ancient India-Greeks, Huns, Scythains and others-who conquered parts of India and created kingdoms were integrated in the Kshatriya Varna (warrior castes). But probably the Aryan policy was not to integrate original Indian communities within them and therefore many aristocratic and warrior communities that were in India before the Aryans did not get the Kshatriya status. Most of the communities that were in India before the arrival of the Aryans were integrated in the Sudra Varna or were made outcast depending on the professions of these communities. Communities who professed non-polluting jobs were integrated in Sudra Varna. And communities who professed polluting professions were made outcasts. The Brahmans are very strict about cleanliness. In the past people believed that diseases can also spread also through air and not only through physical touch. Perhaps because of this reason the untouchables were not only disallowed to touch the high caste communities but they also had to stand at a certain distance from the high castes.

CASTE AND STAGES OF LIFE IN HINDUISM

The pattern of social classes in Hinduism is called the "caste system." The chart shows the major divisions and contents of the system. Basic caste is called *varna*, or "colour." Sub-caste, or *jati*, "birth, life, rank," is a traditional subdivision of *varna*.

The *Bhagavad Gita* says this about the varnas: The works of Brahmins, Kshatriyas, Vaishyas, and Shudras are different, in harmony with the three powers of their born nature. The works of a Brahmin are peace; self-harmony, austerity, and purity; loving-forgiveness and righteousness; vision and wisdom and faith.

These are the works of a Kshatriya: a heroic mind, inner fire, constancy, resourcefulness, courage in battle, generosity and noble leadership. Trade, agriculture and the rearing of cattle is the work of a Vaishya. And the work of the Shudra is service.

There are literally thousands of sub-castes in India, often with particular geographical ranges, occupational specializations, and an administrative or corporate structure. When Mahatma Gandhi wanted to go to England to study law, he had to ask his sub-caste, the Modh Bania, for permission to leave India. ("Bania", means "merchant," and "Gandhi" means "greengrocer"—from *gandha*, "smell, fragrance," in Sanskrit—and that should be enough for a good guess that Gandhi was a Vaishya.) Sometimes it is denied that the varnas are "castes" because, while "true" castes, the jatis, are based on birth, the varnas are based on the theory of the gunas (the "three powers" mentioned in the Gita). This is no more than a rationalization: the varnas came first, and they *are* based on birth. The gunas came later, and provide a poor explanation anyway, since the guna *tamas* is associated with both twice born and once born, caste and outcaste, overlapping the most important religious and social divisions in the system. Nevertheless, the varnas are now divisions at a theoretical level, while the jatis are the way in which caste is embodied for most practical purposes. Jatis themselves can be ranked in relation to each other, and occasionally a question may even be raised about the proper varna to which a particular jati belongs. As jati members change occupations and they rise in prestige, a jati may rarely even be elevated in the varna to which it is regarded as belonging.

Associated with each varna there is a traditional colour. These sound suspiciously like skin colours; and, indeed, there is an expectation in India that higher caste people will have lighter skin—although there are plenty of exceptions (especially in the South of India). This all probably goes back to the original invasion of the Arya, who came from Central Asia and so were undoubtedly light skinned. The people already in India were quite dark, even as today many people in India seem positively black. Apart from skin colour, Indians otherwise have "Caucasian" features—narrow noses, thin lips, etc.—and recent genetic mapping studies seem to show that Indians are more closely related to the people of the Middle East and Europe than to anyone else. Because Untouchables are not a varna, they do not have a traditional colour. I have supplied blue, since this is otherwise not found, and it is traditionally used for the skin colour of Vishnu and his incarnations. Chief among those is *Krishna* whose *name* actually means "black" or "dark," but he is always shown blue rather than with some natural skin colour.

The first three varnas are called the *twice born*. This has *nothing* to do with reincarnation. Being "twice born" means that you *come of age* religiously, making you a member of the Vedic religion, eligible to learn Sanskrit, study the Vedas, and perform Vedic rituals. The "second birth" is thus like Confirmation or a Bar Mitzvah. According to the *Laws of Manu* (whose requirements may not always be observed in modern life), boys are "born again" at specific ages: 8 for Brahmins; 11 for

Kshatriyas; and 12 for Vaishyas. A thread is bestowed at the coming of age to be worn around the waist as the symbol of being twice born. The equivalent of coming of age for girls is marriage. The bestowal of the thread is part of the wedding ceremony. That part of the wedding ritual is even preserved in Jainism. Ancient Iran also had a coming of age ceremony that involved a thread. That and other evidence leads to the speculation that the *three* classes of the twice born are from the original Indo-European social system—the theory of George Dumezil. Even the distant Celts believed in three social classes. The three classes of Plato's *Republic* thus may not have been entirely his idea. Although there must have been a great deal of early intermarriage in India, nowhere did such an Indo-European social system become as rigid a system of *birth* as there. The rigidity may well be due to the influence of the idea of *karma*, that poor birth is morally deserved. According to the *Laws of Manu*, when the twice born come of age, they enter into the four *ashramas* or "stages of life."

1. The first is the *brahmacharya*, or the stage of the student (*brahmacharin*). For boys, the student is supposed to go live with a teacher (*guru*), who is a Brahmin, to learn about Sanskrit, the Vedas, rituals, etc. The *dharma* of a student includes being obedient, respectful, celibate, and nonviolent. "The teacher is God." For girls, the stage of studenthood coincides with that of the householder, and the husband stands in the place of the teacher. Since the boys are supposed to be celibate while students, Gandhi used the term *brahmachari* to mean the celibate practitioner that he thought made the best *Satyagrahi*, the best nonviolent activist.
2. The second stage is the *garhastya*, or the stage of the householder, which is taken far more seriously in Hinduism than in Jainism or Buddhism and is usually regarded as mandatory, like studenthood, although debate continued over the centuries whether or not this stage could be skipped in favour of a later one. This is the stage where the principal *dharma* of the person is performed, whether as priest, warrior, etc., or for women mainly as wife and mother. Arjuna's duty to fight the

battle in the *Bhagavad Gita* comes from his status as a householder. Besides specific duties, there are general duties that pay off the "three debts": (1) a debt to the ancestors that is discharged by marrying and having children; (2) a debt to the gods that is discharged by the household rituals and sacrifices; and (3) a debt to the teacher that is discharged by appropriately teaching one's wife, children, and, for Brahmins, other students. The three debts are sometimes associated with the three Gods of the Trimurti—the ancestor debt with Brahma, the gods debt with Vishnu, and the teacher debt with Shiva.

3. The third stage is the *vanaprastya*, or the stage of the forest dweller. This may be entered into optionally if (ideally) one's hair has become gray, one's skin wrinkled, and grandchildren exist to carry on the family. Husbands and wives may leave their affairs and possessions with their children and retire together to the forest as hermits. This does not involve the complete renunciation of the world, for husbands and wives can still have sex (once a month), and a sacred fire still should be kept and minimal rituals performed. This stage is thus not entirely free of *dharma*. The Forest Treatises were supposed to have been written by or for forest dwellers, who have mostly renounced the world and have begun to consider liberation. I am not aware that forest dwelling is still practiced in the traditional way. The modern alternatives seem to consist of the more stark opposition between householding and becoming a wandering ascetic. Nevertheless, forest dwelling is an institution that doesn't really develop as such in Jainism and Buddhism. The idea that husbands and wives would engage in ascetic practices together, without celibacy, would appear extraordinary. In those terms, it is an unfortunate loss if the institution does not continue in modern Hinduism.
4. The fourth stage is the *sannyasa*, or the stage of the wandering ascetic, the *sannyasin* (or *sadhu*). If a man desires, he may continue on to this stage, but his wife will need to return home; traditionally she cannot stay alone as a forest dweller or wander the highways as an

> ascetic. The *sannyasin* has renounced the world completely, is regarded as dead by his family (the funeral is held), and is finally beyond all *dharma* and caste. When a *sannyasin* enters a Hindu temple, he is not a worshipper but one of the objects of worship. Not even the gods are *sanyasins* (they are householders), and so this is where in Hinduism, as in Jainism and Buddhism, it is possible for human beings to be spiritually superior to the gods. It has long been a matter of dispute in Hinduism whether one need really fulfil the requirements of the *Laws of Manu* (gray hair, etc.) to renounce the world. The Mahabharata says that Brahmins may go directly to Renunciation, but it also says that the three debts must be paid—and the debt to the ancestors could only be paid with husbands and wives living together either as householders or, if renunciates, as forest dwellers (indeed, the Pandavas are all born in that way). There are definitely no such requirements in Jainism or Buddhism. The Buddha left his family right after his wife had a baby, which would put him in the middle of his *dharma* as a householder. Buddhism and Jainism thus developed *monastic* institutions, with monks and nuns, but these did not really develop as such in Hinduism: While wandering ascetics are rather like mendicant monks, we lack monasteries and nuns, and the ascetics are, traditionally, supposed to have already lived something like a normal, lay life.

The four stages of life may, somewhat improbably, be associated with the four parts of the Vedas: the samhitas with the stage of the student, who is particularly obligated to learn them; the Brahmans with the stage of the householder, who is able to regulate his ritual behaviour according to them; the aranyakas with the stage of the forest dweller, who regulates his ritual behaviour according to them and who begins to contemplate liberation; and finally the upanishads with the stage of the wandering ascetic, who is entirely concerned with meditation on the absolute, *Brahman*.

The twice born may account for as much as 48% of Hindus, though I have now seen the number put at more like 18%—quite a difference but more believable. The Shudras (58% of

Hindus) may represent the institutional provision that the Arya made for the people they already found in India. The Shudras thus remain once born, and traditionally were not allowed to learn Sanskrit or study the Vedas—on pain of death. Their *dharma* is to work for the twice born. But even below the Shudras are the Untouchables (24% of Hindus), who are literally "outcastes," without a varna, and were regarded as "untouchable" because they are ritually polluting for caste Hindus. Some Untouchable sub-castes are regarded as so polluted that members are supposed to keep out of sight and do their work at night: They are called "Unseeables."

In India, the term "Untouchable" is now regarded as insulting or politically incorrect (like *Eta* in Japan for the traditional tanners and pariahs). Gandhi's *Harijans* ("children of God") or *Dalits* ("downtrodden") are preferred, though to Americans "Untouchables" would sound more like the gangster-busting federal agent Elliot Ness from the 1920's. Why there are so many Untouchables is unclear, although caste Hindus can be ejected from their jatis and become outcastes and various tribal or formerly tribal people in India may never have been properly integrated into the social system. When Mahatma Gandhi's sub-caste refused him permission to go to England, as noted above, he went anyway and was ejected from the caste. After he returned, his family got him back in, but while in England he was technically an outcaste. Existing tribal people as well as Untouchables are also called the "scheduled castes," since the British drew up a "schedule" listing the castes that they regarded as backwards, underprivileged, or oppressed.

The Untouchables, nevertheless, have their own traditional professions and their own sub-castes. Those professions (unless they can be evaded in the greater social mobility of modern, urban, anonymous life) involve too much pollution to be performed by caste Hindus: (1) dealing with the bodies of dead animals (like the sacred cattle that wander Indian villages) or unclaimed dead humans, (2) tanning leather, from such dead animals, and manufacturing leather goods, and (3) cleaning up the human and animal waste for which in traditional villages there is no sewer system. Mahatma Gandhi referred to the latter euphemistically as "scavenging" but saw in it the most horrible thing imposed on the Untouchables by the caste system.

His requirement on his farms in South Africa that everyone share in such tasks comes up in an early scene in the movie *Gandhi*. Since Gandhi equated suffering with holiness, he saw the Untouchables as hallowed by their miserable treatment and so called them "Harijans" (*Hari=Vishnu*). Later Gandhi went on fasts in the hope of improving the condition of the Untouchables, or at least to avoid their being politically classified as non-Hindus.

Today the status of the Shudras, Untouchables, and other "scheduled castes," and the preferential policies that the Indian government has designed for their advancement ever since Independence, are sources of serious conflict, including suicides, murders, and riots, in Indian society. Meanwhile, however, especially since economic liberalization began in 1991, the social mobility of a modern economy and urban life has begun to disrupt traditional professions, and oppressions, even of Untouchables. Village life and economic stasis were the greatest allies of the caste system, but both are slowly retreating before modernity in an India that finally gave up the Soviet paradigm of economic planning.

VARNA, CASTE, AND OTHER DIVISIONS

Although many other nations are characterized by social inequality, perhaps nowhere else in the world has inequality been so elaborately constructed as in the Indian institution of caste. Caste has long existed in India, but in the modern period it has been severely criticized by both Indian and foreign observers. Although some educated Indians tell non-Indians that caste has been abolished or that "no one pays attention to caste anymore," such statements do not reflect reality. Caste has undergone significant change since independence, but it still involves hundreds of millions of people.

In its preamble, India's constitution forbids negative public discrimination on the basis of caste. However, caste ranking and caste-based interaction have occurred for centuries and will continue to do so well into the foreseeable future, more in the countryside than in urban settings and more in the realms of kinship and marriage than in less personal interactions. Castes are ranked, named, endogamous (in-marrying) groups, membership in which is achieved by birth. There are thousands of castes and sub-castes in India, and these large kinship-based groups are fundamental to South Asian social structure. Each caste is part of a locally based system of interdependence with other groups, involving occupational specialization, and is linked in complex ways with networks that stretch across regions and throughout the nation.

The word *caste* derives from the Portuguese *casta*, meaning breed, race, or kind. Among the Indian terms that are sometimes translated as caste are *varna*, *jati*, *jat*, *biradri*, and *samaj*. All of these terms refer to ranked groups of various sizes and breadth. *Varna*, or colour, actually refers to large divisions that include various castes; the other terms include castes and subdivisions of castes sometimes called sub-castes. Many castes are traditionally associated with an occupation, such as high-ranking Brahmans; middle-ranking farmer and artisan groups, such as potters, barbers, and carpenters; and very low-ranking "Untouchable" leatherworkers, butchers, launderers, and latrine cleaners.

There is some correlation between ritual rank on the caste hierarchy and economic prosperity. Members of higher-ranking castes tend, on the whole, to be more prosperous than members of lower-ranking castes. Many lower-caste people live in conditions of great poverty and social disadvantage. According to the Rig Veda, sacred texts that date back to oral traditions of more than 3,000 years ago, progenitors of the four ranked *varna* groups sprang from various parts of the body of the primordial man, which Brahma created from clay. Each group had a function in sustaining the life of society—the social body. Brahmans, or priests, were created from the mouth. They were to provide for the intellectual and spiritual needs of the community. Kshatriyas, warriors and rulers, were derived from the arms. Their role was to rule and to protect others. Vaishyas—landowners and merchants—sprang from the thighs, and were entrusted with the care of commerce and agriculture. Shudras—artisans and servants—came from the feet. Their task was to perform all manual labour.

Later conceptualized was a fifth category, "Untouchable" menials, relegated to carrying out very menial and polluting work related to bodily decay and dirt. Since 1935 "Untouchables" have been known as Scheduled Castes, referring to their listing on government rosters, or schedules. They are also often called by Mohandas Karamchand (Mahatma) Gandhi's term Harijans, or "Children of God." Although the term *Untouchable* appears in literature produced by these low-ranking castes, in the 1990s, many politically conscious members of these groups prefer to refer to themselves as Dalit, a Hindi word meaning oppressed or downtrodden. According to the 1991 census, there were 138 million Scheduled Caste members in India, approximately 16 percent of the total population.

The first four *varnas* apparently existed in the ancient Aryan society of northern India. Some historians say that these categories were originally somewhat fluid functional groups, not castes. A greater degree of fixity gradually developed, resulting in the complex ranking systems of medieval India that essentially continue in the late twentieth century.

Although a *varna* is not a caste, when directly asked for their caste affiliation, particularly when the questioner is a Westerner, many Indians will reply with a *varna* name. Pressed further, they may respond with a much more specific name of a caste, or *jati*, which falls within that *varna*. For example, a Brahman may specify that he is a member of a named caste group, such as a Jijotiya Brahman, or a Smartha Brahman, and so on. Within such castes, people may further belong to smaller sub-caste categories and to specific clans and lineages. These finer designations are particularly relevant when marriages are being arranged and often appear in newspaper matrimonial advertisements. Members of a caste are typically spread out over a region, with representatives living in hundreds of settlements. In any small village, there may be representatives of a few or even a score or more castes.

Numerous groups usually called tribes (often referred to as Scheduled Tribes) are also integrated into the caste system to varying degrees. Some tribes live separately from others—particularly in the far northeast and in the forested centre of the country, where tribes are more like ethnic groups than castes. Some tribes are themselves divided into groups similar to sub-castes. In regions where members of tribes live in peasant villages with nontribal peoples, they are usually considered members of separate castes ranking low on the hierarchical scale.

Inequalities among castes are considered by the Hindu faithful to be part of the divinely ordained natural order and are expressed in terms of purity and pollution. Within a village, relative rank is most graphically expressed at a wedding or death feast, when all residents of the village are invited. At the home of a high-ranking caste member, food is prepared by a member of a caste from whom all can accept cooked food (usually by a Brahman). Diners are seated in lines; members of a single caste sit next to each other in a row, and members of other castes sit in perpendicular or parallel rows at some distance. Members of Dalit castes, such as Leatherworkers and Sweepers, may be seated far from the other diners—even out in an alley. Farther away, at the edge of the feeding area, a Sweeper may wait with a large basket to receive discarded leavings tossed in by other diners. Eating food contaminated by contact with the saliva of others not of the same family is considered far too polluting to be practiced by members of any other castes. Generally, feasts and ceremonies given by Dalits are not attended by higher-ranking castes.

Among Muslims, although status differences prevail, brotherhood may be stressed. A Muslim feast usually includes a cloth laid either on clean ground or on a table, with all Muslims, rich and poor, dining from plates placed on the same cloth. Muslims who wish to provide hospitality to observant Hindus, however, must make separate arrangements for a high-caste Hindu cook and ritually pure foods and dining area.

Castes that fall within the top four ranked *varnas* are sometimes referred to as the "clean castes," with Dalits considered "unclean." Castes of the top three ranked *varnas* are often designated "twice-born," in reference to the ritual initiation undergone by male members, in which investiture with the Hindu sacred thread constitutes a kind of ritual rebirth. Non-Hindu castelike groups generally fall outside these designations.

Each caste is believed by devout Hindus to have its own dharma, or divinely ordained code of proper conduct. Accordingly, there is often a high degree of tolerance for divergent lifestyles among different castes. Brahmans are usually expected to be nonviolent and spiritual, according with their traditional roles as vegetarian teetotaller priests. Kshatriyas are supposed to be strong, as fighters and rulers should be, with a taste for aggression, eating meat, and drinking alcohol. Vaishyas are stereotyped as adept businessmen, in accord with their traditional activities in commerce. Shudras are often described by others as tolerably pleasant but expectably somewhat base in behaviour, whereas Dalits—especially Sweepers—are often regarded by others as followers of vulgar life-styles. Conversely, lower-caste people often view people of high rank as haughty and unfeeling.

The chastity of women is strongly related to caste status. Generally, the higher ranking the caste, the more sexual control its women are expected to exhibit. Brahman brides should be virginal, faithful to one husband, and celibate in widowhood. By contrast, a Sweeper bride may or may not be a virgin, extramarital affairs may be tolerated, and, if widowed or divorced, the woman is encouraged to remarry. For the higher castes, such control of female sexuality helps ensure purity of lineage—of crucial importance to maintenance of high status. Among Muslims, too, high status is strongly correlated with female chastity.

Within castes explicit standards are maintained. Transgressions may be dealt with by a caste council, meeting periodically to adjudicate issues relevant to the caste. Such councils are usually formed of groups of elders, almost always males. Punishments such as fines and outcasting, either temporary or permanent, can be enforced. In rare cases, a person is excommunicated from the caste for gross infractions of caste rules. An example of such an infraction might be marrying or openly cohabiting with a mate of a caste lower than one's own; such behaviour would usually result in the higher-caste person dropping to the status of the lower-caste person.

Activities such as farming or trading can be carried out by anyone, but usually only members of the appropriate castes act as priests, barbers, potters, weavers, and other skilled artisans, whose occupational skills are handed down in families from one generation to another. As with other key features of Indian social structure, occupational specialization is believed to be in accord with the divinely ordained order of the universe.

The existence of rigid ranking is supernaturally validated through the idea of rebirth according to a person's karma, the sum of an individual's deeds in this life and in past lives. After death, a person's life is judged by divine forces, and rebirth is assigned in a high or a low place, depending upon what is deserved. This supernatural sanction can never be neglected, because it brings a person to his or her position in the caste hierarchy, relevant to every transaction involving food or drink, speaking, or touching.

In past decades, Dalits in certain areas (especially in parts of the south) had to display extreme deference to high-status people, physically keeping their distance—lest their touch or even their shadow pollute others—wearing neither shoes nor any upper body covering (even for women) in the presence of the upper castes. The lowest-ranking had to jingle a little bell in warning of their polluting approach. In much of India, Dalits were prohibited from entering temples, using wells from which the "clean" castes drew their water, or even attending schools. In past centuries, dire punishments were prescribed for Dalits who read or even heard sacred texts.

Such degrading discrimination was made illegal under legislation passed during British rule and was protested against by pre-independence reform movements led by Mahatma Gandhi and Bhimrao Ramji (B.R.) Ambedkar, a Dalit leader. Dalits agitated for the right to enter Hindu temples and to use village wells and effectively pressed for the enactment of stronger laws opposing disabilities imposed on them. After independence, Ambedkar almost single-handedly wrote India's constitution, including key provisions barring caste-based discrimination. Nonetheless, discriminatory treatment of Dalits remains a factor in daily life, especially in villages, as the end of the twentieth century approaches.

In modern times, as in the past, it is virtually impossible for an individual to raise his own status by falsely claiming to be a member of a higher-ranked caste. Such a ruse might work for a time in a place where the person is unknown, but no one would dine with or intermarry with such a person or his offspring until the claim was validated through kinship networks. Rising on the ritual hierarchy can only be achieved by a caste as a group, over a long period of time, principally by adopting behaviour patterns of higher-ranked groups. This process, known as Sanskritization, has been described by M.N. Srinivas and others. An example of such behaviour is that of some Leatherworker castes adopting a policy of not eating beef, in the hope that abstaining from the defiling practice of consuming the flesh of sacred bovines would enhance their castes' status. Increased economic prosperity for much of a caste greatly aids in the process of improving rank .

CASE OF INDIA'S 'UNTOUCHABLES'

More than one-sixth of India's population, some 160 million people, live a precarious existence, shunned by much of society because of their rank as "untouchables" or Dalits-literally meaning "broken" people-at the bottom of India's caste system. Dalits are discriminated against, denied access to land, forced to work in degrading conditions, and routinely abused at the hands of the police and of higher-caste groups that enjoy the state's protection. In what has been called India's "hidden apartheid," entire villages in many Indian states remain completely segregated by caste. National legislation and constitutional protections serve only to mask the social realities of discrimination and violence faced by those living below the "pollution line."

For most of the world caste remains an ancient cultural artefact and untouchability a long eradicated practice. This paper attempts to shift the debate on caste and on broader issues pertaining to socially institutionalised discrimination. It begins with a brief description of the characteristics and mechanisms of caste discrimination and a summary overview of the Indian government's response. It then attempts to dismantle those misperceptions that have allowed the system to survive, and comments on the barriers that keep the international community from effectively intervening against a practice that relegates millions of people to a lifetime of segregation, discrimination, and violence.

India's caste system is perhaps the world's longest surviving social hierarchy. A defining feature of Hinduism, caste encompasses a complex ordering of social groups on the basis of ritual purity. A person is considered a member of the caste into which he or she is born and remains within that caste until death, although the particular ranking of that caste may vary among regions and over time. Differences in status are traditionally justified by the religious doctrine of karma, a belief that one's place in life is determined by one's deeds in previous lifetimes. Traditional scholarship has described this more than 2,000-year-old system within the context of the four principal varnas, or large caste categories. In order of precedence these are the Brahmins (priests and teachers), the Ksyatriyas (rulers and soldiers), the Vaishyas (merchants and traders), and the Shudras (labourers and artisans). A fifth category falls outside the varna system and consists of those known as "untouchables" or Dalits; they are often assigned tasks too ritually polluting to merit inclusion within the traditional varna system.

Within the four principal castes, there are thousands of sub-castes, also called jatis; endogamous groups that are further divided along occupational, sectarian, regional, and linguistic lines. Collectively all of these are sometimes referred to as "caste Hindus" or those falling within the caste system. The Dalits are described as varna-sankara: they are "outside the system"-so inferior to other castes that they are deemed polluting and therefore "untouchable." Even as outcasts, they themselves are divided into further sub-castes and practice untouchability against those ranked below; the discrimination is wholly internalised. Although "untouchability" was abolished under Article 17 of the Indian constitution, the practice continues to determine the socioeconomic and religious standing of those at the bottom of the caste hierarchy. Whereas the first four varnas are free to choose and change their occupation, Dalits have generally been confined to the occupational structures into which they are born.

With little land of their own to cultivate, Dalit men, women, and children numbering in the tens of millions work as agricultural labourers for a few kilograms of rice or less than US$1 a day. Most live on the brink of destitution, barely able to feed their families and unable to send their children to school or break away from cycles of debt bondage that are passed on from generation to generation. At the end of day they return to a hut in their Dalit colony with no electricity, kilometres away from the nearest water source, and segregated from all non-Dalits, known as caste Hindus. They are forbidden by caste Hindus to enter places of worship, to draw water from public wells, or to wear shoes in caste Hindu presence. They are made to dig the village graves, dispose of dead animals, clean human waste with their bare hands, and to wash and use separate tea tumblers at neighbourhood tea stalls, all because-due to their caste status-they are deemed polluting and therefore untouchable.

In November 1999, after a cyclone slammed into the eastern state of Orissa, killing thousands and rendering millions homeless, the government brought in 200 Dalit manual scavengers from New Delhi, and planned to bring 500 more from other parts of Orissa, to load animal carcasses onto hand-drawn carts and take them away to be burned. Government officials had offered local upper-caste residents more than the daily minimum wage for each animal burned but they refused citing the decayed conditions of the carcasses and the fact that the task was beneath them: they had "some self-respect left." Even in times of natural disaster, the laws of purity and pollution prevail and the government moves quickly to accommodate the prejudice. At all levels, and under all circumstances, the discrimination is institutionalised.

Dalit women face the triple burden of caste, class, and gender. Dalit girls have been forced to become prostitutes for upper-caste patrons and village priests. Sexual abuse and other forms of violence against women are used by landlords and the police to inflict political "lessons" and crush dissent within the community. According to a Tamil Nadu state government official, the raping of Dalit women exposes the hypocrisy of the caste system as "no one practices untouchability when it comes to sex." Like other Indian women whose relatives are sought by the police, Dalit women have also been arrested and tortured in custody as a means of punishing their male relatives who are hiding from the authorities.

Any attempt to defy the social order is met with physical or economic retaliation. According to the most recent figures available, between 1994 and 1996 a total of 98,349 cases were registered with the police nationwide as crimes and atrocities against Dalits. Given that Dalits are both reluctant and unable (for lack of police cooperation) to report crimes against themselves, the actual number of abuses is presumably much higher. Whether the clashes are social, economic, or political in nature, they are premised on the same basic principle: any attempt to alter village customs or to demand land, increased wages, or political rights sets off a chain of events and leads to social boycotts and acts of retaliatory violence on the part of those most threatened by changes in the status quo. Dalit communities as a whole are summarily punished for individual transgressions; Dalits are cut off from their land and employment, women endure physical attacks, and letter of the law is rarely enforced. Most of the conflicts take place within very narrow segments of the caste hierarchy, between the poor and the not so poor, the landless labourer and the marginal landowner. The differences lie in the considerable amount of leverage that the higher-caste Hindus or non-Dalits are able to wield over local police, district administrations, and even the state government. A theme that is almost universal in its application, it illustrates a crucial aspect of identity politics: one's identity as a person belonging to a certain caste is perceived not only by one's absolute rank but also by the relative treatment meted out to communities that are ranked below.

Building on constitutional provisions, the government of India has pursued a two-pronged approach to narrowing the gap between the socioeconomic status of the Dalit population and the national average. The first approach involves regulatory measures designed to ensure that relevant legal provisions are adequately implemented, enforced, and monitored; the second focuses on increasing the self-sufficiency of the Dalit population through financial assistance for self-employment activities and through development programs to increase education and skills.

The protective component of this two-pronged strategy includes the implementation of legal provisions contained in state and central government legislation, and reservations or quotas in the arenas of government employment and higher education. India's policy of reservations is an attempt by the central government to remedy past injustices related to low-caste status. To allow for proportional representation in certain state and federal institutions, the constitution reserves 22.5 percent of seats in federal government jobs, state legislatures, the Lower House of parliament, and educational institutions for scheduled castes and scheduled tribes. Though some have benefited the reservation policy has not been successfully implemented and has yet to achieve its desired effect. Moreover, most of the landless and illiterate Dalits in the country are not in a position to avail themselves of any of their constitutional privileges. Controversy over the reservations scheme has also allowed the debate to predictably stagnate around the distribution of privilege, taking the focus away from violations of basic rights. India's policy of economic liberalisation is also having an effect on Dalits and their livelihood. As the public sector shrinks due to privatisation, the reservations model is affecting-and able to assist-fewer people, inasmuch as government-related jobs are being drastically reduced. Globalisation has also led to coastal lands increasingly being acquired by multinationals (via the central government) for aquaculture projects. Dalits are the main labourers and tenants of coastal land areas and are increasingly being forced to leave these areas-to live as displaced people, for the most part-as foreign investment rises.

The persistence of caste-based prejudices and the denial of access to land, education, and political power have all contributed to an atmosphere of increasing intolerance. Violence against Dalits, which has steadily climbed since 1994, is only the most extreme form of that intolerance. In 1989 the Scheduled Castes and Scheduled Tribes (Prevention of Atrocities) Act was enacted to prevent and punish caste-based abuses, to establish special courts for the trial of such offences, and to provide for victim relief and rehabilitation. Its enactment represented an acknowledgement on the part of the government that abuses, in their most degrading and violent forms, were still perpetrated against Dalits decades after independence.

A look at the offences made punishable by the act provides a glimpse into the retaliatory or customarily degrading treatment Dalits may receive. They include forcing members of a scheduled caste or scheduled tribe to drink or eat any inedible or obnoxious substance; dumping excreta, waste matter, carcasses or any other obnoxious substance in their premises or neighbourhood; forcibly removing clothes and parading them naked or with painted face or body; interfering with their rights to land; compelling a member of a scheduled caste or scheduled tribe into forms of forced or bonded labour; corrupting or fouling the water of any spring, reservoir or any other source ordinarily used by scheduled castes or scheduled tribes; denying right of passage to a place of public resort; and using a position of dominance to exploit a scheduled caste or scheduled tribe woman sexually.

The potential of the law to bring about social change has been hampered by institutional prejudice and police corruption, with the result that many offences are not registered. Ignorance of procedures or a lack of knowledge of the act itself has also affected implementation. Even when cases are registered, the absence of special courts to try them can delay prosecutions for up to three to four years. Some state governments dominated by higher castes have even attempted to repeal the legislation altogether. Much like other "social welfare" legislation in India, the act remains a paper tiger with little actual effect.

The existence of constitutionally mandated quotas and a large body of legislation and administrative agency mandates assigned exclusively to deal with the plight of Dalits is held up by the government as a panacea to problems of discrimination. These so-called remedies have also shifted attention away from the institutional nature of caste prejudice. It would be difficult to convince the Dalits of Dholapur district, Rajasthan, that after over fifty years of independence, government intervention had made a difference. In April 1998, a Dalit of the area was assaulted by an upper-caste family who forcibly pierced his nostril, drew a string through his nose, paraded him around the village, and tied him to a cattle post-all because he refused to sell bidis (hand-rolled cigarettes) on credit to the nephew of the upper-caste village chief. The message sent from the judiciary on caste discrimination is equally grim: in July 1998 in the state of Uttar Pradesh, an Allahabad High Court judge had his chambers "purified with Ganga jal" (water from the River Ganges), because it had earlier been occupied by a Dalit judge.

India's distinction as the "world's largest democracy" also helps to mask the abuses. For Dalits throughout the country who suffer from de facto disenfranchisement, democracy has not been a self-fulfilling prophecy. During elections, those unpersuaded by typical electioneering are routinely threatened and beaten by political party strongmen in order to compel them to vote for certain candidates. Already under the thumb of local landlords and police officials, Dalit villagers who do not comply have been murdered, beaten, and harassed. Dalits who have contested political office in village councils and municipalities through seats that have been constitutionally "reserved" for them have been threatened with physical abuse and even death in order to get them to withdraw from the campaign. In Tamil Nadu in June 1997, a newly elected Dalit village council president was beheaded by caste Hindus displaced from their once secure elected positions. In 1999, a Dalit woman from Uttar Pradesh considered contesting elections. She was gang-raped and subsequently beaten and murdered as a lesson to other villagers not to disturb the status quo. As with most cases of violence against Dalits, the culprits have yet to be convicted.

Political mobilisation that has resulted in the emergence of powerful interest groups and political parties among middle- and low-caste groups throughout India since the mid-1980s has also largely bypassed Dalits. Dalits are courted by all political parties but generally forgotten once elections are over. The expanding power base of low-caste political parties, the election of low-caste chief ministers to state governments, and even the appointment of a Dalit as president of India in July 1997 all signal the increasing prominence of Dalits in the political landscape but cumulatively have yet to yield any significant benefit for the majority of Dalits. Laws on land reform and protection for Dalits remain unimplemented in most of India's twenty-five states.

Political parties have frequently fashioned their manifestos and campaign slogans around the need for "upliftment" of these marginalised sectors, while political leaders, mostly drawn from higher castes, offer the promise of equal status and equal rights. However, the laws have benefited very few and, due to a lack of political will, development programs and welfare projects designed to improve economic conditions for Dalits have generally had little effect. Dalits rarely break free from bondage or economic exploitation by upper-caste landowners.

Equally insidious, though not as apparent, is the fact that Dalits are denied their place in the public consciousness. The plight of India's "untouchables" elicits only sporadic attention within the country. Public outrage over large-scale incidents of violence or particularly egregious examples of discrimination fades quickly, and the state is under little pressure to undertake more meaningful reforms. Despite ambitious calls for action by central and state governments in the aftermath publicity of massacres and police raids, the Indian authorities have shown little commitment to resolving the root causes of caste conflicts. Society as a whole has turned a blind eye to the institutional character of caste-based abuse and discrimination. Laws are openly flouted, police allegiance is routinely up for sale, and society continues to sanction what the legislature defines as crimes. In the eastern state of Bihar, for example, the first person to be convicted under a decadesold law combating child labour was in 1998.

A loss of faith in the state machinery and increasing intolerance of their abusive treatment has led many Dalit communities into organised movements to claim their rights. In response, state and private actors have engaged in a pattern of repression to preserve the status quo. Unable to find sustainable alliances within, and in an effort to counter their invisibility at home, Dalit movements have from time to time turned outward to look for parallels in struggles abroad. During the 1970s, for example, the Dalit Panthers emerged outside the framework of recognised political parties and aligned themselves ideologically to the Black Panther movement in the United States. During the same period, Dalit literature, painting, and theatre challenged the very premise and nature of established art forms and their depiction of society and religion. Many of these new Dalit artists formed the first generation of the Dalit Panther movement that sought to wage an organised struggle against the varna system. Dalit Panthers visited atrocity sites, organised marches and rallies in villages, and raised slogans of direct militant action against their upper-caste aggressors.

The determined stance of the Dalit Panthers served to arouse and unite many Dalits, particularly Dalit youth and students. The defeat of ruling party candidates and the boycott of elections in some areas forced the government to take notice of the movement: Panther leaders were often harassed and removed from districts for speaking out against the government and Hindu religion. They also became frequent targets of police brutality and arbitrary detentions. Disagreements over the future of the movement and inclusion of other caste groups ultimately led to a dispersal of Dalit Panther leadership. The former aggressiveness and militancy of the Dalit Panthers has for the most part dissipated, though small splinter groups or groups that have adopted the name still survive.

In the 1960s, leftist guerrilla organisations with Marxist, Leninist, and Maoist orientations began advocating the use of violence to achieve land redistribution. By 1970, these so-called Naxalites had initiated a series of peasant uprisings to seize land, burn property records, and assassinate exploitative landlords and others identified as "class enemies" in large areas of the countryside stretching from West Bengal to the southern state of Kerala. Although the Naxalite insurgency was brought to an end in most parts of the country by a brutal police crackdown designed to eliminate the militants and their supporters, the movement continues to survive, albeit with some splits and regroupings, in the rural areas of West Bengal, Orissa, Andhra Pradesh, and Bihar. Higher-caste landlords in Bihar have organised private militias to counter the Naxalite threat. These militias, or senas, also target Dalit villagers believed to be sympathetic to Naxalites. Senas are believed responsible for the murders of many hundreds of Dalits in Bihar since 1987.

Though offshoots of militant movements still thrive in many parts of the country, the strategy for the actualisation of rights has in the past fifteen years undergone a major shift. Beginning in the 1980s, a handful of Dalit organisations began turning to the United Nations as a possible forum for the mobilisation of international support and condemnation of caste-based abuses. However, the difficulty of slotting caste-based abuses into standard categories of human rights violations, and the prevalence of constitutional and legislative protections at the national level, has allowed these abuses to escape international scrutiny. The government of India has consistently asserted that the caste issue does not fall within the mandate of various "race"-based UNHCHR bodies. The government has also refused to allow relevant working groups and special rapporteurs to gain access to the country. In turn, the response of the international community has been superficial at best. Dalit activists now find themselves struggling to overcome their invisibility abroad. Though caste identity is used as a justification for segregation and exploitation, the discrimination is so entrenched that the victims' shared membership in lower-caste communities is often ignored by upper-caste families and international bodies alike. While the world was united in its condemnation of increasing attacks on India's Christian community this past year, for example, it ignored a significant underlying cause: a majority of Christians in India are Dalits and tribals for whom conversion offers a partial escape from untouchability and exploitation. Conversions are therefore threatening to the social and economic status quo.

Like evaluating the symptoms without diagnosing the disease, most international interventions have also overlooked the fact that Dalits, numbering in the tens of millions, comprise the majority of those driven to bonded labour, manual scavenging, and forced prostitution, under conditions that violate national law and their basic human rights. Despite their mandate of reaching the "poorest of the poor," international development institutions have yet to understand that for those at the bottom of its hierarchy, caste is a determinative factor for the attainment of social, political, civil, and economic rights.

Which strategies then are likely to be effective in reforming socially institutionalised discrimination? Part of the answer lies in supporting the work of grassroots Dalit and human rights activists throughout the country who for many years have assumed many state-like functions and have stepped in where the administration has failed. The second part is to involve the international community in forcing the government to remedy its failures.

In 1998, the National Campaign for Dalit Human Rights was born out of an initiative of grassroots Dalit activists in eight Indian states. Many of these activists were involved in the drafting of over forty recommendations to the government of India and the international community that are contained in a Human Rights Watch report on caste violence released earlier this year. The campaign, which has since expanded to include fourteen states and eleven countries, seeks to mobilise a national coalition that operates at the grassroots level while eliciting the participation of the international community in its struggle. Still, there are other prejudices to be overcome before such participation can be ensured. Internationally, the cyclone in India received little attention in comparison to other recent tragedies of similar or lesser magnitude. Like disparities in responding to crises in Europe and Africa, the "otherness" of those most vividly affected by violence, disaster, or day-to-day deprivation, eases the decision not to respond. When the victims of attacks, even massacres, are non-Christian Dalits, the news barely breaks into international headlines.

Interventions on caste discrimination, if any, have been limited to inquiries regarding the mechanisms of protection offered by the state, without asking for evidence of their effective implementation (which, generally speaking, is a recurring problem in the nature of international intervention on race and ethnicity matters). The Indian government needs to place a priority on strengthening institutional mechanisms aimed at addressing issues of violence and discrimination. But it also needs the active support of-and pressure from-the United Nations, multilateral financial institutions, trading partners, and national and international non-governmental organisations to eradicate the pervasive problem of caste-based abuse. Will the international community respond or even apply the necessary pressure to stimulate domestic political will? Or will it continue to deny Dalits and others their place in the public consciousness? Entrenched forms of discrimination stemming from the world's longest surviving system of social hierarchy may offer some lessons as we prepare for a global forum on modern day "racism." The first and most obvious is to look beyond race as the only arbiter of rights. The second is to look beyond democracy, affirmative action, and the existence of domestic legislation as sufficient guarantors of basic freedoms. The third is to recognise the resilience and adaptability of ancient custom to contemporary global trends. The fourth is to scrutinise the discrimination inherent in the international community's decision to act, and more importantly, in its failure to respond.

2

Ambedkar's View of Caste

AMBEDKAR'S SEMINAL EXPERIENCES OF CASTE

Although Indian society is fragmented into castes, there has been some change due to the movement of Dr. Ambedkar and other reformers. Some of his followers have benefited in terms of education and wealth due to his efforts. However, the change is not striking, and many are still subjected to hatred and perish in poverty. Caste-based violence continues to be an all pervading phenomenon. Even after the abolition of untouchability by law, practices, such as inhuman treatment, raping untouchable women and so forth, still occur in India.

The situation at the time of Dr. Ambedkar was worse, and he personally experienced the caste system in its most inhuman form, being born into and brought up in an untouchable family. A few seminal experiences awakened him to reality of the caste system. The first took place in Goregaon when Dr. Ambedkar was a boy of nine. He was to visit his father along with his brother. The location of his father's work place was far from the railway station, and no cart man was willing to take them on a bullock cart. One cart man agreed with the condition that the boys would have to drive the cart while he would sit behind. Throughout this escapade which lasted through the night, the boys went hungry because they could not get pure water to drink, even though they had plenty of food. Their inability to get water was of course due to the fact that untouchables were barred from using public wells.

This incident had a very important place in Dr. Ambedkar's life and it left an indelible impression on his mind. His worst experience of the caste system took place in Baroda when he was to become the Military Secretary to the Baroda State. He could not get accommodation in Baroda because he was an untouchable, though highly educated. He found a quarter in a Parsi boarding house and assumed a Parsi name. At work, the Brahman clerks and subordinates kept their distance and threw files and papers on him to avoid his touch. Even in the club, he was only allowed to sit in the corner and was not allowed to take part in games. No clear assignment was given to him, though he was a Military Secretary. When the Parsis discovered his identity, they besieged his boarding house and threatened to beat him. Eventually, the owner expelled him and he had to leave Baroda. The third seminal experience took place in Chalisgaon, where no horse carriage driver was willing to take Dr. Ambedkar from the railway station to the place where a meeting was to be held.

After a long wait, a carriage was finally brought. The driver and he were the only two occupants of the carriage. The carriage had not gone 200 paces when there was almost a collision with a motor car. Dr. Ambedkar was surprised that the driver, who was paid for hire every day, should have been so inexperienced. The accident was averted only because of the loud shout of a policeman. They somehow arrived at the culvert on a river. Around it there were no walls as there are on a bridge. The carriage was thrown down on the stone pavement of the culvert, and the horse and the carriage fell down from the culvert into the river. So heavy was the fall that Dr. Ambedkar was knocked senseless. As a result of this he received several injuries. His leg was fractured and he was disabled for several days. On inquiry, Dr. Ambedkar was told the real facts. The delay at the railway station was due to the fact that the carriage drivers were not prepared to drive with a passenger who was an untouchable. They felt it was beneath their dignity. The Mahar untouchables could not tolerate that their leader should walk to their quarters. A compromise was therefore arrived at: the owner of a carriage would give it on hire but not drive. Although they could not find someone to drive it, the Mahars thought this to be a happy solution, evidently forgetting that the safety of the passenger was more important than the maintenance of his dignity. It was then that Dr.

Ambedkar learned that even a menial Hindu carriage driver looked upon himself as superior to any untouchable even if that person be a barrister-at-law like Dr. Ambedkar.

There are many more incidences such as these from Dr. Ambedkar's life. These few, however, are sufficient for any person to understand the suffering experienced due to the practice of untouchability and caste. Many people in contemporary India still suffer from this system of graded inequality. They are living the life of degraded human beings. In the end we must ask why is it necessary that they have to suffer so much and occupy such positions in the social system?

Ambedkar's Analysis of Caste

Understanding the origin, genesis and mechanism of caste in India is a very complex problem. Many able minds have tried to penetrate it, including Dr. Ambedkar who began work on this issue as early as 1916. He attempted to link the many chains in the history of India in order to show how the caste system evolved. In Dr. Ambedkar's understanding, the prime factor responsible for the evolution of the system of untouchability was the religious persecution of Buddhists, while other social-psychological factors are secondary. The existence of caste in India is due to the notion of inequality imposed by religion, which gives rise to social and cultural practices and prejudices. If these social and cultural practices cease, caste could be annihilated. This is a simple formulation of the quite complex issue of caste.

The life and work of the Buddha marks the flowering of the axial period in India in the sixth century BCE. This period was one of great turmoil as smaller tribal societies were transforming into larger settled ones and eventually mighty empires. It has been shown that these smaller, pre-imperial societies were not based on a graded system of inequality or caste (Chakravarti, 1987). This is not to say that there was no class system. Further, these societies often exhibited unethical and immoral aspects, like incest, alcoholism, war mongering, and the savage practice of ritual sacrifice. Thus the revolutionary role of the Buddha was in first clearly proclaiming that the happiness of humans and society lies in ethics and not in rituals. Dr. Ambedkar understood the Buddha's awakening under the bodhi tree as a true revolution. "It was as great a revolution as the French Revolution. Though it began as a religious revolution, it became more than a religious revolution. It became a social and political revolution."

The Buddha's revolution which culminated in the emergence of the mighty empire of Ashoka (r. 270-232 B. C.) further strengthened the Buddhist worldview based on liberty, equality, and fraternity; a universal message that went beyond the Indian subcontinent. Under Ashoka, equality of punishment irrespective of the social standing of the criminal emerged. The priestly class was given the same treatment as that of the common people. Although Ashoka prevented worship of clan deities (kula devata) which served as the basis of income for the Brahmins, he was ecumenical and promoted inter-religious tolerance. He did not persecute the Brahmins, yet the Brahmans lost their social prestige as the majority of the people abandoned the animal sacrifices that the Brahmans officiated. The rule of law was established, and even animals received good treatment, as noted by the famous Chinese pilgrim, Hsuan Tsang.

In Revolution and Counterrevolution in Ancient India, Dr. Ambedkar described that after the establishment of the rule of law, the Brahmins lived as a depressed class for the nearly 140 years of the Mauryan Empire. Pushyamitra Sunga of the Samvedi Brahmin clan then conspired to destroy Buddhism as the state religion and to make the Brahmins the sovereign rulers of India with the political power of the state behind it through murdering Ashoka's grandson, Emperor Brhadratha, in 185 BC. After his accession, Pushyamitra launched a violent and virulent campaign of persecution against Buddhists and Buddhism. Thus, the counter-revolution against Buddhism began with the emergence of the Brahmins under the Sunga Dynasty.

At the same time, various major Brahmanical texts were written in order to counter Buddhism. According to Dr. Ambedkar, these texts are the true sources of inequality and were largely post-Mauryan developments. For example, Dr. Ambedkar showed that the Code of Manu (Manu Smriti) was written by Sumati Bharagava after Psuhyamitra's revolt in 185 BC. The Code of Manu, which served as the law of inequality, was drafted and enforced with the newly acquired state power by the Brahmins, while the myth of the first cosmic being

Purusha, which tells of the divine origin of caste, was interpolated into the Rig-Veda. According to Dr. Ambedkar, the Manu Smriti, the Bhagavad Gita, Shankaracharya's Vedanta, the Mahabharata, the Ramayana and the Puranas are all post-Mauryan texts which serve as sources of inequality.

It should be noted, however, that the Buddhists of ancient India did not accept this worldview all at once-perhaps they never did as is evident from the continuous struggle between the Brahmans and the untouchables (former Buddhists) of modern India. The hatred and contempt preached by the Brahmins was directed against Buddhists in particular and not against other groups. After the Mauryan Period, most Indians who had upheld Buddhism slipped back into Brahmanised Hinduism. Other Indians who did not became untouchables, like the "Broken Men." The "Broken Men", according to Dr. Ambedkar, were the remaining peoples of broken and defeated tribal groups of ancient India. Dr. Ambedkar wrote about this concept of "Broken Men" and how they came into being when the primitive societies were breaking up and transforming into the larger settled societies of imperial India. Brahmanism never tried to absorb these Buddhists into the caste system but rather shut them right out of it by making them untouchables and all that stood for, like no education, no means of economic development, etc. Untouchability was thus only born sometime around 400 AD, as these "Broken Men" were not able to abandon beef eating when cow killing was made a capital offence by the Gupta kings. In this way, the cow politics of present day India has its roots in the counterrevolution of the Brahmans against the Buddhists. Untouchability was thus born out of the struggle for supremacy between Buddhism and Brahmanism on a variety of levels from political power to social convention.

This is not to say that Buddhism was destroyed all at once. The struggle went on until the Muslim invasion in 1200 C.E.. The Muslim invasions played a decisive role as the Muslim invaders killed Buddhist monks or caused them to flee India. According to Dr. Ambedkar, "Religion like any other ideology can be attained only by propaganda. If propaganda fails, religion must disappear. The priestly class, however detestable it may be, is necessary to the sustenance of religion. For it is by its propaganda that religion is kept up. Without the priestly class religion must disappear." Due to this onslaught, the Buddhist Sangha in India underwent a great change in its composition. A disorganized system of married clergy with families who were called aryas developed. They took the place of the bhikkhus and began to cater to the religious needs of the general community. They eventually attained the status of bhikkhus through the performance of some sacraments. They officiated at religious ceremonies, but at the same time, in addition to their profession of priesthood, they earned their livelihood through such avocations as masonry, painting, sculpting, gold smithing, and carpentry. These artisan-priests, who were in later times larger in number than the bhikkhus, became the religious guides of the people. Their avocations left them little time and desire for the acquisition of learning, for deep thinking, or for devotion to meditation and other spiritual exercises. They could not be expected to raise Buddhism to a higher position through their endeavours, nor could they check its course towards ruin through the introduction of salutary reforms. It is obvious that this new Buddhist priesthood had neither prestige nor learning and was a poor match for the rival Brahmins (BAWS III, 151-437).

The upheaval caused by the Muslim invaders in the Buddhist Community lasted for a while. However, the Muslims did not destroy or challenge its principles or doctrines, which governed the spiritual life of the people. On the other hand, the Brahmanic invasion changed the principles which Buddhism had preached for centuries as universal ones of a spiritual life. According to Dr. Ambedkar, the Brahmanic invasion of Buddhist India is significant but usually neglected by the historians of India. Buddhist India is not a myth or construction of Dr. Ambedkar. This is supported by material evidence. However, the concept of Vedic India or the Golden Vedic Age is truly a construction of recent times by Hindu Nationalists. The neo-Brahmanism of the post-Mauryan period brought the real changes in the political and social structure.

Through the medieval and colonial periods, the struggle against Brahmanism continued, though it was very much weakened due to the forces of time. The saint-poets of the 14th century onwards, such as Kabir, Nanadnar, Chokamela, and Tukaram, came from untouchable castes or backward classes and reflect "Buddhist" sentiments. Their teaching is marked with anti-caste and anti-Bramhanistic ideas. They ridiculed the Vedas and the religious texts of the Brahminism. They praised the ideals of liberty, equality and fraternity. This influenced Untouchables in south India who also realized in the beginning of the twentieth century that they were Buddhists and began their now well documented movement (G. Aloysius, 2004).

This deep-seated caste based hatred is responsible for most of the problems and evils in India today, including the degradation of women. The creative energy of the country is imprisoned in the caste system. The life and mission of Dr. Ambedkar was to annihilate caste and create a new society based on the principles of liberty, equality, and fraternity. He also knew that the solution lies in making people aware of their social history and why they are condemned to such a life. He wanted to usher India into an era of enlightenment, or "Right Enlightenment". (Nanda, 2002). This enlightened vision is the preface and key to everything else in conquering ignorance (the origin of suffering) and in the higher life (the end of suffering). For developing this enlightened vision, Dr. Ambedkar felt one needs to realize and understand the law of causality (paticca samuppada) or dhamma, "This is, that is; with the arising of this, that arises. This is not, that is not. With the cessation of this, that ceases."

THE NEW BUDDHISM

Dr. Ambedkar likened Indian society to an orange. If one removes the artificial rind of Hinduism, what remains is a fragmented society with mutually conflicting groups called the castes that run into 6000 in kind. Ambedkar did not strive for positional change in the whole system of graded inequality. He wanted to bring structural change to Indian society. He concluded that the contemporary state of degradation in India was due to the triumph of Brahmanism over Buddhism-the victory of a worldview which sanctifies a graded inequality amongst living beings over one which prizes ethical conduct towards all such beings.

David Brazier in his thought-provoking book, The New Buddhism, raises some very important points by questioning what the real project of the Buddha was after his enlightenment. He stresses that the Buddha had a vision of an ideal society which he shared with his disciples and thus awakened them to the reality of the world. This vision he termed as bodhi, that is, awakened vision. This vision of an awakened society moved the Buddha to turn the wheel of the Dhamma and to express his enlightenment experience to others to make this awakened society a reality (Brazier, 2001). Dr. Ambedkar also challenged traditional Buddhist positions and views. While he accepted that the Buddha was centrally concerned with suffering and the end of suffering, he did not define suffering based on the traditional eight types of suffering. His set of sufferings includes suffering due to humans own wrong-doing and suffering due to inequality to other humans. In The Buddha and His Dhamma, he reformulates the life and teachings of the Buddha so that they can speak to contemporary Indian society and modern world. For him, the function of the Dhamma is twofold. That is to purify one's mind and to reconstruct world. In short, the purpose of the Dhamma is to transform an individual into a Buddha and to transform the world into a sangha. In the preface to The Buddha and His Dhamma, Dr. Ambedkar speaks of the purpose of the Dhamma as the creation of Dhamma Rajya, an ideal society based on liberty, equality and fraternity. It is clear that Dr. Ambedkar was trying to revive the Buddha's original project of the reconstruction of world. He called this vision Navayana or the New Buddhism, which is a universal model applicable to all societies.

STEPS TOWARDS AN AWAKENED SOCIETY

In the early years, Dr. Ambedkar was still struggling with his spirituality and slowly defining for himself this awakened vision. Therefore, most of his work for the liberation of his people came within a framework of activism concerning laws, committees, and commissions in the British India. For example, he gave evidence before the Southborough Committee for franchise and representation to the Indian legislatures in 1919. This was his first successful campaign without any mandate from his people. He successfully gained representation for depressed classes in the legislative assembly in Bombay. He was invited to participate in the Round Table Conference during 1932-1934 in order to discuss the future constitution of India, which he subsequently drafted. At this conference, he clashed with Gandhi, who denied the independent political rights of untouchables by deliberately trying to keep them in the fold of Hinduism. He also submitted a memorandum to the Cabinet Mission Plan in 1946 on behalf of the All India Scheduled Caste Federation (AISCF) in order to guarantee civil and political rights for them in free India.

The limited effect of such work within the system led Dr. Ambedkar to increasingly work outside of it as well. He began initiating mass protest movements, such as the Mahad Water Tank Movement (1927), and the Kalaram Temple Entry Movement (1934). He consciously created conditions for the illiterate people around him to become aware of the reality of the caste system. These conditions included writing books addressing various issues, editing several newspapers, launching political parties, and forming social organizations.

After clashing with Gandhi on the issue of the political empowerment of untouchables, Dr. Ambedkar realized the futility of changing the minds of the high caste Hindus. Although Gandhi outwardly showed his commitment to the untouchables, his real purpose appears to have been political. He wanted to ensure numerical power to Hindus (i.e. high-caste Hindus) vis-a-vis Muslims.

These events led Ambedkar to renounce the systemic container of Hinduism. On May 30-31, 1936 at Dadar in Mumbai, he delivered a lengthy speech entitled What way Liberty? In this historic speech, he detailed the path leading towards liberty and gave a call to conversion. He did not make it clear as to which religion he was going to convert. However, at the end of this speech, he gave a clarion call to his people, which echoed the teaching of the Buddha, to be your own light and refuge: While thinking over what message should I give you on this occasion, I recollected the message given by the Lord Buddha to his Bhikkhu Sangha just before his mahaparinirvana and which has been quoted in Mahaparinibbana Sutta: Once the Bhagwan, after having recovered from illness, was resting on a seat under a tree and his disciple venerable Ananda went to the Buddha. Having saluted, he sat beside him and said, I have seen the Lord in illness as well as in happiness. But from the present illness of the Lord, my body has become heavy like lead, my mind is not is peace. I cannot concentrate on the Dhamma, but I feel consolation and satisfaction that the Lord will not attain the parinibbana until a message is given to the Sangha.

Then the Lord replied, Ananda! What does the Sangha expect from me? Ananda, I have preached the Dhamma with an open heart, without concealing anything. The Tathagata has not kept anything concealed as some other teachers do. So Ananda, what more can the Tathagata tell the Bhikkhu Sangha. So Ananda, be self illuminating like the sun. Do not be dependent for light like the Earth. Believe in yourself, do not be dependent on others. Be truthful. Always take refuge in the truth and do not surrender to anyone. I also take refuge in the words of the Buddha to be your own guide. Take refuge in your own reason. Do not listen to the advice of others. Do not succumb to others. Be truthful and take refuge in the truth. Never surrender to anything. If you keep in mind this message of Lord Buddha at this juncture, I am sure, your decision will not be wrong.

In order to realize an awakened society, Dr. Ambedkar saw than an inner revolution among his people needed to take place in tandem with the social and political work of gaining equal rights for untouchables. This internal revolution he found in the act of conversion from the dependency and subservience of being an untouchable in Hinduism to the independence and empowerment of a Buddhist identity and complete development as a human being. In this way, Dr. Ambedkar began to develop a vision for his people in order to make them realize the importance of the Buddha Dhamma. He saw that religious reformation is often a precursor to political emancipation. In his Annihilation of Caste, he cited such examples in the revolutions of Protestant Europe, the first Mauryan ruler Chandragupta, and the contemporary revolution of Guru Nanak and the Sikhs in Punjab. He concluded that the emancipation of the mind is a necessary preliminary for the political emancipation of the people.

VISION OF DHAMMA

Dhamma is the perfection of life: The Buddha and His Dhamma, Dr. Ambedkar describes the path of the bodhisattva and presents the sublime teaching of non-attachment through quotes from the dialogue between the Buddha and Subhuti in the Diamond Sutra. In this sutra, the six perfections (paramita) of giving, morality, patience, energy, meditation, and wisdom are taught as not only practices for the individual but also ones to instigate others to do. Dhamma is to live in Nibbana: Dr. Ambedkar strongly affirmed the nature of Nibbana as experienced here in this life and in this world.

He wrote that the Buddha clearly rejected notions of Nibbana held by other schools of thought at the time. Specifically, the Buddha saw that the Brahmanistic and Upanishadic notions of the salvation of a soul made Nibbana into a goal achieved after death. Dr. Ambedkar quotes the famous Fire Sermon (Adittapariyaya Sutta, S.iv.19) to show how the Buddha's notion of the extinction of the passions, and not physical death, made Nibbana into a much more practical this-worldly goal. Nibbana or awakened vision tells one of the difficulties in the realization of the Eight-Fold Path.

The chief of these difficulties are the five fetters (samyojana) or five underlying tendencies (anusaya). The third fetter of dependence on the efficacy of rites and ceremonies is especially important in this context. Dr. Ambedkar felt that no good resolutions, however firm, will lead to anything unless we shed ritualism. By ritualism, he meant the belief that outward acts associated with priestly power and holy ceremony can afford one assistance of some kind. It is only when we have overcome our ties to salvific ritual, that humans can be said to have fairly entered the stream of liberation and have a chance to sooner or later win victory.

Dhamma is Karma-the instrument of moral order: Dr. Ambedkar clearly stated that the moral order or the world (kamma niyama) does not depend on a creator god or any other gods. The moral order may be good or bad but this depends on humans and nothing else. The Buddha discovered that the world (loka) revolves due to karma. There are three worlds: the sensual world, the form-ish world, and the formless world. The state of Nibbana, where the law of karma is not operative, is a way of being and acting beyond these worlds. However, the world in which most of us live most of the time is the world of sensual pleasures. The mental states in the sensual world are destructive because enormous strife and suffering come about due to competition for sensual desires. This world is made up of sounds, forms, colours, tastes, tactile objects, ideas, concepts etc. Sometimes, the ideas or concepts are just imposed by society, such as caste or graded inequality in India.

Caste as a consciousness comes into being due to social practices and conventions and is wrong view (miccha ditthi). It is a mental and social conditioning whereby the individual is crushed. Individuals have little or no choice. Clearly, this goes against the Buddha's teaching of karma and the power of intention (cetana). The intention or mental state behind an action indicates its moral quality and action per se does not determine the nature of karma. As mental states precede actions by body and speech, positive mental states lead to positive actions of body and speech and negative mental states lead to negative actions of body and speech. Thus, the law of karma emphasizes personal responsibility and positive action, not passivity to harmful social conventions. In this way, it clearly does not support that the idea that birth in a lower caste is the deserved result of one's unwholesome past actions.

PURIFICATION OF MIND, BODY AND SPEECH

Thus Dr. Ambedkar made it explicit that purification of mind, body and speech is the Dhamma. Dr. Ambedkar emphasized the training of mind in meditation, as did the Buddha, for developing intention or thought, which leads to right states of consciousness. He paraphrases the Sallekha Sutta (M.i.40):

You are to expunge by resolving that, though others may be harmful, you will be harmless.

That though others may kill, you will never kill.

That though others may steal, you will not.

That though others may not lead the higher life, you will.

That though others may lie, traduce, denounce, or prattle, you will not.

That though others may be covetous, you will covet not.

That though others may be malignant, you will not be malignant.

That though others may be given over to wrong views, wrong aims, wrong speech, wrong actions, and wrong concentration, you must follow (the Noble Eightfold Path in) right outlook, right aims, right speech, right actions, right mode of livelihood, right effort, right mind-fulness and right concentration.

That though others are wrong about the truth and wrong about deliverance, you will be right about truth and right about deliverance. That though others may be possessed by sloth and torpor, you will free yourselves therefrom. That though others may be puffed up, you will be humble-minded. That though others may be perplexed by doubts, you will be free from them.

That though others may harbour wrath, malevolence, envy, jealousy, niggardliness, avarice, hypocrisy, deceit, imperviousness, arrogance, forwardness, association with bad friends, slackness, unbelief, shamelessness, unscrupulousness, lack of instruction, inertness, bewilderment, and unwisdom, you will be the reverse of all these things.

That though others may clutch at and hug the temporal nor loose their hold thereon, you will clutch and hug the things that are not temporal, and will ensue renunciation.

I say it is the development of thought which is so efficacious for right states of consciousness, not to speak of act and speech. And therefore, Cunda, there must be developed the thought to all the foregoing resolves I have detailed.

This sutta can be interpreted as one's own resolve to transform oneself into a Buddha even when the world around is steeped with various vices.

Morality and Ethics (sila)-the bridge between the individual and the social or the foundation of a just society.

The highest realization in Buddhism is the emancipation of the mind, which Dr. Ambedkar also understood as liberty. The antithesis of liberty is slavery. According to the Buddha, there are two kinds of slavery: inner and outer. A certain deity asked the Buddha:

The inner tangle and the outer tangle.
This generation is entangled in a tangle.
And so I ask of Gautama this question:
Who succeeds in disentangling this tangle?

The Buddha replied:

When a wise man, established in Virtue
Develops Consciousness and Understanding
Then as a Bhikkhu ardent and sagacious
He succeeds in disentangling this tangle. (S.i.13)

Liberty is freedom from any control and in return demands no will to control others. The ethics of Buddhism ensures this freedom from control. Therefore, sila is the foundation of a just society. It is universal and not marked with sectarian feeling. If it does, it will only protect the group interest, and according to Dr. Ambedkar will become anti-social. Sila is right or ethical behaviour by one person towards another. Thus Dr. Ambedkar wrote that religion is personal, while Dhamma as the practice of sila is interpersonal. Therefore, society cannot do without Dhamma or righteousness.

In this way, Dr. Ambedkar clearly shows an understanding of the difference between the type of morality belonging to personal power and threat and the type belonging to collective power and personal responsibility. He makes the observation that the former type belongs to religion, which is concerned with the relation between humans and God. This type of morality helps to maintain peace and order and "is attached and detached as the occasion requires" to protect the interests of a particular group (Sangharakshita, 1986:156). In the latter understanding of morality, Ambedkar speaks not of religion but of Dhamma:

Morality is Dhamma and Dhamma is Morality. Morality and Dhamma arise from the direct necessity for man to love man. It is not to please God that man has to be moral. It is for his own good that man has to love man. (Sangharakshita, 1986:156)

This Dhamma is the universal morality which protects the weak from the strong and which safeguards the growth of the individual. It gives common models, standards, and rules. Finally, it ensures that liberty and equality can be established.

The only remedy lies in making fraternity universally effective. What is fraternity? It is nothing but another name for the brotherhood of men which is another name for morality. This is why the Buddha preached that Dhamma is morality and as Dhamma is sacred so is morality. (Sangharakshita, 1986:157)

This morality, however, is not just a set of ideals, but part of the threefold training of the mind in morality, concentration, and wisdom. For Dr. Ambedkar, training in sila is formalized for non-monastics in the practice of the five basic precepts (pancasila) and the taking of refuge in a ceremony called diksha.

In the institutionalization of the diksha ceremony for untouchables converting to Buddhism, Ambedkar included taking the five precepts as well as twenty-two additional vows. Dr. Ambedkar made this ceremony of taking refuge central to his vision of a new Buddhist identity for the lay Buddhist movement he led among untouchables. He recognized the fundamental need of a very conscious statement of Buddhist identity for his community as it renounced Hinduism and embraced Buddhism. In order to face the oppressive system of caste society in India, this new Buddhist identity could not be fuzzy or passive, especially since there was no monastic order to lead and defend the community. He also felt a strong lay community was imperative to re-establishing a proper ordained community in India, since he saw the existing monastic order, especially in Theravada countries, as corrupt (Sangharakshita, 1986:123).

AMBEDKAR VIEWS ON UNTOUCHABILITY

It is usual to hear all those who feel moved by the deplorable condition of the Untouchables unburden themselves by uttering the cry "We must do something for the Untouchables". One seldom hears any of the persons interested in the problem saying 'Let us do something to change the Touchable Hindu'. It is invariably assumed that the object to be reclaimed is the Untouchables. If there is to be a Mission, it must be to the Untouchables and if the Untouchables can be cured, untouchability will vanish. Nothing requires to be done to the Touchable. He is sound in mind, manners and morals. He is whole, there is nothing wrong with him. Is this assumption correct? Whether correct or not, the Hindus like to cling to it. The assumption has the supreme merit of satisfying themselves that they are not responsible for the problem of the Untouchables.

Like the Hindus the Gentiles also do not admit that the Jewish problem is in essence a Gentile problem. The observations of Louis Goulding on the subject are therefore very illuminating. In order to show how the Jewish problem is in its essence a Gentile problem, he says: "I beg leave to give a very homely instance of the sense in which I consider the Jewish Problem in essence a Gentile Problem. A close acquaintance of mine is a certain Irish terrier of mixed pedigree, the dog Paddy, who is to my friend John Smith as the apple of both his eyes. Paddy dislikes Scotch terriers; it is enough for one to pass within twenty yards of Paddy to deafen the neighbourhood with challenges and insults. It is a practice which John Smith deplores, which, therefore, he does his best to check—all the more as the objects of Paddy's detestation are often inoffensive creatures, who seldom speak first. Despite all his affection for Paddy, he considers, as I do, that Paddy's unmannerly behaviour is due to some measure of original sin in Paddy. It has not yet been suggested to us that what is here involved is a Scotch Terrier Problem and that when Paddy attacks a neighbour who is peacefully engaged in inspecting the evening smells it is the neighbour who should be arraigned for inciting to attack by the fact of his existence."

There is here a complete analogy between the Jewish Problem and the problem of the Untouchables. What Paddy is to the Scotch Terrier, the Gentile is to the Jews, and the Hindu is to the Untouchables. But there is one aspect in which the Jewish Problem stands in contrast to the Gentile Problem. The Jews and the Gentiles are separated by an antagonism of the creeds. The Jewish creed is opposed to that of the Gentile creed. The Hindus and the Untouchables are not separated by any such antagonism. They have a common creed and observe the same cults. The second explanation is that the Jews wish to remain separate from the Gentiles. While the first explanation is chauvinistic the second seems to be founded on historical truth. Many attempts have been made in the past by the Gentiles to assimilate the Jews. But the Jews have always resisted them. Two instances of this may be referred.

The first instance relates to the Napoleonic regime. After the National Assembly of France had agreed to the declaration of the 'Rights of man' to the Jews, the Jewish question was again reopened by the guild merchants and religious reactionaries of Alsace. Napoleon resolved to submit the question to the consideration of the Jews themselves. He convened an Assembly of Jewish Notables of France, Germany and Italy in order to ascertain whether the principles of Judaism were compatible with the requirements of citizenship as he wished to fuse the Jewish element with the dominant population. The Assembly consisting of III deputies, met in the Town Hall of Paris on the 25th of July 1806, and was required to frame replies to twelve questions relating mainly to the possibility of Jewish patriotism, the permissibility of inter-marriage between Jew and Non-Jew, and the legality of usury.

So pleased was Napoleon with the pronouncements of the Assembly that he summoned a Sanhedrin after the model of the ancient council of Jerusalem to convert them into the decree of a Legislative body. The Sanhedrin, comprising of 71 deputies from France, Germany, Holland and Italy met under the presidency of Rabbi Sinzheim, of Strassburg on 9th February 1807, and adopted a sort of Charter which exhorted the Jews to look upon France as their fatherland, to regard its citizens as their brethren, and to speak its language, and which also pressed toleration of marriages between Jews and Christians while declaring that they could not be sanctioned by the synagogue. It will be noted that the Jews refused to sanction intermarriages between Jews and non-Jews. They only agreed to tolerate them.

The second instance relates to what happened when the Batavian Republic was established in 1795. The more energetic members of the Jewish community pressed for a removal of the many disabilities under which they laboured. But the demand for the fuller rights of citizenship made by the progressive Jews was at first, strangely enough, opposed by the leaders of the Amsterdam community, who feared that civil equality would militate against the conservation of Judaism and declared that their co-religionists renounced their rights of citizenship in obedience to the dictates of their faith. This shows that the Jews preferred to live-as strangers rather than as members of the community.

Whatever the value of their explanations the Gentiles have at least realized that there rests upon them a responsibility to show cause for their unnatural attitude towards the Jews. The Hindu has never realised this responsibility of justifying his treatment of the Untouchables. The responsibility of the Hindus is much greater because there is no plausible explanation he can offer in justification of untouchability. He cannot say that the Untouchable is a leper or a mortal wretch who must be shunned. He cannot say that between him and the Untouchables, there is a gulf due to religious antagonism which is not possible to bridge. Nor can he plead that it is the Untouchable who does not wish to assimilate with the Hindus. But that is not the case with the Untouchables. They too are in a different sense an eternal people who are separate from the rest. But this separateness, their segregation is not the result of their wish. They are punished not because they do not want to mix. They are punished because they want to be one with the Hindus. In other words, though the problem of the Jews and of the Untouchables is similar in nature—inasmuch as the problem is created by others—it is essentially different. The Jew's case is one of the voluntary isolation. The case of the Untouchables is that of compulsory segregation. Untouchability is an infliction and not a choice.

SLAVES AND UNTOUCHABLES

Far from being ashamed of untouchability, the Hindus try to defend it. The line of their defence is that the Hindus have never upheld slavery as other nations have done and that in any case, untouchability is not worse than slavery. This argument was used by no less a person than the late Lala Lajpat Rai in his book called 'Unhappy India'. It would have been unnecessary to waste one's time in refuting this countercharge had it not been that on account of its plausibility the world at large not having witnessed anything worse than slavery is likely to believe that untouchability cannot be worse than slavery.

The first reply to the countercharge is that it is quite untrue that slavery was not recognised by the Hindus. Slavery is a very ancient institution of the Hindus. It is recognised by Manu, the Hindu lawgiver and has been elaborated and systematised by the other Smriti writers who followed Manu. Slavery among the Hindus was never merely ancient institution, which functioned, only in some hoary past. It was an institution which continued throughout Indian history down to the year 1843 and if it had not been abolished by the British Government by law in that year, it might have continued even today.

As to the relative merits of slavery and untouchability, the best way to meet the countercharge is to compare and contrast untouchability with slavery as it existed in ancient Rome and in modern America. What was the *de facto* condition of the slaves in the Roman Empire? The best description I know of is to be found in Mr. Barrow's *Slavery in the Roman Empire.* Says' Mr. Barrow: "Hitherto, it is the repulsive side of household slavery that has been sketched. There is also another aspect. The literature reveals the vast household as normal. It is, of course, the exception. Large slave staffs undoubtedly existed, and they are generally to be found in Rome. In Italy and the Provinces there was less need of display; many of the staff of the Villa were engaged in productive work connected with land and its produce. The old-fashioned relationship between foreman and slave remained there; the slave was often a fellow worker. The kindliness of Pliny towards his staff is well known. It is in no spirit of self-righteousness, and in no wish to appear in a favourable light in the eyes of the future generations which he hoped would read his letters that he tells of his distress at the illness and death of his slaves. The household (or Pliny) is the slaves' republic. Pliny's account of his treatment of his slaves is sometimes regarded as so much in advance of general or even occasional practice as to be valueless as evidence.

There is no reason for this attitude. From reasons both of display and genuine literary interest, the rich families attached to their households, slaves trained in literature and art. Clavisices Sabinus is said by Seneda to have had eleven slaves taught to recite Homer, Hesioid, and nine lyric poets by heart. 'Book cases would be cheaper', said a rude friend. 'No, what the household knows the master knows' was the answer. But, apart from such abuses, educated slaves must have been a necessity in the absence of printing;.... The busy lawyer, the dilettante poet, the philosopher and educated gentlemen of literary tastes and need of copyists and readers and secretaries. Such men were naturally linguistic also; a *librarius* who dies at the age of twenty boasts that he was 'literatus Graecis Latinis'. *Amanuenses* were common enough; librarians are to be found in public and private libraries.... Shorthand writing was in common use under the Empire, and slave *Notarii* were regularly employed. Many freemen, rhetoricians and grammarians are collected by Snetonius in a special treatise. Verrius Flaccus was tutor to Austus's grandsons, and at death was publicly honoured by a statue. Scribonius Aphrodisius was the slave and disciple of Orbilius and was afterwards freed by Scribenia. Hyginus was librarian of the Palatine Library, in which office he was followed by Julius Modestus, his own freeman. We hear of freemen historians of a slave philosopher who was encouraged to argue with his master, friends of slaves and freed architects. Freemen as doctors occur frequently in the inscriptions, some of them specialists, they had been trained in big households as slaves, as is shown by one or two examples; after Manumission they rose to eminence and became notorious for their high fees.'" The tastes of some section of society demanded that dancer, singers, musicians, mountebanks, variety artists, athletic trainers and messieurs should be forthcoming. All these are to be found in slavery often trained by teachers who had acquired some reputation."

The age of Augustus was the beginning of a period of commercial and industrial expansion.... Slaves had indeed been employed (in arts and crafts) before, but the sudden growth of trade.... their employment in numbers that would otherwise have been unnecessary. Romans engaged more freely and more openly in various forms of commercial and industrial venture. Yet, even so, the agent became more important, for commercial activities became more widespread; and such agents were almost necessarily slaves.... (this is so) because the bonds of slavery (are elastic). (They could be) so relaxed as to offer an incentive to the slave to work by the prospect of wealth and freedom, and so tightened as to provide a guarantee to the master against loss from the misconduct of his slave.

In business contracts between slave and master or third person seem to have been common, and the work thus done, and no doubt, the profits were considerable.... Renting of land to the slave has already been noticed.... and in industry much the same system was used in various forms; the master might lease a bank, or a business of the use of a ship, the terms being a fixed return or the slave being paid on a commission basis.

The earnings of the slave became in law his peculium was saved it might be used to a variety of purpose. No doubt in many cases this fund was expended in providing food or pleasure. But peculium must not be regarded merely as petty savings, casually earned and idly spent. The slave who made his master's business yield profits, to his own profit too, very often, had a keen sense of the best use to make up his own money. Often he reinvested it in his master's business or in enterprises entirely unrelated to it. He could enter into business relations with his master, from whom he came to be regarded as entirely distinct, or he could make contracts with a third person. He could even have procurators to manage his own property and interests. And so with the peculium may be found not only land, houses, shops, but rights and claims.

The activities of slaves in commerce are innumerable; numbers of them are shopkeepers selling every variety of food, bread, meat, salt, fish, wine, vegetables, beans, lupine-seed, honey, curd, ham, ducks and fresh fish; others deal in clothing—sandals, shoes, gowns and mantles. In Rome, they plied their trade in the neighbourhood of the Circus Mamimus, or the Porticus Trigemimus; or the Esquiline Market, or the Great Mart (on the Caolian Hill) or the Suburra .... The extent to which slave secretaries and agents acted for their masters is shown very clearly in the receipts found in the house of Caecillius Jucundus at Pompei.

That the State should possess slaves is not surprising; war, after all, was the affair of the State and the captive might well be State-property. What is surprising is the remarkable use made of public slaves under the Empire and the extraordinary social position occupied by them.... "'Public slave' came to mean before the Empire a slave of the State employed in its many offices, and the term implied a given occupation and often social position. The work of slaves of the State, slaves of the townships, and slaves of Caesar comprises much of what would now fall to parts of the higher and the whole of the lower branches of the civil services and of the servants of Municipal Corporations, working both with head and hands.... In the subordinate levels (of the Treasury) there worked numbers of clerks and financial officers, all freedmen and slaves. The business dealt with must have been of vast range.... The Mint.... the immediate head was a knight, in charge of the minting processes.... a freedman was placed; under him served freedmen and slaves.... From one branch of State service, at any rate, slaves were rigorously excluded, except on one or two occasions of exceptional stress. They were not allowed to fight in the Army because not thought worthy of honour. Doubtless other motives were present also; it would be dangerous experiment to train too many slaves systematically in the use of Arms. If, however, slaves served rarely in the fighting line, they are regularly to be found in great numbers behind it employed as servants, and in the commissariat and transport. In the fleet slaves were common enough."

Let us turn to the *de facto* position of the Negro in the United States during the period in which he was slave in the eye of the law. Here are some facts which shed a good deal of light on his position: "Lafayette himself had observed that white and black seamen and soldiers had fought and messed together in the Revolution without bitter difference. Down in Granville County, North Carolina, a full blooded Negro, John Chavis, educated in Princeton University, was conducting a private school for white students and was a licentiate under the local Presbytery, preaching to white congregations in the State.

One of his pupils became Governor of North Carolina, another the State's most prominent Whig senator. Two of his pupils were sons of the Chief Justice of North Carolina. The father of the founder of the greatest military Academy of the State attended his school and boarded in his home..... Slave labour was used for all kinds of work and the more intelligent of the Negro slaves were trained as artisans to be used and leased. Slave artisans would bring twice as much as an ordinary field hand in the market.

Master craftsmen owned their staff. Some masters, as the system became more involved, hired slaves to their slave artisans. Many slave artisans purchased their freedom by the savings allowed them above the normal labour expected." "The advertisements for runaways and sales are an index to this skill. They received the same or better wages than the poor white labourer and with the influence of the master got the best jobs. The Contractors for masons' and carpenters' work in Athens, Georgia in 1838 were petitioned to stop showing preference to Negro labourers. "The white man is the only real, legal, moral, and civil proprietor of this country and state. The right of his proprietorship reached from the date of the studies of those whitemen, Copernicus and Galileo, who indicated the sphericity of the earth; which sphericity hinted to another white man, Columbus, the possibility by a westerly course of sailing, of finding land. Hence by whitemen alone was this continent discovered, the whitemen alone, aye, those to whom you decline to give money for bread or clothes for their famishing families, in the logical manner of withholding work from them defending Negroes too in the bargain."

In Atlanta in 1858 a petition signed by 2 white mechanics and labourers sought protection against the black slave artisans of masters who resided in other sections. The very next year sundry white citizens were aggrieved that the City Council tolerated a Negro dentist to remain and operate in their midst. 'In justice to ourselves and the community it ought to be abated. We, the residents of Atlanta, appeal to you for justice'. A Census of free Negroes in Richmond County, Georgia, in 1819 showed carpenters, barbers, boatcorkers, saddlers, spinners, millwrights, holsters, weavers, harness makers, sawmill attendants and steamboat pilots.

A Negro shoemaker made by hand the boots in which President Munrow was inaugurated. Harriet Martineau marvelled at the slave workmanship in the delicately tiled floors of Thomas Jefferson's home at Monticello. There still stands in the big house of the old plantation, heavy marks of the hands of these Negro craftsmen, strong mansions built of timber hewn from the original oak and pinned together by wooden pins. Negro women skilled in spinning and weaving worked in the mills. Buckingham in 1839 found them in Athens, Georgia, working alongside with white girls without apparent repugnance or objection.

Negro craftsmen in the South, slave and free fared better than their brothers in the North. In 1856 in Philadelphia, of 1637 Negro craftsmen recorded, less than two-thirds could use their trades; 'because of hostile prejudice'. The Irish who were pouring into America from the very beginning of the nineteenth century were being used in the North on approximately the same motives of preference, which governed Negro slavery. 'An Irish Catholic, it was argued in their favour, seldom attempts to rise to a higher condition than that in which he is placed, while the Negro often makes the attempt with success. Had not the old Puritan Oliver Cromwell, while the traffic in black slaves was on, sold all the Irish not killed in the Drogheda Massacre, into Barbados? Free and fugitive Negroes in New York and Pennsylvania were in constant conflict with this group and the bitter hostility showed itself most violently in the draft riots of the New York. These Hibernians controlled the hod carrying and the common labour jobs, opposing every approach of the Negro as a menace to their slight hold upon America and upon a means of livelihood."

Such was the *de facto* condition of the Roman slave and the American Negro slave. Is there anything in the condition of the Untouchables of India which is comparable with the condition of the Roman slave and the American Negro slave? It would not be unfair to take the same period of time for comparing the condition of the Untouchables with that of the slaves under the Roman Empire. But I am prepared to allow the comparison of the condition of the slaves in the Roman Empire to be made with the condition of the Untouchables of the present day. It is a comparison between the worst of one side and the best of the other, for the present times are supposed to be the golden age for the Untouchables. How does the *de facto* condition of the Untouchables compare with the *de facto* condition of the slaves? How many Untouchables are engaged as the slaves in Rome were, in professions such as those of Librarians, Amanuenses, Shorthand writers? How many Untouchables are engaged, as the slaves in Rome were, in such intellectual occupations as those of rhetoricians, grammarians, philosophers, tutors, doctors and artists? How many Untouchables are engaged, as the slaves in Rome? Can any Hindu dare to give an affirmative answer to anyone of these queries?

The Untouchables are completely shut out from any of these avenues in which the slaves found so large a place. This proves how futile is the line of defence adopted by the Hindus to justify untouchability. The pity of the matter is that most people condemn slavery simply because they hold that for one man or class to have by law the power of life and death over another is wrong. They forget that there can be cruel oppression, tyranny, and persecution, with the train of misery, disappointment and desperation even when there is no slavery. Those who will take note of the facts stated above relating to the *de facto* condition of the slaves will admit that it is idle to condemn slavery lightly or hurriedly on the mere *de jure* conception of it. What the law permits is not always evidence of the practices prevalent in society. Many a slave would readily have admitted that they owed everything to slavery, and many did so whether they would have admitted it or not.

Slavery, it must be admitted, is not a free social order. But can untouchability be described as a free social order? The Hindus who came forward to defend untouchability no doubt claim that it is. They, however, forget that there are differences between untouchability and slavery, which makes untouchability a worse type of an unfree social order. Slavery was never obligatory. But untouchability is obligatory. A person is *permitted* to hold another as his slave. There is no compulsion on him if he does not want to. But an Untouchable has no option. Once he is born an Untouchable, he is subject to all the disabilities of an Untouchable. The law of slavery permitted emancipation. Once a slave always a slave was not the fate of the slave. In untouchability there is no escape. Once an Untouchable always an Untouchable.

The other difference is that untouchability is an indirect and therefore the worst form of slavery. A deprivation of a man's freedom by an open and direct way is a preferable form of enslavement. It makes the slave conscious of his enslavement and to become conscious of slavery is the first and most important step in the battle for freedom. But if a man is deprived of his liberty indirectly he has no consciousness of his enslavement. Untouchability is an indirect form of slavery. To tell an Untouchable 'you are free, you are a citizen, you have all the rights of a citizen', and to tighten the rope in such a way as to leave him no opportunity to realise the ideal is a cruel deception. It is enslavement without making the Untouchables conscious of their enslavement. It is slavery though it is untouchability. It is real though it is indirect. It is enduring because it is unconscious. Of the two orders, untouchability is beyond doubt the worse.

Neither slavery nor untouchability is a free social order. But if a distinction is to be made—and there is no doubt that there is distinction between the two—the test is whether education, virtue, happiness, culture, and wealth is possible within slavery or within untouchability. Judged by this test it is beyond controversy that slavery is hundred times better than untouchability. In slavery there is room for education, virtue, happiness, culture, or wealth. In untouchability there is none.

Untouchability has none of the advantages of an unfree social order such as slavery. It has all the disadvantages of a free social order. In an unfree social order such as slavery there is the advantage of apprenticeship in a business, craft or art or what Prof. Mures calls 'an initiation into a higher culture'. Neither the crushing of untouchability nor the refusal of personal growth was necessary inherent in slavery, especially slavery as it existed in Roman Empire. It is therefore over hasty to say that slavery is better than untouchability.

This training, this initiation of culture was undoubtedly a great benefit to the slave. Equally it involved considerable cost to the master to train his slave, to initiate him into culture. 'There can have been little supply of slaves educated or trained before enslavement. The alternative was to train them when young slaves in domestic work or in skilled craft, as was indeed done to some extent before the Empire, by Cato, the Elder, for example. The training was done by his owner and his existing staff.... indeed the household of the rich contained special pedagogue for this purpose. Such training took many forms, industry, trade, arts and letters'.

The reason why the master took so much trouble to train the slave and to initiate him in the higher forms of labour and culture was undoubtedly the motive of gain. A skilled slave as an item was more valuable than an unskilled slave. If sold, he would fetch better price, if hired out he would bring in more wages. It was therefore an investment to the owner to train his slave.

In an unfree social order, such as slavery, the duty to maintain the slave in life and the body falls upon the master. The slave was relieved of all responsibility in respect of his food, his clothes and his shelter. All this, the master was bound to provide. This was, of course, no burden because the slave earned more than his keep. But a security for boarding and lodging is not always possible for every freeman, as all wage earners now know to their cost. Work is not always available even to those who are ready to toil and a workman cannot escape the rule according to which he gets no bread if he finds no work. This rule—no work no bread—has no applicability to the slave. It is the duty of the master to find bread and also to find work. If the master fails to find work, the slave does not forfeit his right to bread. The ebbs and tides of business, the booms and depressions are vicissitudes through which all free wage earners have to go. But they do not affect the slave. They may affect his master. But the slave is free from them. He gets his bread, perhaps the same bread, but bread whether it is boom or whether it is depression.

In an unfree social order, such as slavery, the master is bound to take great care of the health and well being of the slave: The slave was property of the master. But this very disadvantage gave the slave an advantage over a freeman. Being property and therefore valuable, the master for sheer self-interest took great care of the health and well-being of the slave In Rome, the slaves were never employed on marshy and malarial land. On such a land only freemen were employed. Cato advises Roman farmers never to employ slaves on marshy and malarial land. This seems strange. But a little examination will show that this was quite natural. Slave was valuable property and as such a prudent man who knows his interest will not expose his valuable possession to the ravages of malaria. The same care need not be taken in the case of freeman because he is not valuable property. This consideration resulted into the great advantage of the slave. He was cared for as no one was.

Untouchability has none of the three advantages of the unfree social order mentioned above. The Untouchable has no entry in the higher arts of civilisation and no way open to a life of culture. He must only sweep. He must do nothing else. Untouchability carries no security as to livelihood. None from the Hindus is responsible for the feeding, housing and clothing of the Untouchable. The health of the Untouchable is the care of nobody. Indeed, the death of an Untouchable is regarded as a good riddance. There is a Hindu proverb, which says 'The Untouchable is dead and the fear of pollution has vanished'.

On the other hand, untouchability has all the disadvantages of a free social order. In a free social order the responsibility for survival in the struggle for existence lies on the individual. This responsibility is one of the greatest disadvantages of a free social order. Whether an individual is able to carry out this responsibility depends upon fair start, equal opportunity and square deal. The Untouchable, while he is a free individual, had neither fair start, nor equal opportunity nor square deal. From this point of view, untouchability is not only worse than slavery but is positively cruel as compared to slavery. In slavery, the master has the obligation to find work for the slave. In a system of free labour workers have to compete with workers for obtaining work. In this scramble for work what chances has the Untouchable for a fair deal? To put it shortly, in this competition with the scales always weighing against him by reason of his social stigma he is the last to be employed and the first to be fired. Untouchability is cruelty as compared to slavery because it throws upon the Untouchables the responsibility for maintaining himself without opening to him fully all the ways of earning a living.

To sum up, the Untouchables unlike the slaves are owned by the Hindus for purposes which further their interests and are disowned by them, when owning them places them under burden. The Untouchables can claim none of the advantages of an unfree social order and are left to bear all the disadvantages of a free social order.

TOUCHABLES V/S UNTOUCHABLES

A relationship of touchables against untouchables may cause surprise. Such a surprise will not be altogether without reason. The touchables are not one uniform body of people. They are themselves divided into innumerable castes. Each Hindu is conscious of the caste to which he belongs. Given this heterogeneity it does seem that to include all the touchable castes into one group and put them as forming a block against the untouchables is to create a division which can have no meaning. But although this division of touchables against untouchables may require explanation, the division so far as modern India is concerned is real and substantial.

The explanation of how the touchables have now become one block and are conscious of their being different from the untouchables means nothing but recounting the mutual relationship of the four Varnas.

At the outset it must be borne in mind that those who like Mr. Gandhi accept the Chaturvarna as an ideal form of society, either do not know the history of the mutual relations of the four Varnas or are cherishing an illusion or conjuring up a vision for purposes which they are out to serve. For, the fact is that the four Varnas never formed a society based on loving brotherhood or on economic organisation based on cooperative effort. The four Varnas were animated by nothing but a spirit of animosity towards one another. There would not be the slightest exaggeration to say that the social history of the Hindus is a history not merely of class struggle but class war fought with such bitterness that even the Marxist will find it difficult to cite parallel cases to match.

It seems that the first class struggle took place between the Brahmins, Kshatriyas and Vaishyas on the one hand and the Sudras on the other. In Katyayana's Srauta Sutras, it is said, that men with the exception of those whose members are defective, who have not read the Veda, eunuchs, and Sudras, have a right to sacrifice. It is Brahmanas, Rajanyas and Vaishyas (only who) according to the Veda (possess this privilege)". We are told by Manu that *(Quotation not given in the MS.)*. Manu also says that *(Quotation not given in the MS.)*. Compare with this the following instances and statements relating to the status of the Sudra occurring in the Vedic literature of a period earlier than Manu and even earlier than Katyayana. Prof. Max Muller calls attention to two instances showing that Sudras were admitted to great sacrifices such as *"gavedhukacharu"*. One is that of Rathakara and the other of Nishadasthapati, both Sudras.

It might however be supposed that this was a concession made to the exceptional men from the Sudras. That it was not a mere concession but a right enjoyed by the Sudras is beyond question. In the Satapatha Brahmana which is a part of the Veda, the formula for the Brahmin Priest to call the sacrificer to come and make the oblation is given. He is asked to say *ehi,* come, in the case of a Brahman; *Agahi* 'come hither', in the case of a Vaishya; *Adrava,* 'hasten hither' in the case of a Kshatriya and *Adhava,* 'run hither' in the case of a Sudra. This passage is of very great importance. It shows that the Sudra had at one time the right to sacrifice. Otherwise a form of address for a Sudra sacrificer could not have found a place in the Vedic precept. If the Sudra had a right to sacrifice, they also must have had a right to study the Vedas.

For, according to Katyayana, only those who had the right to read the Vedas were entitled to perform the sacrifice. That the Sudras were at one time entitled to read the Vedas is a fact which is well supported by tradition which is referred to in the Shanti Parva of the Mahabharata, where the sage Bhrigu answers the question "How is Varna to be determined?" in the following terms: "There is no difference of castes; this world, having been at first created by Brahma entirely Brahmanic, became (afterwards) separated into castes in consequence of works. 6940. Those Brahmans (lit. twice born men), who were fond of sensual pleasure, fiery, irascible, prone to violence, who had forsaken their duty, and were red-limbed, fell into the condition of Kshatriyas. Those Brahmans, who derived their livelihood from kine, who were yellow, who subsisted by agriculture, and who neglected to practise their duties, entered into the state of Vaisyas. Those Brahmans, who were addicted to mischief and falsehood, who were covetous, who lived by all kinds of works, who were black and had fallen from purity, sank into the condition of Sudras. Being separated from each other by these works, the Brahmans became divided into different castes. Duty and the rites of sacrifice have not been always forbidden to (any of) them. Such are four classes for whom the Brahmanic Sarasvati was at first designed by Brahma, but who through their cupidity fell into ignorance."

Interpreting the word "Brahmanic" Sarasvati the Commentator says: "Sarasvati, consisting of the Veda, was formerly designed by Brahma for all the four castes; but the Sudras having through cupidity fallen into 'ignorance i.e. of darkness,' lost their right to the Veda."

After the Sudra was reduced came the turn of the Vaishya. The bitterest class war took place between the Brahmins and the Kashatriyas. The classical literature of the Hindus abounds in reference to class wars between these two Varnas. First was the conflict between the Brahmins and King Vena. "There was formerly a Prajapati (lord of creatures), a protector of righteousness, called Anga, of the race of Atri, and resembling him in power. His son was the Prajapati Vena, who was but indifferently skilled in duty, and was born of Sunitha, the daughter of Mritya. This son of the daughter of Kala (death), owing to the taint derived from his maternal grandfather, threw his duties behind his back and lived in covetousness under the influence of desire. This king established an irreligious system of conduct; transgressing the ordinances of the Veda, he was devoted to lawlessness. In his reign men lived without study of the sacred books and without the vashatkara, and the gods had no Soma-libations to drink at sacrifices. 'I', he declared, 'am the object, and the performer of sacrifice, and the sacrifice itself, it is to me that sacrifice should be presented, and oblations offered. 'This transgressor of the rules of duty, who arrogated to himself what was not his due, was then addressed by all the great rishis, headed by Marichi: 'We are about to consecrate ourselves for a ceremony which shall last for many years, practice not unrighteousness, o Vena; this is not the eternal rule of duty. Thou art in very deed a Prajapati of Atri's race, and thou hast engaged to protect thy subjects. 'The foolish Vena, ignorant of what was right, laughingly answered those great rishis who had so addressed him: 'Who but myself is the ordainer of duty? Or who ought I to obey? Who on earth equals me in sacred knowledge, in prowess, in austere fervour, in truth? Yet who are deluded and senseless know not that I am the source of all beings and duties. Hesitate not to believe that I, if I willed, could burn up the earth, or deluge it with water, or close up heaven and earth'. When owing to his delusion and arrogance Vena could not be governed, then the mighty rishis becoming incensed, seized the vigorous and struggling king, and rubbed his left thigh. From this thigh, so rubbed, was produced a black man, very short in stature, who, being alarmed, stood with joined hands. Seeing that he was agitated, Atri said to him 'Sit down" (nishida). He became the founder of the race of the Nishadas, and also progenitor of the Dhivaras (fisherman), who sprang from the corruption of Vena. So too were produced from him the other inhabitants of the Vindhya range, the Tukharas and Turnburas, who are prone to lawlessness. Then the mighty sages, excited and incensed, again rubbed the right hand of Vena, as men do the Arani wood, and from it arose Pritha, respondent in body, glowing like the manifested Agni."

"The son of Vena (Prithu) then, with joined hands, addressed the great rishis: 'A very slender understanding for perceiving the principles of duty has been given to me by nature; tell me truly how I must employ it. Doubt not that I shall perform whatever you shall declare to me as my duty, and its object.' Then those gods and great rishis said to him: 'Whatever duty is enjoined perform it, without hesitation, disregarding what thou may est like or dislike, looking on all creatures with an equal eye, putting far from the lust, anger, cupidity, and pride. Restrain by the strength of thin arm all those men who swerve from righteousness, having a constant regard to duty. And in thought, act, and word take upon thyself, and continually renew, the engagement to protect the terrestrial Brahman (Veda or Brahmans?)...... And promise that thou wilt exempt the Brahmans from punishment, and preserve society from the confusion of Castes'. The son of Vena then replied to the gods, headed by the rishis: 'The great Brahmans, the chief of men, shall be reverenced by me'. 'So be it,' rejoined those declares of the Veda. Sukra, the depository of divine knowledge, became his purohita: the Balakhilyas and Sarasvetyas his ministers; and the venerable Garga, the great rishi, his astrologer. "The second conflict took place between the Brahmins and the Kshatriya king Pururavas. A brief reference to it occurs in the Adiparva of the Mahabharata.

"Subsequently the wise Pururavas was born of 11, who, as we have heard, was both his father and his mother. Ruling over thirteen islands of the ocean, and surrounded by being who were all superhuman, himself a man of great renown, Pururavas, intoxicated by his prowess, engaged in a conflict with the Brahmans, and robbed them of their jewels, although they loudly remonstrated. Sanatkumara came from Brahma's heaven, and addressed to him an admonition, which, however, he did not regard. Being then straightway cursed by the incensed rishis, he perished, this covetous monarch, who, through pride of power, had lost his understanding. This glorious being (virat), accompanied by Urvasi, brought down for the performance of sacred rites the fires which existed in the heaven of the Gandharvas, properly distributed into three."

A third collision is reported to have occurred between the Brahmins and King Nahusha. The story is given in great details in the Udyogaparva of the Mahabharata. It is there recorded: "After his slaughter of the demon Vrittra, Indra became alarmed at the idea of having taken the life of a Brahmin (for Vrittra was regarded as such), and hid himself in waters. In consequence of the disappearance of the king of gods, all affairs, celestial as well as terrestrial, fell into confusion. The rishis and gods then applied to Nahusha to be their king. After at first excusing himself on the plea of want of power, Nahusha at length, in compliance with their solicitations, accepted the high function. Up to the period of his elevation he had led a virtuous life, but he now became addicted to amusement and sensual pleasure; and even aspired to the possession of Indrani, Indra's wife, whom he had happened to see.

The queen resorted to the Angiras Vrihaspati, the preceptor of the gods, who engaged to protect her. Nahusha was greatly incensed on hearing of this interference; but the gods endeavoured to pacify him, and pointed out the immorality of—appropriating another person's wife. Nahusha, however, would listen to no remonstrance, and insisted that in his adulterous designs he was no worse than Indra himself; 373. The renowned Ahalya, a rishi's wife, was formerly corrupted by Indra in her husband's lifetime; Why was he not prevented by you? 374.

And many barbarous acts, and unrighteous deeds, and frauds, were perpetrated of old by Indra; Why was he not prevented by you? The gods, urged by Nahusha, then went to bring Indrani; but Vrihaspati would not give her up. At his recommendation, however, she solicited Nahusha for some delay, till she should ascertain what had become of her husband. This request was granted.

The gods next applied to Vishnu on behalf of Indra; and Vishnu promised that if Indra would sacrifice to him, he should be purged from his guilt, and recovers his dominion, while Nahusha would be destroyed. Indra sacrificed accordingly: and the result is thus told; "Having divided the guilt of Brahmanicide among trees, rivers, mountains, the earth, women, and the elements, Vasava (Indra), lord of the gods, became freed from suffering and sin, and self-governed." Nahusha was by this means, shaken from his place. But (unless this is said by way of prelepsis, or there is some confusion in the narrative) he must have speedily regained his position, as we are told that Indra was again ruined,, and became invisible.

Indrani now went in search of her husband; and by the help of Upasruti (the goddess of night and reveller of secrets) discovered him existing in a very subtle form in the stem of a lotus growing in a lake situated in a continent within an ocean north of the Himalaya. She made known to him the wicked intention of Nahusha, and entreated him to exert his power, rescue her from danger, and resume his dominion. Indra declined any immediate interposition on the plea of Nahusha's superior strength; but suggested to his wife a device by which the usurper might be hurled from his position.

She was recommended to say to Nahusha that "if he would visit her on a celestial vehicle borne by rishis, she would with pleasure submit herself to him". The question of the gods accordingly went to Nahusha, by whom she was graciously received, and made this proposal: "I desire for thee, king of the gods, a vehicle hitherto unknown, such as neither Vishnu, nor Rudra, nor the ashuras, nor the rakshases employ. Let the eminent rishis, all united, bear thee, lord, in a car: this idea pleases me". Nahusha receives favourably this appeal to his vanity, and in the course of his reply thus gives utterance to his self-congratulation: "He is a personage of no mean prowess who makes the munis his bearers.

I am a fervid devotee of great might, lord of the past, the future and the present. If I were angry the world would no longer stand; on me everything depends.... Wherefore, O goddess, I shall, without doubt, carry out what you propose. The seven rishis, and all the Brahman-rishis, shall carry me. Behold beautiful goddess, my majesty, and my prosperity." The narrative goes on: "Accordingly this wicked being, irreligious, violent, intoxicated by the force of conceit, and arbitrary in his conduct, attached to his car the rishis, who submitted to his commands, and compelled them to bear him ".

Indrani then again resorts to Vrihaspati, who assures her that vengeance will soon overtake Nahusha for his presumption: and promises that he will himself perform a sacrifice with a view to the destruction of the oppressor, and the discovery of Indra's lurking place. Agni is then sent to discover and bring Indra to Vrihaspati; and the latter, on Indra's arrival, informs him of all that had occurred during his absence. While Indra with Kuvera, Yama, Soma, and Varuna, was devising means for the destruction of Nahusha, the sage Agastya came up, congratulated Indra on the fall of his rival, and proceeded to relate how it had occurred. Wearied with carrying the sinner Nahusha, the eminent divine rishis, and the spotless brahman-rishis asked that divine personage Nahusha (to solve) a difficulty; "Dost thou, a Vasava, most excellent of conquerors, regard as authoritative or not those Brahmana texts which are recited at the immolation of kine?' 'No', replied Nahusha, whose understanding was enveloped in darkness. The rishis rejoined: 'Engaged in unrighteousness, thou attainest not unto righteousness: these texts, which were formerly uttered by great rishis, are regarded by us as authoritative.' The (proceeds Agastya) disputing with the munis, Nahusha, impelled by unrighteousness, touched me on the head with his foot. In consequence of this the king's glory was smitten and his prosperity departed. When he had instantly become agitated and oppressed with fear, I said to him, 'Since thou, O fool, contemnest that sacred text, always held in honour, which has been composed by former sages, and employed by brahman-rishis, and has touched my head with thy foot, and employest the Brahma—like and irresistible rishis as bearers to carry thee, therefore, shorn of thy lustre and all thy merit exhausted, sink down, sinner, degraded from heaven to earth. For then thousand years thou shalt crawl in the form of a huge serpent. When that period is completed, thou shalt again ascend to heaven'. So fell that wicked wretch from the sovereignty of the gods."

Next there is reference to the conflict between King Nimi and the Brahmins. The Vishnu Puran relates the story as follows: "Nimi had requested the Brahman-rishi Vashishtha to officiate at a sacrifice, which was to last a thousand years, Vashishtha in reply pleaded a pre-engagement to Indra for five hundred years, but promised to return at the end of that period. The king made no remark, and Vashishtha went away, supposing that he had assented to this arrangement. On his return, however, the priest discovered that Nimi had retained Gautama (who was, equally with Vashishtha a Brahman-rishi) and others to perform the sacrifice; and being incensed at the neglect to give him notice of what was intended, he cursed the king, who was then asleep, to lose his corporeal form. When Nimi awoke and learnt that he had been cursed without any previous warning, he retorted, by uttering a similar curse on Vashishtha, and then died. "In consequence of this curse "(proceeds Vishnu Purana, iv. 5, 6)" the vigour of Vashishtha entered into the vigour of

Mitra and Varuna. Vashishtha, however, received from them another body when their seed had fallen from them at the sight of Urvashi". Nimi's body was embalmed. At the close of the sacrifice which he had begun, the gods were willing, on the intercession of the priests, to restore him to life, but he declined the offer, and was placed by the deities, according to his desire, in the eyes of all living creatures. It is in consequence of this fact that they are always opening the shutting (Nimishas means "the twinkling of the eye")".

Manu mentions another conflict between the Brahmins and King Sumukha. But of this no details are available. These are instances of conflict between the Brahmins and the Kshatriya Kings. From this it must not be supposed that the Brahmins and the Kshatriyas as two classes did not clash. That there were clashes between these two classes as distinguished from conflicts with kings is abundantly proved by material the historic value of which cannot be doubted. Reference may be made to three events.

First is the contest between the Vishvamitra the Kshatriya and Vashishtha the Brahmin. The issue between the two was whether a Kshatriya can claim Brahminhood. The story is told in Ramayana and is as follows: "There was formerly, we are told, a king called Kusa, son of Prajapati, who had a son called Kushanabha, who was father of Gadhi, the father of Vishvamitra. The latter ruled the earth for many thousand years. On one occasion, when he was making a circuit of the earth, he came to Vashishtha's hermitage, the pleasant abode of many saints, sages, and holy devotees, where, after at first declining he allowed himself to be hospitably entertained with his followers by the son of Brahma. Vishvamitra, however, coveting the wondrous cow, which had supplied all the dainties of the feast, first of all asked that she should be given to him in exchange for a hundred thousand common cows, adding that "she was a gem, that gems were the property of the king, and that, therefore, the cow was his by right". On this price being refused the king advances immensely in his offers, but all without effect. He then proceeds-very ungratefully and tyrannically, it must be allowed to have the cow removed by force, but she breaks away from his attendants, and rushes back to her master, complaining that he was deserting her. He replies that he was not deserting her, but that the king was much more powerful than he. She answers, "Men do not ascribe strength to a Kshatriya: the Brahmans are stronger. The Strength of Brahmans is divine, and superior to that of Kshatriya. Thy strength is immeasurable. Vishvamitra, though of great vigour, is not more powerful than thou. Thy energy is invincible. Commission me, who have been acquired by thy Brahmanical power, and I will destroy the pride, and force, and attempt of this wicked prince". She accordingly by her bellowing creates hundreds of Pahalvas, who destroy the entire host of Vishvamitra, but are slain by him in their turn. Sakas and Yavans, of great power and valour, and well armed, were then produced, who consumed the king's soldiers, but were routed by him."

The cow then calls into existence by her bellowing, and from different parts of her body, other warriors of various tribes, who again destroyed Vishvamitra's entire army, foot soldiers, elephants, horses, chariots, and all. A hundred of the monarch's sons, armed with various weapons, then rushed in great fury on Vashishtha, but were all reduced to ashes in a moment by the blast of that sage's mouth. Vishvamitra, being thus utterly vanquished and humbled, appointed one of his son to be regent, and travelled to the Himalaya, where he betook himself to austerities, and thereby obtained a vision of Mahadeva, who at his desire revealed to him the science of arms in all its branches, and gave him celestial weapons with which, elated and full of pride, he consumed the hermitage of Vashishtha, and put its inhabitants to flight.

Vashishtha then threatens Vishvamitra and uplifts his Brahmanical mace. Vishvamitra too, raises his fiery weapon and calls out to his adversary to stand. Vashishtha bids him to show his strength, and boasts that he will soon humble his pride. He asks: "What comparison is there between a Kshatriya's might, and the great might of a Brahman? Behold, thou contemptible Kshatriya, my divine Brahmanical power. The dreadful fiery weapon uplifted by the son of Gadhi was then quenched by the rod of the Brahman, as fire is by water." Many and various other celestial missiles, as the nooses of Brahma, Kala (time), and Varuna, the discuss of Vishnu, and the trident of Shiva, were hurled by Vishvamitra at his antagonist, but the son of Brahma swallowed them up in his all-devouring mace.

Finally, to the intense consternation of all the gods, the warrior shot off the terrific weapon of Brahma (brahmastra): but this was equally ineffectual against the Brahmanical sage.

Vashishtha had now assumed a direful appearance: "Jets of fire mingled with smoke darted from the pores of his body; the Brahmanical mace blazed in his hand like a smokeless mundane conflagration, or a second sceptre of Yama." Being appeased, however by the munis, who proclaimed his superiority to his rival, the sage stayed his vengeance; and Vishvamitra exclaimed with a groan: "Shame on a Kshatriya's strength: the strength of a Brahman's might alone is strength: by the single Brahmanical mace all my weapons have been destroyed." No alternative now remains, to the humiliated monarch, but either to acquiesce in this helpless inferiority, or to work out his own elevation to the Brahmanical order. He embraces the latter alternative: "Having pondered well this defeat, I shall betake myself, with composed senses and mind, to strenuous austere fervour, which shall exalt me to the rank of a Brahman".

Intensely vexed and mortified, groaning and full of hatred against his enemy, he travelled with his queen to the south, and carried his resolution into effect; and we are first of all told that three sons Havishyanda, Madhusyanda, and Dridhanetra were born to him. At the end of a thousands years Brahma appeared, and announced that he had conquered the heaven of royal sages (rajarshis); and, in consequence of his austere fervour, he was recognised as having attained that rank. Vishvamitra, however, was ashamed, grieved, and incensed at the offer of so very inadequate a reward, and exclaimed; "I have practised intense austerity, and the gods and rishis regard me only as a rajarshi.

Austerities, it appears, are altogether fruitless". Notwithstanding this disappointment, he had ascended one grade, and forthwith recommenced his work of mortification. "At this point of time his austerities were interrupted by the following occurrences: King Trisanku, one of Ikshvaku's descendants, had conceived the design of celebrating a sacrifice by virtue of which he should ascend bodily to heaven. As Vashishtha, on being summoned, declared that the thing was impossible (asakyam), Trisanku travelled to the south, where the sage's hundred sons were engaged in austerities, and applied to them to do what their father had declined. Though he addressed them with the greatest reverence and humility, and added that "the Ikshvaku regarded their family-priests as their highest resource in difficulties, and that, after their father, he himself looked to them as his tutelary deities "he received from the haughty priests the following rebuke for his presumption: "Asakyam" "Fool, thou hast been refused by thy truth speaking preceptor.

How is it that, disregarding his authority, thou has resorted to another school (sakha). The family priest is the highest oracle of all the Ikshvakus; and the command of those veracious personages cannot be transgressed. Vashishtha, the divine rishi, has declared that 'the thing cannot be'; and how can we undertake thy sacrifice? Thou art foolish king; return to thy capital. The divine (Vashishtha) is competent to act as priest of the three worlds; how can we shew him disrespect?" Trisanku then gave them to understand that as his preceptor and "his preceptor's sons had declined compliance with his requests, he should think of some other expedient."

In consequence of his venturing to express this presumptuous intention, they condemned him by their imprecation to become a Chandala. As this curse soon took effect, and the unhappy king's form was changed into that of a degraded outcast, he resorted to Vishvamitra (who, as we have seen, was also dwelling at this period in the south), enlarging on his own virtues and piety, and bewailing his fate. Vishvamitra commiserated his condition, and promised to sacrifice on his behalf, and exalt him to heaven in the same Chandala-form to which he had been condemned by his preceptor's curse. "Heaven is now as good as in thy possession, since thou hast resorted to the son of Kusika".

He then directed that preparations should be made for the sacrifice, and that all the rishis, including the family of Vashishtha, should be invited to the ceremony. The disciples of Vishvamitra, who had conveyed his message, reported the result on their return in these words: "Having heard your message, all the Brahmans are assembling in all the countries, and have arrived, excepting Mahodaya (Vashishtha). Hear what dreadful words those hundred Vashishthas, their voices quivering with rage, have uttered: 'How can the gods and rishis consume the oblation at the sacrifice of that man, especially if he be a Chandala, for whom a Kshatriya is officiating priest? How can illustrious Brahmans ascend to heaven, after eating the food of a Chandala, and being entertained by Vishvamitra?"

These ruthless words all Vashishthas, together with Mahodaya, uttered, their eyes inflamed with anger. Vishvamitra, who was greatly incensed on receiving this message, by a curse doomed the sons of Vashishtha to be reduced to ashes, and reborn as degraded outcasts (mritapah) for seven hundred births, and Mahodaya to become a Nishada. Knowing that this curse had taken effect, Vishvamitra thereafter eulogizing Trisanku, proposed to the assembled rishis that the sacrifice should be celebrated. To this they assented, being actuated by fear of the terrible sage's wrath.

Vishvamitra himself officiated at the sacrifice as yajakas; and the other rishis as priests (ritvijah) with other functions) performed all the ceremonies. Vishvamitra next invited the gods to partake of the oblations: "When, however, the deities did not come to receive their portions, Vishvamitra became full of wrath, and raising aloft the sacrificial ladle, thus addressed Trisanku: 'Behold, O monarch, the power of austere fervour acquired by my own efforts. I myself, by my own energy, will conduct thee to heaven. Ascend to that celestial region which is so arduous to attain in an earthly body. I have surely earned some reward of my austerity' "Trisanku ascended instantly to heaven in the sight of munis. Indra, however, ordered him to be gone, as person who, having incurred the curse of his spiritual preceptors, was unfit for the abode of the celestials; and to fall down headlong to earth. He accordingly began to descend, invoking loudly, as he fell the help of his spiritual patron.

Vishvamitra, greatly incensed, called out to him to stop: "Then by the power of his divine knowledge and austere fervour created, like another Prajapati, other Seven Rishis (a constellation so called) in the southern part of the sky. Having proceeded to this quarter of the heavens, the renowned sage, in the midst of the rishis, formed another garland of stars, being overcome with fury. Exclaiming, 'I will create another Indra, or the world shall have no Indra at all,' he began, in his rage, to call gods also into being. The rishis, gods (Suras), and Ashuras now became seriously alarmed and said to Vishvamitra, in a conciliatory tone, that Trisanku, "as he had been cursed by his preceptors, should not be admitted bodily into heaven, until he had undergone some lustration".

The sage replied that he had given a promise to Trisanku, and appealed to the gods to permit his protege to remain bodily in heaven and the newly created stars to retain their places in perpetuity. The gods agreed that "these numerous stars should remain, but beyond the Sun's path, and that Trisanku, like an immortal, with his head downwards should shine among them, and be followed by them," adding "that his object would be thus attained, and his renown secured, and he would be like a dweller in heaven". Thus was this great dispute adjusted by a compromise, which Vishvamitra accepted.

This story of Trisanku, it will have been observed, differs materially from the one quoted above from the Harivarnsa; but brings out more distinctly the character of the conflict between Vashishtha and Vishvamitra. "When all the gods and rishis had departed at the conclusion of the sacrifice, Vishvamitra said to his attendant devotees; "This has been a great interruption (to our austerities) which has occurred in the southern region: we must proceed in another direction to continue our penances". He accordingly went to a forest in the west, and began his austerities anew. Here the narrative is again interrupted by the introduction of another story, that of king Ambarisha, king of Ayodhya, who was, according to the Ramayana, the twentyeighth in descent from Ikshvaku, and the twentysecond from Trisanku.

Vishvamitra is nevertheless represented as flourishing contemporaneously with both of these princes. The story relates that Ambarisha was engaged in performing a sacrifice, when Indra carried away the victim. The priest said that this ill-omened event had occurred owing to the king's bad administration; and would call for a great expiation, unless a human victim could be produced. After a long search the royal rishi (Ambarisha) came upon the Brahman-rishi Richika, a descendant of Bhrigu, and asked him to sell one of his sons for a victim, at the price of a hundred thousand cows. Richika answered that he would not sell his eldest son; and his wife added that she would not sell the youngest: "eldest sons," she observed, "being generally the favourites of their fathers, and youngest sons of their mothers". The second son, Sunassepa, then said that in that case he regarded himself as the one who was to be sold, and desired the king to remove him. The hundred thousand cows, with the millions of gold-pieces and heaps of jewels, were paid down, and Sunassepa carried away.

As they were passing through Puskara Sunassepa beheld his maternal uncle Vishvamitra who was engaged in austerities there with other rishis, threw himself into his arms, and implored his assistance, urging his orphan, friendless, and helpless state, as claims on the sage's benevolence. Vishvamitra soothed him; and pressed his own sons to offer themselves as victims in the room of Sunassepa. This proposition met with no favour from Madhushyanda and the other sons of the royal hermit, who answered with haughtiness and derision: "How is it that thou sacrifices thine own sons, and seeks to rescue those of others? We look upon this as wrong, and like the eating of one's own flesh". The sage was exceedingly wroth at this disregard of his injunction, and doomed his sons to be born in the most degraded classes, like Vasishtha's sons, and to eat dog's flesh, for a thousand years. He then said to Sunassepa: "When thou art bound with hallowed cords decked with a red garland, and anointed with ungents, and fastened to the sacrificial post of Vishnu, then address thyself to Agni, and sing these two divine verses (gathas), at the sacrifice of Ambarisha; then shall thou attain the fulfilment (of thy desire)".

Being furnished with the two gathas, Sunassepa proposed at once to king Ambarisha that they should set out for their destination. When bound at the stake to be immolated, dressed in a red garment, "he celebrated the two gods, Indra and his younger brother (Vishnu), with the excellent verses. The thousand-eyed (Indra) was pleased with the secret hymn, and bestowed long life on Sunassepa". King Ambarisha also received great benefits from this sacrifice. Vishvamitra meanwhile proceeded with his austerities, which he prolonged for a thousand years.

At the end of this time the gods came to allot his reward; and Brahma announced that he had attained the rank of a rishi, thus apparently advancing an additional step. Dissatisfied, as it would seem, with this, the sage commenced his task of penance anew. After a length of time he beheld the nymph

(Apsara) Menka, who had come to bathe in the lake of Pushkara. She flashed on his view, unequalled in her radiant beauty, like lightning in a cloud. He was smitten by her charms, invited her to be his companion in his hermitage, and for ten years remained a slave to her witchery, to the great prejudice of his austerities. At length he became ashamed of this ignoble subjection, and full of indignation at what he believed to be a device of the gods to disturb his devotion; and, dismissing the nymph with gentle accents, he departed for the northern mountains, where he practised severe austerities for a thousand years on the banks of the Kausiki river.

The gods became alarmed at the progress he was making, and decided that he should be dignified with the appellation of great rishi (maharshi); and Brahma, giving effect to the general opinion of the deities, announced that he had conferred that rank upon him. Joining his hands and bowing his head, Visvamitra replied that he should consider himself to have indeed completely subdued his senses, if the incomparable title of Brahman-rishi were conferred upon him. Brahma informed him in answer, that he had not yet acquired the power of perfectly controlling his senses; but should make further efforts with that view.

The sage then began to put himself through a yet more rigorous course of austerities, standing with his arms erect, without support, feeding on air, in summer exposed to five fires (*i.e.* one on each of four sides, and the sun overhead), in the rainy season remaining unsheltered from the wet, and in winter lying on a watery couch night and day.

This he continued for a thousand years. At last Indra and the other deities became greatly distressed at the idea of the merit he was storing up, and the power which he was thereby acquiring; and the chief of the celestials desired the nymph Rambha to go and bewitch him by her blandishments. She expressed great reluctance to expose herself to the wrath of the formidable muni, but obeyed the repeated injunction of Indra, who promised that he and Kandarpa (the god of love) should stand by her, and assumed her most attractive aspect with the view of overcoming the sage's impassability. He, however, suspected this design, and becoming greatly incensed, he dommed the nymph by a curse to be turned into stone and to continue in that state for a thousand years. The curse took effect, and Kandarpa and Indra slunk away. In this way, though he resisted the allurements of sensual love, he lost the whole fruit of his austerities by yielding to anger; and had to begin his work over again. He resolved to check his irascibility, to remain silent, not even to breathe for hundreds of years; to dry up his body; and to fast and stop his breath till he had obtained the coveted character of a Brahman. He then left the Himalaya and travelled to the east, where he underwent a dreadful exercise, unequalled in the whole history of austerities, maintaining silence, according to a vow, for a thousand years. At the end of this time he had attained to perfection, and although thwarted by many obstacles, he remained unmoved by anger.

On the expiration of this course of austerity, he prepared some food to eat; which Indra, coming in the form of a Brahman, begged that he would give him. Visvarnitra did so, and though he had none left for himself, and was obliged to remain fasting, he said nothing to the Brahman, on account of his vow of silence. As he continued to suspend his breath, smoke issued from his head, to the great consternation and distress of the three worlds.

The gods, rishis, etc., then addressed Brahma: "The great muni Vishvamitra has been allured and provoked in various ways, but still advances in his sanctity. If his wish is not conceded, he will destroy the three worlds by the force of his austerity. All the regions of the universe are confounded, no light anywhere shines; all the oceans are tossed, and the mountains crumble, the earth quakes, and the wind blows confusedly.

We cannot, O Brahma, guarantee that mankind shall not become atheistic..... Before the great and glorious sage of fiery form resolves to destroy (everything) let him be propitiated." The gods, headed by Brahma, then addressed Vishvamitra: "Hail Brahman rishi, we are gratified by thy austerities; O Kausika, thou hast, through their intesity, attained to Brahmanhood. I, O Brahman, associated with the Maruts, confer on thee long life.

May every blessing attend thee; depart wherever thou wilt.' The sage, delighted, made his obeisance to the gods, and said:

'If I have obtained Brahmanhood, and long life, then let the mystic monosyllable (omkara) and the sacrificial formula (vashatkara) and the Vedas recognise me in that capacity.

And let Vashishtha, the son of Brahma, the most eminent of those who are skilled in the Kshattra-veda, and the Brahma-veda (the knowledge of the Kshatriya and the Brahmanical disciplines), address me similarly.'..... Accordingly Vashishtha, being propitiated by the gods, became reconciled to Vishvamitra, and recognised his claim to all the prerogatives of a Brahman rishi..... Vishvamitra, too, having attained the Brahmanical rank, paid all honour to Vashishtha." The second event has reference to the slaughter of the Brahmins by the Kshatriyas. It is related in the Adiparva of the Mahabharata from which the following account is taken: There was a king named Kritvirya, by whose liberality the Bhrigus, learned in the Vedas, who officiated as his priests, had been greatly enriched with corn and money. After he had gone to heaven, his descendants were in want of money, and came to beg for a supply from the Bhrigus, of whose wealth they were aware. Some of the latter hid their money under ground, others bestowed it on Brahmans, being afraid of the Kshatriyas, while others again gave these last what they wanted. It happened, however, that a Kshatriya, while digging the ground, discovered some money buried in the house of a Bhrigu. The Kshatriyas then assembled and saw this treasure, and, being incensed, slew in consequence all the Bhrigus, whom they regarded with contempt, down to the children in the womb. The widows, however, fled to the Himalaya mountains. One of them concealed her unborn child in her thigh. The Kshatriyas, hearing of its existence from a Brahmani informant, sought to kill it; but it issued forth from its mother's thigh with lustre, and blinded the persecutors. After wandering about bewildered among the mountains for a time, they humbly supplicated the mother of the child for the restoration of their sight; but she referred them to her wonderful infant Aurva into whom the whole Veda, with its Veda Vyas had entered, as the person who (in requisition of the slaughter of his relatives) had robbed them of their eyesight, and who alone could restore it.

They accordingly had recourse to him, and their eyesight was restored. Aurva, however, meditated the destruction of all living creatures, in revenge for the slaughter of the Bhrigus, and entered on a course of austerities which alarmed both gods, ashuras, and men; but his progenitors (Pitris) themselves appeared, and sought to turn him from his purpose by saying that they had no desire to be revenged on the Kshatriyas: "It was not from weakness that the devout Bhrigus overlooked the massacre perpetrated by the murderous Kshatriyas. When we became distressed by old age, we ourselves desired to be slaughtered by them. The money which was buried by some one in a Bhrigu's house was placed there for the purpose of exciting hatred, by those who wished to provoke the Kshatriyas. For what had me, who were desiring heaven, to do with money?" They added that they hit upon this device because they did not wish to be guilty of suicide, and concluded by calling upon Aurva to restrain his wrath; and abstain from the sin he was meditating: "Destroy not the Kshatriyas, O son, nor the seven worlds.

Suppress thy kindled anger which nullifies the power of austere-fervour." Aurva, however, replies that he cannot allow his threat to remain unexecuted. His anger, unless wreaked upon some other object, will, he says, consume himself. And he argues on grounds of justice, expediency, and duty, against the clemency, which his progenitors recommend. He is, however, persuaded by the Pitris to throw the fire of his anger into the sea, where they say it will find exercise in assailing the watery element, and in this way his threat will be fulfilled." The third event has reference to the slaughter of the Kshatriyas by the Brahmins. This story is told in several places in the Mahabharata.

The magnificent and mighty Kartavirya, possessing a thousand arms, was lord of this whole world, living in Mahishmati. This Haihaya of unquestioned valour ruled over the whole sea-girt earth, with its oceans and continents". He obtained boons from the muni Dattatreya, a thousand arms whenever he should go into battle power to make the conquest of the whole earth, a disposition to rule it with justice and the promise of instruction from the virtuous in the event of his going astray.

"Then ascending his chariot glorious as the resplendent sun, he exclaimed in the intoxication of his prowess, 'Who is like me in fortitude, courage, fame, heroism, energy, and vigour?' At the end of this speech a bodiless voice in the sky addressed him: 'Thou knowest not, O fool, that a Brahman is better than a Kshatriya. It is with the help of the Brahman that the

Kshatriya rules his subjects.' Arjuna answers: 'If I am pleased, I can create, or, if displeased, annihilate, living beings; and no Brahman is superior to me in act, thought or word. The first proposition is that the Brahmans are superior; the second that the Kshatriyas are superior; both of these thou hast stated with their grounds, but there is a difference between them (in point of force). The Brahmans are dependent on the Kshatriyas and not the Kshatriyas are beaten up by the Brahmans, who wait upon them, and only make the Vedas a pretence.

Justice, the protection of the people, has its seat in the Kshatriyas. From them the Brahmans derived their livelihood; how then can the latter be superior? I always keep in subjection to myself those Brahmans, the chief of all beings, who subsist on alms, and who have a high opinion of them selves. For truth was spoken by that female the Gayatri in the sky. I shall subdue all those unruly Brahmans clad in hides. No one in the three worlds, god or man can hurl me from my royal authority; wherefore I am superior to any Brahman. Now shall I turn the world in which Brahmans have the upper hand into a place where Kshatriyas shall have the upper hand; for no one dares to encounter my force in battle.' Hearing this speech of Arjuna, the female roving in the night became alarmed. Then Vayu hovering in the air, said to Arjuna: 'Abandon this sinful disposition, and do obeisance to the Brahmans. If thou shalt do them wrong, thy kingdom shall be convulsed.

They will subdue thee: those powerful men will humble thee, and expel thee from thy country." The king asks him, 'Who art thou?' Vayu replies, 'I am Vayu, the messenger of the gods, and tell thee what is for thy benefit.' Arjuna rejoins, 'Oh, thou displayest today a great warmth of devotion to the Brahmans. But say that a Brahman is like (any other) earth-born creature." This king came into conflict with Parashuram the son of a Brahman sage Jamadagni. The history of this conflict is as follows: "There lived a king of Kanyakubja, called Gadhi, who had a daughter named Satyavati. The marriage of this princess to the rishi Richika, and the birth of Jamadagni, are then told in nearly the same way as above narrated. Jamadagni and Satyavati had five sons, the youngest of whom was the redoubtable Parashuram. By his father's command he kills his mother (who, by the indulgence of impure desire, had fallen from her previous sanctity), after the four elder sons had refused this matricidal offence, and had in consequence been deprived of reason by their father's curse. At Parashuram's desire, however, his mother is restored by his father to life, and his brothers to reason; and he himself is absolved from all the guilt of murder; and obtains the boon of invincibility and long life from his father. His history now begins to be connected with that of king Arjuna (or Kartavirya). The latter had come to Jamadagni's hermitage, and had been respectfully received by his wife; but he had requited this honour by carrying away by force the calf of the sage's sacrificial cow, and breaking down his lofty trees. On being informed of this violence, Parasurama was filled with indignation, attacked Arjuna, cut off his thousand arms, and slew him. Arjuna's sons, in return, slew the peaceful sage Jamadagni, in the absence of Parasurama."

"Rama, after performing, on his return, his father's funeral obsequies, vowed to destroy the whole Kshatriya race; and executed his threat by killing first Arjuna's sons and their followers. Twenty one times did he sweep away all the Kshatriyas from the earth, and formed five lakes of blood in Samantapanchaka; in which he satiated the manes of the Bhrigus, and beheld face to face (his grandfather), Richika, who addressed himself to Rama. The latter gratified Indra by offering to him a grand sacrifice, and gave the earth to the officiating priests. He bestowed also a golden altar, ten fathoms long and nine highs, on the mighty Kasyapa. This, by his permission, the Brahmans divided among themselves, deriving thence the name of Khandavavanas. Having given away the earth to Kasyapa, Parasurama himself dwells on the mountain Mahendra. Thus did enmity arise between him and Kshatriyas, and thus was the earth conquered by Rama of boundless might."

The Kshatriyas who were slain by Parashuram are described in the Dronaparvan of the Mahabharata as of various provinces, *viz.*, Kasmiras, Darads, Kuntis, Ksudrakas, Malavas, Angas, Vangas, Kalingas, Videhas, Tamraliptakas, Marttikavatas, Sivis and other Rajanyas. The means by which the Kshattriya race was restored is also told as part of this story of annihilation of the Kshatriyas by the Brahmins. It is said: "Having one and twenty times swept away all the Kshatriyas from the earth, the son of Jamadagni engaged in austerities on Mahendra the most excellent of mountains. After he had cleared the world of Kshatriyas, their widows came to the Brahmans, praying for offspring. The religious Brahmans, free from any impulse of lust, cohabited at the proper seasons with these women, who in consequence became pregnant, and brought forth-valiant Kshatriya boys and girls, to continue the Kshatriya stock. Thus was the Kshatriya race virtuously begotten by Brahmans on Kshatriya women, and became multiplied and long-lived. Thence there arose four castes inferior to the Brahmans."

3

Caste, Class and Power in Indian Political System

PARTY SYSTEM AND WOMEN'S REPRESENTATION

India is a bicameral parliamentary democracy, with a strong multiparty political system. The lower house is called the Lok Sabha (Peoples' Assembly) and has 545 members. The upper house is called the Rajya Sabha (State Assembly) with 250 members. In 1991, women constituted 5.2 per cent of the membership of the Lok Sabha and 9.8 per cent of the membership of the Rajya Sabha. This was lower than the preceding 1989 parliament. The election results in 1996 showed a further decline in women's representation, but in the 1999 election, 8.8 per cent of parliamentarians were women. This trend is worrying given the recent state-led initiatives to ensure women's representation in political institutions. One of the reasons for the low representation may be the strength of the party system itself, which can lead to the marginalization of issue-based politics, or to an expropriation of movements that are based on single issues. The women's movement in India has had to confront this issue. Indian political parties are, however, organizationally weak and dependent on local elites. This might be a second factor for the resistance to implementation of gender-sensitive political initiatives.

Women's Movement and the Issue of Representation

The demand for greater representation of women in political institutions in India was not taken up in a systematic way until the setting up of the Committee on the Status of Women in India (CSWI) which published its report in 1976. Before this the focus of the growing women's movement had been on improving women's socioeconomic position. The CSWI report suggested that women's representation in political institutions, especially at the grass-roots level, needed to be increased through a policy of reservation of seats for women. In 1988, the National Perspective Plan for Women suggested that a 30 per cent quota for women be introduced at all levels of elective bodies. Women's groups insisted that reservation be restricted to the panchayat (village council) level to encourage grass-roots participation in politics. The consensus around this demand resulted in the adoption of the 73rd and 74th amendments to the Indian Constitution in 1993.

In 1995, the question of quotas was raised again, but this time the focus was women in parliament. Initially, most political parties agreed to this proposition. But soon doubts surfaced. When the bill addressing this issue was introduced in the Eleventh Parliament in 1997, several parties and groups raised objections. The objections focused around two main issues: first, the issue of overlapping quotas for women in general and those for women of the lower castes; second, the issue of elitism. Most women's groups felt that the caste issue was a divisive one for women. Also, many felt uneasy about giving special privileges to elite women by ensuring seats for them in the parliament, while they had previously supported quotas for women at the grass-roots level of the panchayats. To date, the amendment has not been passed by parliament. However, the current government of the Hindu nationalist Bharatiya Janata Party (BJP) has committed itself to introducing another quota bill for women in parliament.

Profile of Women in the Indian Parliament

The 39 women representatives in the 1991-1996 Indian Parliament were mostly middle-class, professional women, with little or no links to the women's movement. A significant number of them accessed politics through their families, some through student and civil rights movements and some as a result of state initiatives aimed at increasing representation from the lower castes. The majority of women in the Indian

Parliament are elite women. While their public role challenges some stereotypes, their class position often allows them a far greater range of options than are available to poorer women.

Gender and Caste in Parliament

Caste has been an important feature of Indian public and political life. Most of the women MPs in the Tenth Parliament were members of the higher castes. For example, there were six women from the Brahmin caste. This represents a sizeable 17.14 per cent of the women MPs, while Brahmins comprise only 5.52 per cent of the population. However, it is important to guard against making an easy correlation between caste and political representation. For example, of the six women who are Brahmins, two are MPs from the Communist Party of India. In both cases the caste factor is less important than their privileged class backgrounds. Further, both were products of political movements, the nationalist struggle and the anti-emergency movement. The number of women who are able to avail of India's caste-based reservation system remains small. While 22 per cent of the parliamentary seats were reserved for the Scheduled Castes, women occupied only 4.1 per cent of the reserved seats. Two women MPs were from what are called the Scheduled Tribes. However, out of 39 women MPs in the Tenth Lok Sabha (representing seven per cent of the total), 14 per cent were from the Scheduled Castes. Two women MPs belonged to the "backward" castes and represented open constituencies. Caste, therefore, affects the profile, loyalties and work of representatives in the Indian Parliament.

Class, Social Position and Gender in Public Life

Out of the 39 women MPs in the 1991-1996 Lok Sabha, 32 had postgraduate qualifications; in the Rajya Sabha 14 out of the 17 women were graduates. The class position of these women is obviously more important to their educational levels than caste. Only one out of the seven lower caste women MPs was not a graduate and the one Scheduled Caste woman MP in the Rajya Sabha had postgraduate education. The levels of education are also reflected in the professional profiles of these women. Thirty per cent of women MPs in the Rajya Sabha for example were lawyers and 25 per cent in the Lok Sabha were either teachers or lecturers. The class from which most of the women MPs come is perhaps the most important factor in their successful inclusion into the political system.

Most of the women MPs (about 65 per cent) were between their late 30s and 60s and therefore did not have the responsibility of bringing up a young family. Given the almost universal marriage pattern that exists in India, the figure for unmarried MPs is extraordinarily high and indicates the social pressures on women who join public life. For those who are married, the pressures of public life are eased a bit by their class situation. Most MPs are able to afford paid help in the home. In many cases the joint family system, or at least strong family support, also helps. However, the constraints of family life continue to be real concerns even for privileged women.

Women have different strategies to cope with these constraints. If the family has accepted a woman's career in politics, she can negotiate with her family. This is more likely if the family is an elite political family with more than one member participating in politics. If the woman was already active in political life before she married, she can face tremendous pressures from her husband's family to conform to a traditional role that allows little scope for pursuing an active political career. A woman politician's options in this case are either to conform to the expectations of the family and retreat from public life, or to leave the family in pursuit of an uncertain future in party politics. In the latter case, the lack of family support and the stigma of divorce are a clear disadvantage for a woman in politics.

Class also mediates the influence of religion. With only one woman Muslim MP in the Rajya Sabha and one in the Lok Sabha, Muslim women are significantly under-represented. Dr. Najma Heptullah, who was also the Deputy Speaker of the Rajya Sabha, is from an elite class and educational background and enjoys support for her work from both her natal and marital family. Margaret Alva, a Christian, a former Minister of State and Founder Chair of the National Commission for Women of India, is from a similar background. In both cases the families were involved in the national movement, were influenced by liberal ideology and were highly educated. Thus, the majority of women in the Indian Parliament are elite women. While their public role challenges some stereotypes, their class position often allows them far greater range of options than are available to poorer women.

Accessing the System: Surprisingly, active participation in the women's movement has not been one of the entry routes into formal party politics for women MPs. "Male equivalence"-the assumption that women access political life with the support, backing and contacts of the family, in particular that of the husband-has been a dominant explanation for how women enter political life.

Kinship or More?: "Male equivalence" has been a dominant explanation for how women access political life. The assumption here is that women access political life with the support, backing and contacts of the family, in particular that of the husband. In the sample of 15 women surveyed, 1/3 of the women MPs, for example, have "family support" in the background. However, in a well-argued critique of this theory, Carol Wolkowitz points out that "male equivalence" is an inadequate conceptual framework. First, because it is the public sphere (e.g. state institutions, press and political discourse) that has to be negotiated if the family decision to put forward a woman in politics is to succeed, it is not a private, but a public matter. Second, in many cases the husbands do not support the candidature of the wife at all. It is the pressure of party political bosses that forces the issue in many cases. The centralized system of distribution of seats in mass political parties helps in this context. A party's concern with levels of representation of certain groups within its ranks and consequences for legitimacy of the party among the under-represented groups might be the motive for including women.

Social and Political Movements: Together with "kinship link" and state initiatives, an important factor impacting on women's access to political life seems to be social and political movements. These movements have created windows of opportunity and some women have been able to take advantage of these opportunities to access political life. For example, the national movement was an important mobilizer of women. Gandhi's contribution to bringing women into politics is well-documented; the left movement also mobilized women. Women's organizations were constituted under the umbrella and control of the party-the Mahila Congress and the All India Women's

Federation (CPI). However, none of the women interviewed in this survey had strong links with the women's wing of their party prior to their entry into parliamentary politics. The civil rights and anti-emergency movement led by Jaiprakash Narayana (JP) in 1975-1977 was an important political movement that brought students to the forefront of national politics. Many women, both on the right and on the left wing, joined this movement and continued on in politics.

Finally, in the context of current politics in India, fundamentalist and communal parties are mobilizing women. One of the most charismatic woman MPs is Uma Bharti, the product of the rise of Hindu militancy in Indian politics. She is the member of the Vishwa Hindu Parishad, a mobilizational wing of the BJP and a "preacher" of Hindu texts by profession. She was at the forefront of the movement that brought down the Babri Mosque in Ayodhya.

Political Leadership and Quotas

Quotas for women as a strategy for accessing the political arena has growing support among women MPs, despite the fact that very few have accessed the system through this route; most women are still firm believers in the meritocratic argument.

The influence of individual national leaders is also an important factor that militates against the "male equivalence" theory. While Indira Gandhi, for example, did little to promote women's representation in politics, Rajiv Gandhi accepted the principle of reservation of seats for women. He initiated measures that had a direct impact on the inclusion of women in politics, e.g., the 1993 provision for reservation of 33 per cent of elected seats on village panchayats for women. As we have mentioned, the ability to take advantage of such reservations is mediated by class, ethnicity and caste. However, the support of the state and state/political leaders can be important to women who want to access the political system. Quotas for women as a strategy for accessing the political arena has growing support among women MPs, despite the fact that very few have accessed the system through that route and are firm believers in the meritocratic argument. Most women MPs have supported the 81st Amendment, which would ensure a 33 per cent quota for women in parliament, even though party discipline has not allowed them to vote for this. This issue highlights the constraints that the party system poses for women politicians.

Gender and Public Power: What do Women MPs do?: Out of the 20 Congress women MPs in the 1991-1996 Lok Sabha, none was a Cabinet Minister; two were Ministers of State; and two were Deputy Ministers of State. In the Rajya Sabha, out of seven Congress women MPs, one is a Minister of State. The portfolios of these ministers included, human resource development, civil aviation and tourism, health and family welfare and personnel and public grievances. All these are generally regarded as "soft portfolios"; this does not, however, take away from the responsibility that these women ministers have. One Congress woman MP is the Deputy Chairperson of the Rajya Sabha. At the level of the party, one MP was on the disciplinary committee of the party and one was the President of the Mahila Congress. Among BJP women, the one Rajya Sabha member was the spokesperson on the economy and general political line of the party. Of the 10 members of the Lok Sabha, one was one of the vice-presidents of the party and two were on the National Executive Committee of their party. Women's representation in the parliament, while important on the grounds of social justice and legitimacy of the political system, does not easily translate into improved representation of women's various interests.

The system of institutional incentives and disincentives at the level of the party and parliament impact on the issues that women espouse in parliament. Most women MPs interviewed did not have women's issues high on their list of interests. Rather, they wanted to be on committees relating to economy, international relations and trade. As ambitious women these MPs want to be where power and influence converge.

The Accountability Question: One of the important issues for any discussion on gender and representation has to deal with the constituency that women represent. As there are no "women's only" constituencies, women MPs are not accountable to women as women. And yet, when issues regarding women are raised in the parliament, these women are expected to and do participate in the debates. Issues such as the welfare of women and violence against women are particularly important in uniting women MPs. These issues are discussed in the "ladies room" in the parliament. However, as all the MPs questioned made clear, they are "party women first"; the party whip is rarely flouted. Most women MPs interviewed did not have women's issues high on their list of interests. Rather, they wanted to be on the more influential committees relating to the economy, international relations and trade.

Some women MPs are also asked by the party leadership to get involved in the women's wing of the party. While the women MPs do not necessarily see this role as an enhancement of their status within the party, some have made a success of this role and as a result gained influence with the leadership of the party.

As "party women" with political ambitions, women MPs respond to the institutional incentives and disincentives that are placed on them. All these factors limit the potential of these women MPs for representing the interests of Indian women across a range of issues. As a result there seems to be little regular contact between women's groups and women MPs. The exception here is of course the women's wing of political parties that do liaise with women MPs. This does allow the possibility of women MPs becoming conduits between the party's leadership and its women members. They are also consulted from time to time by the party leadership on issues regarding the family and women's rights. But nonparty women's groups do not seem to approach women MPs.

Women's representation in the parliament, while important on the grounds of social justice and legitimacy of the political system, does not easily translate into improved representation of women's various interests. While we cannot assume that more women in public offices would mean a better deal for women in general, there are important reasons for demanding greater representation of women in political life. First is the intuitive one: the greater the number of women in public office, articulating interests and seen to be wielding power, the more the gender hierarchy in public life could become disrupted. Without sufficiently visible, if not proportionate, presence in the political system-"threshold representation"12-a group's ability to influence either policy-making, or indeed the political culture framing the representative system, is limited. This fact is confirmed by the various other contributions in this volume.

Further, the fact that these women are largely elite women might mean that the impact that they have on public consciousness might be disproportionately large in relation to their numbers. Second and more important, we could explore the strategies that women employ to access the public sphere in the context of a patriarchal sociopolitical system. These women have been successful in subverting the boundaries of gender and in operating in a very aggressive male-dominated sphere. Could other women learn from this example? The problem here is, of course, precisely that these women are an elite. The class from which most of these women come is perhaps the most important factor in their successful inclusion into the political system. We can, however, examine whether sociopolitical movements provide opportunities for women to use certain strategies that might be able to subvert the gender hierarchy in politics. Finally, we can explore the dynamics between institutional and grass-roots politics. As this study demonstrates, the "politicization of gender" in the Indian political system is due largely to the success of the women's movement.

There has been limited interaction between women representatives and the women's movement-one of the important areas of weakness behind the effectiveness of women MPs and the women's movement.

Women representatives have thus benefited from this success of the women's movement. However, there has been limited interaction between women representatives and the women's movement-one of the important areas of weakness behind both the effectiveness of women MPs as well as that of the women's movement. This is, perhaps, the issue that the women's movement needs to address as part of its expanding agenda in the 21st century.

CASTE POLITICS IN INDIA

Caste is one of the major factors in politics of India. Independent India has seen intense debates over reverse discrimination, caste-based quotas and reservations.

Before 1980s: Mahatma Gandhi, B. R. Ambedkar and Jawaharlal Nehru had radically different approaches to caste esp. over constitutional politics and the status of "untouchables". Till the mid-1970s, the politics of independent India was largely dominated by economic issues and questions of corruption. But since 1980s, caste has emerged as a major issue.

Mandal Commission: The Mandal Commission was established in 1979 by the Janata Party government under Prime Minister Morarji Desai with a mandate to "identify the socially or educationally backward". The Commission was set up to consider the question of seat reservations and quotas for people to redress caste discrimination, and used eleven social, economic, and educational indicators to determine "backwardness." In 1980, the commission's report affirmed the affirmative action practice under Indian law whereby members of lower castes (known as Other Backward Classes and Scheduled Castes and Tribes) were given exclusive access to a certain portion of government jobs and slots in public universities, and recommended changes to these quotas, increasing them by 27% to 49.5%. L R Naik, the only Dalit member in the Mandal Commission refused to sign the Mandal recommendations, as he feared that well-to-do OBCs would corner all the benefits of reservation.

A decade after the commission gave its report, V. P. Singh, the Prime Minister at the time, tried to implement its recommendations in 1989. The criticism was sharp and colleges across the country held massive protests against it. Many alleged that the politicians were trying to cash on caste-based reservations for purely pragmatic electoral purposes. Rajiv Goswami, student of Delhi University, threatened self-immolation in protest of the government's actions. His act further sparked a series of self-immolations by other college students and led to a formidable movement against job reservations for Backward Castes in India.

Votebank Politics: Many political parties in India have openly indulged in caste-based votebank politics.

In 1990s, many parties Bahujan Samaj Party (BSP), the Samajwadi Party and the Janata Dal started claiming that they are representing the backward castes. Many such parties, relying primarily on Backward Classes' support, often in alliance with Dalits and Muslims, rose to power in Indian states. At the same time, many Dalit leaders and intellectuals started realizing that the main Dalit oppressors were so-called Other Backward Classes, and formed their own parties, such as the Indian Justice Party.

The Congress (I) in Maharashtra long relied on OBCs' backing for its political success. Bharatiya Janata Party has also showcased its Dalit and OBC leaders to prove that it is not an upper-caste party. Bangaru Laxman, the former BJP president (2001-2002) was a former Dalit. Sanyasin Uma Bharati, former CM of Madhya Pradesh, who belongs to OBC caste, was a former BJP leader. In 2006 Arjun Singh cabinet minister for MHRD of the UPA government was accused of playing caste politics when he introduced reservations for OBCs in educational institutions all around. In Tamil Nadu, the Anti Hindu DMK party rose to power under the canard of "Brahmin oppression", resulting in reverse discrimination against the upper caste Brahmins. Many Brahmins have alleged that Tamil Brahmins (Iyers, Iyengars etc.) have left the state, due to a "hostile atmosphere" prevalent against upper castes in the region.

Criticism: Back in 1950s, B. R. Ambedkar had criticized the use of caste as a political plank. He anticipated the limitations of using caste as a political resource and instead, emphasized on eliminating the concept of caste from the society.

CASTE, RACE, POLITICS

The arguments in this paper are set out in two stages. I will first point out why caste should not be seen as another variant of race. If this position is sustained then it follows that casteism is not racism under a different name. In the second section I hope to demonstrate the political consequences, some quite damaging, if caste were to be equated with race.

For a long time anthropologists and sociologists felt that the 'caste-is-race' thesis was dead and buried. Obviously, it was not given a decent enough burial for it surfaced again in the context of the United Nations conference on racism held in Durban in August 2001. The heat and dust raised during the Durban conference necessitates a return to some of the points made much earlier in scholarly contributions on caste. Though, on occasion, the professional academic might get a sense of deja vu while going through this paper, the fact that the parallelisms between caste and race are still compelling enough for many political activists demonstrates that something was obviously missing in previous presentations. In my view, the best way to nail down the caste-is-race thesis is to logically show how this equation is politically misleading if not, in fact, dangerous. To do so it is ineluctable that the distinction between caste and race be made more fulsomely than before, keeping in mind all the while that this exercise has clear political implications.

Why is caste so often mistaken to be another kind of racism? There are two reasons for this. One is a misreading of Vedic texts inspired by the distinction made by early Indologists between fair Aryans and dark Dravidians. The other reason for equating caste with race comes about because there are some similarities between the ways blacks were treated in southern United States, or in apartheid Africa, and the treatment meted out to so-called 'untouchables' in caste Hindu society.

There is no doubt that people known as the Aryans came to India around 1,500 BC in successive waves and settled down in the Indo-Gangetic plains. But there is no unambiguous evidence to suggest that these in-migrating Aryans were physically of a different sort from those who were already living in this region. What is clear, however, is that the Aryans who came across the mountains brought in a different language that was quite distinct from the families of languages spoken by the people who were earlier inhabitants in the land mass which we now identify as India.

There also appears to be good reason to believe that Aryans met with some resistance from autochthonous peoples of this region. It is, however, far from clear whether Aryans overcame such opposition by superior military might, or by ideological warfare, or by hard-nosed diplomacy. The evidence seems to suggest a combination of all three.

Early European Indologists took a shine to the notion that fair Aryans conquered dark Dravidians in remote history probably because it justified such a re-enactment in colonial India. But what is more surprising is the alacrity with which some Indian intellectuals internalized this position and began to draw racial lines of distinction within Hindu society.

There is a well-worn sociological clichz which says that the dominated people often appropriate aesthetic standards of the superior community. This seems to have happened in India as well. Thus, those from Punjab and the northern regions proudly took on the mantle of being Aryans and distanced themselves from the darker people of the southern provinces of India as they considered them to be Dravidians. Even a staunch Hindu nationalist like Bankim Chandra felt a sense of pride in the belief that superior Aryan blood coursed through his veins.

Those from the South, not to be undone by all this, began demonizing Aryans and all those who claimed ancestry from them. This was how the Dravida Kazhagam and later Dravid Munnetra Kazhagam rationalized their demands for secession from the Indian union several decades ago. So the caste is race thesis played a politically divisive role during the years of our nationalist struggle against colonialism. If left unattended it will continue to be divisive, though 'racial' opponents may be arraigned differently at different times. But we are already jumping ahead of our presentation.

In terms of empirical detail a lot more is required than has been provided so far if the theory of the racial origin of caste is to be made convincing. The factual evidence given in favour of this point of view is exceedingly exiguous. In fact, the manner in which dark skin and fair skin have been read into Vedic texts is itself highly disputable. What is interpreted as 'fair skin' in the Vedas could easily mean, and most probably did mean, 'light', in which case it was not a matter of skin complexion but of knowledge. The Aryans then distinguished themselves from others not by their complexion, but by their belief that they were in possession of superior knowledge and wisdom. They were the carriers of light, and that is how they dispelled the darkness and ignorance that reigned during pre-Aryan times.

Further, there is only one passage in the Vedas that purportedly depicts the Dravidians as being 'nose-less and bull-lipped'. The Sanskritist, Hans Hock has convincingly demonstrated that this particular sentence in the Vedas has been translated and interpreted in a highly dubious fashion. The same word, viz., anas, can also mean a person of poor speech and not someone who is nose less.

If the Aryans indeed brought in a new language then it is only natural that they should emphasize proper speech and pronunciation (uccharan) to differentiate themselves from those others over whom they ruled, or with whom they had an uneasy relationship. The term bull-lipped can also have a variety of meanings. Remember, the bull is not really looked down upon in India as it is in many European metaphors. The bull in Indian tradition is not seen as dumb and obdurate but strong and determined. So the evidence from the Vedas is far from conclusive. Moreover, what is most striking is that this description of the autochthonous original inhabitants is to be found in only a single passage in the Vedas, and yet so much has been made of it.

It should also be noted in this connection that the term Varna in the Vedas need not necessarily mean skin colour. Varna can also refer to order. Therefore, if there were four Varnas, or two (as in the early Rig Veda), then it signified that the society was stratified along four orders, or two orders, as the case may be. Each order was supposed to have a colour pennant of its own as they represented different phases of the sun's journey around the earth.

The rising sun, the grandest of all, was red, and this was the colour given to the ruling Kshatriyas. Brahmans were signified by the colour white because that was supposed to be the colour of the sun at noon. Vaishyas were yellow because that is the colour the sun took in the East, and finally sudras were blue, for that was the hue of the setting sun. To extrapolate racial segregation from factual material of this order is indeed far-fetched. It will then have to be admitted that even the Vedas concede that Kshatriyas are superior to brahmans as they represent the rising sun. Further, from where does the colour yellow get any material substantiation? Why have yellow or red not received any attention from those who argue in favour of the racial origins of caste? Why are many of us committed to a two race theory and not a four race one? Quite clearly the thesis that caste originated from race is flawed as it is based on flimsy evidence.

The race argument takes a further beating when we study gene distribution and racial measurements along caste lines. Once again no clear pattern emerges between different castes on the basis of the distribution of heavy gamma chains and light kappa chains in their genetic make-up. It has also been pointed out in this context that the presence of African haplotype among some people of North India obviously means that the term

'African' is a misnomer. Much earlier in 1960, Majumdar and Rao conducted a statistical study of so-called race elements in Bengal and came to the interesting conclusion that there were overwhelming physical similarities between high and low castes within the same geographical region. But the story was different between different regions. Upper castes in one area differed a great degree from upper castes in a different geographical locale. The same held true between lower castes in different regions of the country (Majumdar and Rao 1960).

In an influential paper published in 1990 in Current Anthropology, an international team of scholars undertook anthropometric exercises and found no differences between different castes. They took three important measurements, viz., head length, head breadth, and bizygomatic breadth. After examining a wide range of material they came to the conclusion that all efforts 'at typological/"racial" classification should be abandoned' (Majumder, Shanker, et al.).

Interestingly enough the various smritis, like the Yagnavalkyasmriti and the Manusmriti strongly disapprove of marrying outside one's caste. Out of such cases of miscegenation, the smritis argue, that new and despicable castes are formed. Thus the chamars were born out of the union of a vaideha and a nishada. In the case of the lowliest of the low caste, the chandals, something much, much worse is said to have happened. A Brahman woman had sexual relations with a Shudra man and, not surprisingly, therefore, a monster in the shape of a chandal was born. Note, no matter how fanciful and spiteful such origin tales might be, nowhere is it said that the child of such unions is half a vaideha and half a nishada, or half a Brahman and half a Shudra. The miscegenes of such highly despised unions belonged to a different breed altogether, to a completely different caste. Mixed marriages, in such cases, do not result in mixed off-springs but in dangerous and impure outcastes.

This situation changes when we move from caste to race. Children born out of inter-racial unions, however, are socially recognized to carry the strains of both parents and are thus classified as hybrid, mulattos, octoroon, quadroons, and so on. In many racist societies, mulattos and mestizos have greater privileges and occupy a higher rank than other blacks. We will have occasion to return to this when we discuss the differences between the politics of caste and race.

It needs also to be mentioned that it was commonplace to have a black cook or wet nurse in white homes in racially segregated ante bellum southern United States. While blacks were despised they were not considered polluting. Imagine the horror that would be aroused in the home of a traditional privileged caste in India at the very suggestion of an untouchable cook in the kitchen. Thus, while racism at its height might consider blacks to be despicable, it did not regard them as polluting.

Additionally, in a racially segregated society one's sense of identity gets stronger as one moves from the particular to the more general level. In other words, it does not matter if the person is from Belgium, Germany or Holland, as long as the person is white. Any further sub-classification is not necessary and may indeed take away from the power of racial consciousness. Likewise, to be considered black it is not at all important, or relevant, to know whether the person is from Botswana or from Nigeria. If the person is black then that is enough regardless of where the person comes from.

Caste identity works in a reverse direction. Caste loyalties gain in commitment the more localized and particularized they get. It is not enough to be a Brahman but to be a Brahman of a certain endogamous jati, such as the kanyakubja Brahman or chitpavan Brahman or barendra Brahman. In many cases this may not be enough either, and further sub-divisions are necessary. The same holds true for Rajputs, jats and kayasthas, and indeed for all other caste clusters as well. This brings us to the crucial analytical difference between caste and race. Strata based on race are arranged along a continuum of colour. Whites occupy one end and blacks the other of this hierarchical ladder. The colours in between are positioned accordingly along this scale. This is why those who are one-eighth black are superior to those who are one-fourth black and so forth.

In Washington, light-skinned blacks set up an organization called the Bon-Ton Society in the 1930s. To be a member of this society was fairly prestigious for mulattos of various degrees, but they had to pass two qualification tests. Their skin colour had to be lighter than the standard brown paper bag, and when a comb was run through the prospective candidate's hair it was not supposed to meet with any resistance. In Nashville around the same time there existed the Blue Vein Society. This too was formed by light-skinned blacks, and they too wanted it to be quite an exclusive affair. The criterion in this case was that the fine blue criss-cross of veins on the applicant's wrist should be easily discernible.

In the Caribbean, in Latin America, and in the United States there are a range of terms to encompass those who are not black but not quite white either. Harry Hutchinson found eight terms in Brazil distinguishing different shades of black. Charles H. Parrish listed 145 different terms to denote fine shades of colour distinction in the United States. Malcolm X, the famous Black Muslim leader, confessed in his autobiography that he was favoured over his siblings by his mother because he was lighter skinned than them. Melville Herskovitz studied successful black couples in Harlem and found that as many as 56.5% black men married light-skinned women. The really successful black men like Quincy Jones, Justice Clarence Thomas, O.J. Simpson, James Earl Jones, and even the revered Frederick Douglass, all had white trophy wives.

The colour continuum is in many senses objective and demonstrable. There is little point in a black person claiming to be white if the person's skin colour and features do not help to back this claim. On the other hand there are a large number of light-skinned blacks who want to be taken for whites and often succeed in 'passing' off as one. This phenomenon of 'passing' has been widely noticed and commented upon in the United States. Journals such as Ebony, Jet and Essence, which have a predominantly black readership devote pages to help black women solve their 'hair problem'. Straightening one's hair and cosmetically changing the colour of one's eyes are quite well-known among black people in America. In other words, blacks accept white aesthetics and would like to be like them if it was possible. The only way this could happen is through inter-marriage.

This is probably why blacks in America have a low sense of self-esteem, nor have they much use for their heritage. This is also evident in the politics of Louis Farrakan. Farrakan urges blacks to reform themselves, to be caring parents, and to be hard working and diligent breadwinners. If blacks are in a bad way, Farrakan would argue, the prevailing black way of life is certainly not going to help them come out of their misery. The 'black is beautiful' phase is now more or less over in the United States. As many as 72% blacks prefer to be called blacks and not Afro-Americans.

Caste-based stratification displays very different characteristics. To begin with, it is impossible to construct a uniform hierarchy of caste based on the notion of purity and pollution. No caste would acquiesce to its placement among the so-called 'untouchables'. No caste would agree that members of other castes are made up of substances better than theirs. No caste would like its people to marry outside the community. No caste would like to merge its identity with any other caste. No caste accepts that it has originated from a shameful act of miscegenation. Any suggestion of being half-breed is dismissed haughtily across the board by all castes.

It is true that castes try to elevate their social status through a process known as Sanskritization. This term should be handled carefully for it can give rise to certain misinterpretations. It is not at all true that those castes that emulate the lifestyle of powerful Brahmans, or Kshatriyas, or Baniyas want to merge their identity with these castes. The viswakarma brahmans have Sanskritized much of their lifestyle but do not want to marry chitpavan or saraswat or any other kind of Brahman. They want to stay separate but would claim equality with, if not superiority over, other Brahmans and prosperous castes.

Sanskritization does not mean merger with other castes. On the contrary it is a show of defiance and an extraversion of what the caste always believed in an introverted fashion all along. In the past, members of such Sanskritizing castes dare not work out their ambitions, or express them in any way, for fear of being punished by wealthier and powerful castes. But now with democracy and an open market economy such displays of self-assertion are gaining prominence. In Rajasthan till a few decades ago, jats could not wear a turban, carry arms, or ride a horse. Jats today flout all these restrictions against them, but in the 1930s they encountered stiff resistance from Rajputs.

Now that jats lead a lifestyle similar to Rajputs it does not mean that jats want to merge with Rajputs, or 'pass' off as them.

While Sanskritization may involve some amount of emulation of the powerful caste of the region, it is not as if the upwardly mobile Sanskritizing caste is ready to jettison all its earlier beliefs and practices. Castes always differentiate themselves from other castes on multiple fronts: on how they get married, how they conduct their funerary ceremonies, the cuisines they cook and prefer, and even on the basis of gods that they each castes considers to be special to its members. Each caste has a clear idea of which caste it considers to be below it and which ones roughly equal. Endogamy, or marrying within one's jati, is a strict rule that all castes hold dear. It is not at all true that poorer castes are less punctilious in observing their caste norms. Each caste inspires its own variety of caste patriotism for which reason jati puranas, or origin tales, are such an important aspect of their cultural legacy and heritage. All dominated castes explain their subjugation, not on the basis of purity and pollution, but on the basis of lost wars, chicanery and deceit by kinsmen and fair weather friends. Sometimes the gods too are blamed for being fickle, inconstant and temperamental in bestowing their favours.

Unlike the distinctions used to demarcate racial separation, there is no objective indication of which category is to be placed where in the caste hierarchy. As no caste accepts that it is less pure than other castes, though it would easily grant that Brahmans are ritual specialists, there are probably as many hierarchies in practice as there are castes. In the past when the economy was controlled by rural oligarchs and petty potentates, the hierarchy on the ground was the one that was ordained by the superior caste of the region.

Other castes had to acquiesce to this or face brutal consequences. They dared not express their version of the 'true' hierarchy. With the growth in commercialization, urbanization and democracy, poorer castes are becoming bolder and now have the courage to openly express what they have always held dear but dared not manifest in any form in the past.

The distinguishing characteristic of the caste order is the discrete character of its constituent units that resist being forced into a single hierarchical frame. As these castes are discrete and semaphore their separation on multiple fronts, caste competition is built in at various levels. It is only by accepting the reality of multiple hierarchies that we can conceptually make room for the existence of caste politics. If one were to go by the traditional understanding of a single hierarchy of purity/pollution, with Brahmans at the top, then any evidence of caste conflict should have meant the dissolution of the caste order. Nor is it true that caste politics is a recent phenomenon. All through traditional and medieval India castes have fought and slaughtered each other to gain worldly preeminence. Once a caste is politically and economically powerful it can then live out its own believed-in hierarchy. This is as true of the Gujara Pratihara and Rajput kingdoms in medieval India, as it is of jat supremacy in Punjab several centuries later, and of Baniya ascendance in Rajasthan and Gujarat today.

The difference between traditional and modern displays of caste politics is not that there were no power struggles between communities in the past, but that the format for such competition and strife has now changed. Democracy and commerce have created new avenues that were not available to caste antagonists even in early colonial India. If one is to understand caste politics in its vivacity and depth it is necessary to appreciate that in the caste situation there are multiple nodes. Jats are against gujars, together they are against urban castes; kolis are against patidars; thevars oppress pallars or the devendrakula vellalas; the vanniyars torment adi dravidas, even as many of them may be against, or for, Brahmans in their local settings.

Caste alliances such as the KHAM (Kshatriya, Harijan and Muslim) and AJGAR (Ahir, Jat, Gujar and Rajput) are made and then cast aside. New alliances come into being with quite different caste friends and enemies. Even as castes may enter into political alliances, however ephemeral, they do not drop barriers of endogamy, though they may occasionally ease up on inter-dining restrictions.

Race politics gets its charge from the bipolar antagonism between blacks and whites. Half breeds, mestizos or quadroons are of no consequence. They have to align themselves with one side or the other. They cannot form an independent front of their own. In America till about fifty years ago the 'one drop rule' applied. This meant that if a person had as low as one-sixty fourth black blood, then the person was considered black. This is why many who would like to 'pass' as whites cannot easily pull it off. As the Black Panthers put it in America: 'You are either part of the problem or part of the solution.' There is no other alternative.

As castes operate on the basis of separation into discrete categories, which then fashions multiple hierarchies, the single hierarchy principle of race would be quite alien to it. Consequently, caste politics would be imbued with a logic quite different from what obtains in racist politics. It is because many members of India's literati did not quite appreciate this and, perhaps unconsciously, applied the race model to caste politics that they let the Mandal recommendations pass without too much opposition.

In the view of these pro-Mandalites, caste politics in India is really between powerful Brahmans and the oppressed rest, just as in race politics it is whites versus blacks. In fact, Brahmans do not always occupy the top spot in most hierarchies. And whenever Brahmans hold such a position it is because they have economic and political power to match. But this would still be a very small and atypical part of the entire caste and politics scenario. If caste politics is seen only in terms of superior Brahman versus the suffering rest then the atrocities that yadavas inflict on ex-untouchables, what thevars do to pallars, and what Rajputs did to the jats, would be unnoticed and brushed aside. This would impoverish and distort our understanding of caste politics in India and would allow for the intellectual acceptance of dangerous and retrograde policies such as those recommended by the Mandal Commission. The distinctions between the politics of caste and race can and should be made if one is interested in fighting casteism in a concrete and meaningful way. While a radical advocacy of some form of inverted racism may seem feasible to some in the United States, such a stance would make no sense in terms of caste politics in India. In caste politics there is casteism at multiple levels and inversions at one level would leave the rest quite untouched. This is why B.R. Ambedkar saw no future in politics of this sort. He anticipated the limitations of using caste as a perennial political resource and fought instead to extirpate this cultural blot from our society. As there are multiple castes in India, and as many of these castes also occupy, statistically at least, different positions in the economic structure, caste politics often passes off as democratic politics. I have heard it being said that in India we have caste democracy.

It is possible to overlook the inherent drawbacks of caste democracy as there are so many castes occupying different occupational and income positions in society. There is no caste that is dominant in numerical terms, and if the plain game of numbers were to apply then a semblance of democracy may well be arrived at. But at what cost? Caste would be a permanent feature of mobilization, dividing the country on the basis of birth and ascription without giving citizenship a chance to establish itself. Caste then becomes an immutable category.

The reality of caste is, however, very different. Not every Harijan is a leather worker, and not every Brahman is a pandit. There are more harijans employed as agricultural labourers than any other single caste group in Uttar Pradesh. Today many of them are also moving to cities and have jobs far removed from what their predecessors were forced to commit themselves to just a few generations back. When an equation is made between caste and race the suggestion often is that these caste categories are fixed and immutable. But many once upon a time low castes have become Kshatriyas, sudras have become elite pen pushers and, if the tales of doms and mochis are to be believed, then those who were once in positions of power have now fallen into really bad days. If the ignominies heaped on certain castes arise from the occupations they were forced to follow by tradition, then it can be safely said that such a state of affairs no longer holds everywhere with the same degree of consistency. It is very rarely that one can correlate caste and occupation in contemporary India.

Race politics accepts that blacks and whites are immutable categories. In this situation there are two options: inverted racism, or racial representation. In either case one has to work within the framework of race. Black Panthers advocated inverted racism and it did not work. A small minority cannot overturn a majority. What remains problematic, however, is that in inverted racism it is racism that is still triumphant, albeit of another kind. Race representation, the other alternative, accepts that races are here to stay as it is not possible to change the colour of one's skin. Hence, even when there is a question of fairness, the tendency among liberal democrats is to push for a policy that would ensure some kind of proportionate representation in the job market and in educational institutions. In the caste order, how a caste is perceived depends to a very significant extent on what occupation members of that caste follow.

In India it is possible and, indeed, feasible to move from one kind of job to another in one's lifetime, and with greater facility over two to three generations. Over 13% of Grade A services in the Government of India are today occupied by those whose predecessors were once considered untouchables. This percentage is bound to increase in the years to come. In that sense those who are descendents of so-called untouchables are no longer untouchables today. For them, at least, their caste position has changed significantly.

Caste is, therefore, not as immutable a category as race is. This is why the provisions for reservations in the Constitution could think in terms of extirpating caste altogether in the not too distant future. Reservations for scheduled castes and tribes in India were never envisaged in terms of either compensation or retribution, as is the case with affirmative action in America. In racism a person continues to be black no matter what position that person may occupy in terms of status and wealth. But history has shown that though caste mobility may be much more pronounced today, it was not unknown in ancient and medieval India. The reservation policy for scheduled castes is based on giving this latent dynamic a greater fillip by unearthing and releasing talents that were hitherto hidden in these communities. In this process it is not just that these historically disprivileged castes would improve their status, but that society as a whole would benefit from a wider pool of talent that would now be available to it. As the question is not of compensation but of a dynamic transformation of the caste order itself, the system of reservation eventually looks towards a state of affairs when it would make itself redundant.

In race the scenario is quite different. Once a black, always a black. This fixity cannot be transposed to caste politics, without doing a lot of damage to empirical reality. Once a chamar is not always a chamar, once a scavenger is not always a scavenger, and so forth. The vahivanca barots of Gujarat earlier called themselves Kshatriyas but now prefer to be known as Baniyas (Shah and Shroff 1975). Further, as we mentioned earlier, ex-untouchables have never ideologically acquiesced to their own degradation. This is why whenever they are able to improve their economic situation they successfully shed their earlier caste status and moved on.

Once we use the language of race to the caste situation the emphasis shifts from removing the scourge of caste from Indian society to making one's caste identity a fixed political resource. In which case, quite understandably, castes would tend to be viewed as permanent fixtures and caste identities as political assets. The task would then be not so much to eradicate castes but to give proportionate representation to different castes in educational institutions, in jobs, housing, and so on. This again closely resembles the Mandal formula. The current Raj Nath Singh government in Uttar Pradesh is making an even finer distinction among the Other Backward Castes (OBCs). According to his formulation from the 27% reserved seats for OBCs, 5% should go to yadavas, 9% to eight Most Backward Castes such as lodhs, kurmis and jats (sic), and the remaining 13% or so to the 70 other OBCs that remain (Bhambri 2001).

Mandalism encourages this game of numbers and proportionate representation. It does not employ reservations to uproot caste identities in public life, but rather to perpetuate it. Those scheduled caste activists who want to see caste as a form of race should then be prepared for this eventuality. Caste identities, in this case, would always be an important mainstay of public life in India, a self-defeating project for any self-respecting activist.

To sum up, if caste were race then caste politics would be salient only when Brahmans are pitted against the rest. Ahirs, kurmis, thevars, vanniyars, vokkaligas, Rajputs and jats, then do not matter as full bodied entities. If caste were race then the reality and brutality of yadavas marauding in the fields of Bihar would be a bloodless reality and would not have any symbolic energy at all. It has to be a Brahman plot, or a Brahman inspired one, nothing else is of any significance.

Those who have felt the full wrath of non-Brahman superior castes, either in the North or in the South, will never accept such a characterization of caste atrocities. Further, if caste were race, then one's caste identity is fixed, both internally and externally.

There is one similarity, however, between the fight against caste and the fight against race. Ultimately the battle has to be fought and won by those who are victims of such stratified social orders. It is only by empowering the scheduled castes and blacks that casteist and racist prejudices, respectively, are not given the scope to manifest themselves in practice in everyday relations. No amount of consciousness raising can do this job adequately. Only when those that have been hitherto disprivileged have the power and the wherewithal to fight back will sectarian prejudices be halted in their tracks.

MODERNITY AND CASTE POLITICS

Is there really a 'resurgence' of caste? Is it the case that the question of caste has 'suddenly' become important, implying thereby that till now such was not the case? Is the general perception that was aired in the media during the Mandal Commission controversy-that caste was simply resurrected by V. P. Singh—a correct perception? The answer is both 'yes' and 'no'. Yes, because there was a sense in which caste had been banished from public discourse and to that extent, its reappearance is a new phenomenon. No, because this unpseakability of caste in public discourse was limited to civil society, that is, to the domain of the secular modern institutions of society. It had not disappeared from society at large. In another realm, away from the watchful gaze of the modern elite, in the domain of what Partha Chatterjee calls political society, caste was a central category that framed the common ways of seeing and being in the world. The secret story of our modernity is of course, lodged in the first realm, that of civil society, for it is here that we see the mutated upper-caste modern Indian Self, in perpetual denial of caste (and to some extent, religion) in all his/her splendour. There is no denying that this modern 'Self' is really and genuinely modern; it wants to excise that shameful thing called caste from its memory. The upper-caste-turned-modern Self does not ever want to be reminded of this one aspect of his/her inheritance. It can deal with religion, for that is something that 'we all have' whether we are from the West or from the East. But caste is a blot that has affected the psyche of the mutated modern in ways that can be best expressed in Freudian terms: Caste is the suppressed/repressed, the 'unconscious' as it were, of the modern moral Self (the Superego?). Yet, caste is the hidden principle that gives it the access to all kinds of modern privileges precisely because it functions, as Deshpande suggests, as cultural/symbolic capital.

To the oppressed castes, especially the lowest among them-the Dalits or the untouchables-this repression of caste appears as a conspiracy of the Brahminical castes to deprive them of their voice. It appears to them to displace what is their bitter lived experience to another domain-that of class, for instance. The story that the Dalit wants to narrate can only be told with reference to the history of caste oppression. It is there that the secret of their exclusion and cultural mutilation lies. One of the critical elements of the recalcitrance of caste in contemporary Indian politics is, therefore, the search for a past, a cultural legacy, a history and a sense of Self. The oppressive structure of caste functioned, in relation to the Dalits in particular, through their almost complete exclusion from 'society', such as it was. Here I will not go into stories of daily humiliation and degradation that were and have been part of Dalit life, as these are by now fairly well articulated, documented and discussed. I will briefly refer to one aspect of their exclusion: their exclusion from any kind of access to learning-of whatever kind, including elementary skills of reading and writing. The implications of this forced exclusion are far greater than might appear at first glance. This took away from them any possibility of registering their own history, creating their myths and literature, in other words, deprived them of any sense of their own past. It was, therefore, only with the arrival of colonialism and the opening up of public spaces and institutions to the Dalits, if in a limited fashion (because of upper caste opposition) that these became accessible to them. It is, therefore, only in the early twentieth century, strictly speaking, that the Dalits really found their voice in the sense of being able to record their experience of oppression and talk about it publicly. And it was at this precise moment that the mutated upper-caste modern began to legislate a certain modern universalist language, decrying all attempts to talk of caste oppression as 'casteism', a sign of 'backward consciousness'.

There is, therefore, a peculiar ambivalence that marks Dalit politics and discourse today. On the one hand, it invests tremendous faith in modernity because it is really with its onset that possibilities of Dalit emancipation opened up in significant ways; on the other, it exhibits a strong aversion to the dominant, secular-nationalist discourse of modernity in India that it sees as irrevocably 'upper-caste' and the root of the re-institution of upper-caste power over modern institutions.

This ambivalence is visible not only in the field of cultural politics, as it were, but equally in the field of politics as such. In this field, the dynamic is somewhat different but what makes it possible for the Dalit political formations like the Bahujan Samaj Party (BSP), to chart out a course that radically questions the common sense of the secular modern, is its deep distrust of the old nationalist and secular elite. A case in point is the relationship of BSP and much of the Dalit intelligentsia, with the emerging secular political formations, especially in North India. It is well-known that here, in the state of Uttar Pradesh, the Bahujan Samaj Party, has repeatedly gone into an alliance with the main party of the Hindu Right, the Bharatiya Janata Party (BJP). It has formed governments along with the BJP, not only in 1993 and 1997 but also in 2002, in the year of the Gujarat massacres of the Muslims. In this period, when the BJP and its partner organisations of the Sangh family have bared their fascist fangs, leaving nobody in any doubt about their intentions, the BSP entered into an alliance and formed a government with the BJP in UP, and its top leaders even campaigned for it in Gujarat during the subsequent elections.

There are two levels of problems involved here; first, the actual relations between different caste groups and second, the logic of electoral politics. On the face of it, it only seems logical that in order to break upper-caste hegemony there should be a larger alliance of the OBCs and Dalits. This had seemed to be a promising line of action to many leaders of the late nineteenth and early twentieth century, like Jyotiba Phule of Maharashtra and Periyar EVR Ramasamy Naicker of what is today Tamil Nadu. Hence they had advocated the idea of a

'NonBrahmin' unity (Periyar) or a unity of the Shudraatishudras (Phule) in order to challenge the hegemony of the Brahminical elite. And up to a point this did have an impact in the first half of the twentieth century, in so far as the Brahminical stranglehold over society in these two regions was seriously challenged. Even Kanshi Ram, the chief architect of the present Dalit upsurge in North India, believed that his party should not simply be a Dalit party but a party of 'bahujans' (literally, majority); hence the name, Bahujan Samaj Party. The bahujan samaj, in Kanshi Ram's rendering was to be forged through a broad alliance of the Dalits, the backwards and the minorities, particularly the Muslims. Kanshi Ram also saw clearly that the Dalits alone, comprising not more than about 20 per cent of the electorate in any constituency, could not possibly challenge upper-caste dominance. Hence the aggressive slogan of the period of the rise of the Bahujan Samaj Party (BSP): 'Tilak, tarazu aur talwar/inko maro joote chaar (thrash the Brahmin, the Bania and the Rajput with shoes)'. That was the astute strategy that managed to make BSP an important force in its early days.

The problem, however, began after the first alliance of the Bahujan Samaj Party (BSP) and the Samajwadi Party led by Mulayam Singh Yadav, representing the backward castes, formed its government in UP in 1993. Within a short time it became apparent that as soon as the political pact that was forged between the parties moved towards the countryside, sharp conflicts between the two groups began playing themselves out. It was during the panchayat elections that the conflicts became really serious and many Dalit leaders and intellectuals realised that much of their present conflict in the villages was with the dominant backward castes who had consolidated their hold following the post-independence land reforms. In many states, it was these castes, comprising the erstwhile tenants, who had by now become landowners, who were their main oppressors. And they were not willing to change their attitude towards Dalits in everyday matters, even in the face of the political alliance at the state level. In many areas it was they who had been preventing the Dalits even from casting their votes.

More importantly, this was the period of the sharp rise of the Hindu Right. Very soon, this threat of the Sangh combine was to become the most important reference point for all future electoral-political alliances. The parties of the OBCs, represented by Mulayam Singh and Laloo Prashad Yadav in the two most important northern states of UP and Bihar, positioned themselves firmly against the BJP and the Sangh combine. It is worth remembering that in the period of the build-up to the demolition of the Babri Masjid, it was these two leaders who had displayed the most determined opposition to the BJP. Mulayam Singh, in fact, used the entire force of the state machinery during his chief ministership, to prevent the 'kar sevaks' from demolishing the structure of the masjid in November 1990. It was during this same period when L. K. Advani's Rath Yatra entered Bihar, in route to Ayodhya, that Laloo Yadav displayed exemplary courage in arresting Advani, leading to the eventual downfall of the V. P. Singh government of which Laloo was a part. It was in this context that the anti-communal secular front came into existence and the OBC parties naturally acquired a crucial position within it, given their stance. This is where the problems began as far as the BSP and the newly assertive Dalits were concerned. To throw their lot with the secular front unconditionally was to tie their own hands and throw themselves to the wolves. For the conflict with the OBCs in the countryside was now playing itself out in its most aggressive form. The choice was a difficult one and it was aggravated by another circumstance: the BJP, suave and sophisticated, with the self confidence of the classes who have traditionally wielded power, showed a preparedness to play second fiddle to the BSP in a joint government. This was something that the OBC parties and Mulayam Singh Yadav just could not do-they were novices in the game of power as were the Dalit groups. It is quite possible that if Mulayam had made the magnanimous gesture that the BJP repeatedly made, the BSP might still have opted to remain in the secular alliance.

This is where the deep distrust of the common sense of the secular-nationalist, so ingrained in Dalit politics, comes into play. For the BSP did not really have a moment's hesitation in joining forces with the BJP in forming a government and, in a sense, it was to open the floodgates for later realignments where parties like the Telegu Desam Party and the AIADMK and DMK were to enter into alliances with the BJP, in order to form the government at the Centre. Not only did it form governments with the BJP, the BSP in its last round of power-sharing even bent over backwards to help the BJP leaders in the Babri Masjid demolition case. The point here is not simply that the BSP went into a power-sharing alliance with the BJP, for there are enough precedents of many other parties and groups doing the same in different ways, at different times. Even the Left is not entirely free of that taint. In that sense, political opportunism has always been part and parcel of electoral politics in India. The point here is that it entered into this alliance with a clear argument against the dichotomised mode of politics where the 'communalism versus secularism' conflict was presented by the secular front as simple common sense, as if it subsumed all other conflicts and exhausted all other problems. This manner of privileging the 'secular versus communal' conflict in a manner of speaking, presented the secular front as non-negotiable: you had to enter the front only on the terms already set by it. There was no possibility of any negotiation here, especially with regard to the backward caste parties. It is here that despite its history of attempting to build an anti-upper-caste-Hindu alliance, and despite the fact that it sees its project as irreconcilable with the Hindutva project, the BSP displayed its refusal to take any proposition as given and non-negotiable. The sole concern that guided it was whether its move would help its own project of Dalit liberation. As mentioned earlier, on this occasion, the BJP displayed considerable sagacity by agreeing to play a subordinate role in the alliance.

After the recent collapse of the BSP-BJP alliance for the third time, reports coming in from UP nevertheless, indicate that insofar as the Dalit masses of UP are concerned, the experiments have been fruitful in restoring a sense of dignity among them. On the other hand, the upper caste supporters of the BJP, the Rajputs in particular, feel slighted by the way in which lower orders have taken to insubordination and challenged their position during these successive tenures of the alliance. The experiment, whatever its long-term implications for the secular front, reveals the immense complexity that marks the new era of 'caste politics' in India.

4

Social Class, Status and Culture

A social class system differs radically from those systems which we have so far considered. Social classes are *de facto* (not legally or religiously defined and santioned) groups; they are relatively open, not closed. Their basis is indisputably economic, but they are more than economic groups. They are characteristic groups of the industrial societies which have developed since the seventeenth– century. Considerable difficulties arise when the attempt is made to specify the number of social classes, or to define their membership precisely. However, most sociologists would probably agree in recognizing the existence of an upper class (comprising the owners of the major part of the economic resources of a society), a working class (chiefly the industrial wage-earners), and a middle class, or middle classes (a more amorphous group, often treated as a residual category, but including most while collar workers and most members of the liberal professions. In some societies the existence of a fourth class, the peasantry, would be recognized.

Disagreement among sociologists begins generally on the issues of the cohesiveness of the different classes, their role in society, and their future. These problems will be discussed later in considering some theories of social stratification. The different classes, and especially the middle class, have been extensively studied. On the working class, the classical work is G. Briefs, *The Proletariat,* which begins from a Marxist definition and expands it to differentiate more clearly between the working class and the white collar middle class. Subsequently, there was little research in this area until recent years when controversies about the effects of affluence upon the working class stimulated a number of studies, in France, Britain and the USA. General studies of the middle class include C. Wright Mills, *White Collar,* and David Lockwood, *The Blackcoated Worker* (London, 1958); but there have also been many accounts of specific groups within the middle classes, and especially of the liberal professions. In the nature of things it has been less easy to study the upper class, and sociological writing here extends from theoretical and historical studies of elites to studies based upon statistical information about property ownership, income, educational privilege, etc.

The picture of social stratification in industrial societies is compociated by the existence of *status groups* as well as social classes. Max Weber was the first to distinguish rigorously between the two, and the examine their interrelation. 'With some over-simplification one might thus say that "classes" are stratified according to their relation to the production and acquisition of goods; whereas "status groups' are stratified according the principles of their *consumption* of goods as represented by special "styles of life". The notion of social status has been analysed by a number of recent writers, especially by T.H. Marshall. In one essay on this subject Marshall examines the factors which produce differences in status, as well as different types of status—personal, positional, etc. More recently, ha has discussed the changes in social stratification in capitalist societies, and has argued that there has been a shift from class organization to status organization, or as the terms it, from multibonded but unidimensional groups to multidimensional and unibonded groups.

There have been many empirical studies of status groups, especially in terms of occupational differentiation; indeed recent investigions of social stratification and social mobility have been carried out largely in terms of occupational prestige scales. The emphasis, in much recent sociology, upon studies of social status and mobility, reflects a variety of influences. The needs of research have favoured the use of occupational scales, since these facilitate the design and implementation research projects. The predominance of American sociology has been an important influence; in the USA, which is unique among Western industrial societies in having no strong tradition of class organization or ideological conflict, sociologists have naturally been concerned with social stratification in those aspects which do characterize American society—status and mobility. But the singularity of American society has not always been recognized, so that some writers have simply confused status with class, while others have attempted to analyse social stratification in all societies in terms of the American model.

A third influence has been the actual changes in Western societies, resulting in a real abatement, though by no means a disappearance, of class differences and class conflicts. This process of change can only be clearly grasped, however, if the phenomena of class and status are first carefully distinguished and their interrelations then examined. I have discussed this problem briefly elsewhere, and have suggested that : 'Stratification by prestige affects the class system, as Marx conceived it, in two important ways: first, by interposing between the two major classes a range of status groups which bridge the gulf between the extreme positions in the class structure and secondly, by suggesting an entirely different conception of the social hierarchy as a whole, according to which it appears as a continuum of more or less clearly defined status positions, determined by a variety of factors and not simply by property ownership, which is incompatible with the formation of massive social classes and with the existence of a fundamental conflict between classes. The relations between status groups at different levels are relations of competition and emulation, not of conflict. With the growth in numbers of the middle classes, which form an increasing proportion of the whole population, this view of the social hierarchy as a continuum of prestige ranks (or statuses), without any sharp breaks, and thus without any clear lines of conflict between major social groups, has acquired a much greater influence upon social thought and its diffusion has served to check the growth of class consciousness.

The analysis of social stratification in the contemporary Western capitalist societies is complex and difficult. Equal, and perhaps greater, difficulties appear in the study of the second type of modern industrial society, represented by the USSR and some of the People's Democracies. An initial obstacle is the absence of data concerning income distribution, education opportunities, attitudes and group sentiments, in these societies, owing to the lack of any systematic sociological research. Moreover, the social realities are here obscured by the fury of ideological warfare. Orthodox Marxists claim that in the Soviet type countries social classes, or at least a hierarchical system of classes, have been abolished with the abolition of private ownership of the means of production. Critics point to the existence of great economic inequalities, educational privileges, the monopolization of political power by a small elite, and other characteristics which together amount to a system of social stratification. Much of the theoretical controversy turns upon the relationship between class structure and political power and will be discussed again below. From this controversy it emerges clearly that the classical notion of social class, in Marxist and non-Marxist writing, is closely connected with the notion of political power and especially with the concept of a 'ruling class'. This connection, however, may give rise to two different lines of thought: one, the Marxist which makes political power dependent upon economic power, and the other which treats the economy and the polity as interrelated systems each of which may at different times be either 'basis' or 'superstructure'.

These problems indicate the need for renewed study of social stratification. A useful starting point is to be found in the phenomena of political conflict. The social groups involved in such conflict may be either elites or class. In Pareto's sociology, at least in its major concern with the 'governing elite', the terms 'class' and 'elite' were practically synonymous; and it was in the context of his own theory of the 'circulation of elites' that Paareto regarded to notion of class conflict as the most important of Marx's contributions to sociology. More recently, sociologists have used the term 'elite' to refer to smaller and more cohesive groups, which may be more or less closely connected with social classes as traditionally conceived. Raymond Aron has provided on of the best studies of the relationship between elites and social classes. He formulates the problem as one of the relation between social differentiation and political hierarchy in modern societies, and sets out to show that the 'abolition of classes' (in the classical sense of abolishing private ownership of the means of production) will not resolve the problems of social differentiation, formation of elites, and inequalities of political power. There are, indeed, some advantages in the conflicts of elites and classes in capitalist societies, since these restrict the power of the rulers at any particular time.

We may summarize this beif study by saying that the nineteenth century concern with problems of social class was closely associated with a concern about democracy and political power, but that the answers provided did not distinguish clearly enough between the two sets of problems. In the twentieth century sociologists, guided by Max Weber, but more strongly influenced by events themselves, have attempted to study political power directly, and to examine the ways in which elite groups recruit support, conduct political struggles and attain or fail to attain power, as well as the conditions in which a power elite is either controlled or uncontrolled. For such studies, social class is only one element in the situation, though an important one. At the same time, the study of social differentiation and social stratification has been broadened to take account of the phenomena of social status and social mobility which are for the most part only indirectly related to political power, but which are important in other ways.

CLASS CULTURE

Social classes are economic or cultural arrangements of groups in society. Class is an essential object of analysis for sociologists, political scientists, economists, anthropologists and social historians. In the social sciences, social class is often discussed in terms of 'social stratification'. In the modern Western context, stratification typically comprises three layers: upper class, middle class, and lower class. Each class may be further subdivided into smaller classes (e.g. occupational).

The most basic class distinction is between the powerful and the powerless. Social classes with a great deal of power are usually viewed as "the elites" within their own societies. Various social and political theories propose that social classes with greater power attempt to cement their own ranking above the lower classes in the hierarchy to the detriment of the society overall. By contrast, conservatives and structural functionalists have presented class difference as intrinsic to the structure of any society and to that extent ineradicable. In Marxist theory, two basic class divisions owe to the fundamental economic structure of work and property: the proletariat and the bourgeoisie. The capitalists own the means of production, but this effectively includes the proletariat as they are only able to sell their own labour power. These inequalities are normalised and reproduced through cultural ideology. Max Weber critiqued historical materialism (or economic determinism), positing that stratification is not based purely on economic inequalities, but on other status and power differentials. Social class pertaining broadly to material wealth may be distinguished from status class based on honour, prestige, religious affiliation, and so on.

Theorists such as Ralf Dahrendorf have noted the tendency toward an enlarged middle class in modern Western societies, particularly in relation to the necessity of an educated work force in technological economies. Perspectives concerning globalization and neocolonialism, such as dependency theory, suggest this owes to the shift of low-level labourers to developing nations and the Third World. Developed nations have thereby become less directly active in primary industry (e.g. basic manufacturing, agriculture, forestry, mining, etc.) and increasingly involved with "virtual" goods and services. The national concept of "social class" has therefore become increasingly complex and confused.

CAUSES AND OUTCOMES OF SOCIAL CLASS

In so-called non-stratified societies or acephalous societies, there is no concept of social class, power, or hierarchy beyond temporary or limited social statuses. In such societies, every individual has a roughly equal social standing in most situations.

In class societies a person's class status is a type of group membership. Theorists disagree about the elements determining membership, but common features appear in many accounts. Among these are:

- Relationships of production, ownership and consumption
- A common legal status, including ceremonial, occupational and reproductive rights
- Family, kinship or tribal group structures or membership
- Acculturation, including education.

Classes often have a distinct lifestyle that emphasizes their class. The most powerful class in a society often uses markers such as costume, grooming, manners and language codes that mark insiders and outsiders; unique political rights such as honorary titles; and, concepts of social honour or face that are claimed to only be applicable to the in group. But each class has distinctive features, often becoming defining elements of personal identity and uniting factors in group behaviour. French sociologist Pierre Bourdieu suggests a notion of high and low classes with a distinction between bourgeois tastes and sensitivities and the working class tastes and sensitivities.

Race and other large-scale groupings can also influence class standing. The association of particular ethnic groups with class statuses are common in many societies. As a result of conquest or internal ethnic differentiation, a ruling class is often ethnically homogenous and particular races or ethnic groups in some societies are legally or customarily restricted to occupying particular class positions. Which ethnicities are considered as belonging to high or low classes varies from society to society. In modern societies strict legal links between ethnicity and class have been drawn, such as in apartheid, the Caste system in Africa, and in the position of the Burakumin in Japanese society.

A distinction often made is that of Ascribed status versus Achieved status. This deals with difference between obtained class identification, and whether social standing is determined at birth or earned over a lifetime. Achieved statuses are acquired based on merit, skills, abilities, and actions. Examples of achieved status include being a doctor or even being a criminal—the status then determines a set of behaviors and expectations for the individual.

CONSEQUENCES OF CLASS POSITION

Different consumption of social goods is the most visible consequence of class. In modern societies, it manifests as income inequality, though in subsistence societies it manifested as malnutrition and periodic starvation. Although class status is not a causal factor for income, there is consistent data that show those in higher classes have higher incomes than those in lower classes. This inequality still persists when controlling for occupation. The conditions at work vary greatly depending on class. Those in the upper-middle class and middle class enjoy greater freedoms in their occupations. They generally are more respected, enjoy more diversity, and are able to exhibit some authority. Those in lower classes tend to feel more alienated and have lower work satisfaction overall. The physical conditions of the workplace differ greatly between classes. While middle-class workers may "suffer alienating conditions" or "lack of job satisfaction", blue-collar workers suffer alienating, often routine, work with obvious physical health hazards, injury, and even death.

In the more social sphere, class has direct consequences on lifestyle. Lifestyle includes tastes, preferences, and a general style of living. These lifestyles could quite possibly affect educational attainment, and therefore status attainment. Class lifestyle also affects how children are raised. For example, a working-class person is more likely to raise their child to be working class and middle-class children are more likely to be raised to be middle-class. This perpetuates the idea of class for future generations.

Theoretical Models

Theoretical models of class seek to explain how class relationships come into being, and why particular class relationships exist across broadly similar societies.

Marxist

The Marxist conception of class involves a collective group of individuals that share similar economic and social relations relative to each other in society. A class is a group with intrinsic tendencies and interests that are different from, and may be opposed to the interests of other groups in society. For example, it is in the laborer's best interest to maximize wages and benefits and in the capitalist's best interest to maximize profit at the expense of such, leading to a contradiction within the capitalist system, even if the laborers and capitalists themselves are unaware of these class dichotomies.

For Marx, class involves two factors:

Objective Factors

A class shares a common relationship to the means of production. That is, all people in one class make their living in a common way in terms of ownership of the things that produce social goods. A class may own things, own land, own people, be owned, own nothing but their labour. A class will extract tax, produce agriculture, enslave and work others, be enslaved and work, or work for a wage.

Subjective Factors

The members will necessarily have some perception of their similarity and common interest. Marx termed this Class consciousness. Class consciousness is not simply an awareness of one's own class interest (for instance, the maximisation of shareholder value; or, the maximization of the wage with the minimization of the working day), class consciousness also embodies deeply shared views of how society should be organized legally, culturally, socially and politically.

The first criteria divides a society into the owners and non-owners of means of production. In capitalism, these are capitalist (bourgeoisie) and proletariat. Finer divisions can be made, however: the most important subgroup in capitalism being petite bourgeoisie (small bourgeoisie), people who possess their own means of production but utilize it primarily by working on it themselves rather than hiring others to work on it. They include self-employed artisans, small shopkeepers, and many professionals. Jon Elster has found mention in Marx of 15 classes from various historical periods.

A prerequisite for classes is existence of sufficient surplus product. Marxists explain the history of "civilized" societies in terms of a war of classes between those who control production and those who produce the goods or services in society. In the Marxist view of capitalism, this is a conflict between capitalists (bourgeoisie) and wage-workers (the proletariat). For Marxists, class antagonism is rooted in the situation that control over social production necessarily entails control over the class which produces goods—in capitalism this is the exploitation of workers by the bourgeoisie.

Marx himself argued that it was the goal of the proletariat itself to displace the capitalist system with socialism, changing the social relationships underpinning the class system and then developing into a future communist society in which: "..the free development of each is the condition for the free development of all." (Communist Manifesto) This would mark the beginning of a classless society in which human needs rather than profit would be motive for production. In a society with democratic control and production for use, there would be no class, no state and no need for money.

Vladimir Lenin has defined classes as "large groups of people differing from each other by the place they occupy in a historically determined system of social production, by their relation (in most cases fixed and formulated in law) to the means of production, by their role in the social organization of labour, and, consequently, by the dimensions of the share of social wealth of which they dispose and the mode of acquiring it."

Proletarianisation

The most important transformation of society for Marxists has been the massive and rapid growth of the proletariat the last two hundred and fifty years. Starting with agricultural and domestic textile labourers in England and Flanders, more and more occupations only provide a living through wages or salaries.

Private manufacturing, leading to self-employment, is no longer as viable as it was before the industrial revolution, because automation made manufacturing very cheap. Many people who once controlled their own labour-time were converted into proletarians through industrialization. Today groups which in the past subsisted on stipends or private wealth—like doctors, academics or lawyers—are now increasingly working as wage labourers. Marxists call this process proletarianization, and point to it as the major factor in the proletariat being the largest class in current societies in the rich countries of the "first world."

The increasing dissolution of the peasant-lord relationship, initially in the commercially active and industrializing countries, and then in the unindustrialized countries as well, has virtually eliminated the class of peasants. Poor rural labourers still exist, but their current relationship with production is predominantly as landless wage labourers or rural proletarians. The destruction of the peasantry, and its conversion into a rural proletariat, is largely a result of the general proletarianization of all work.

This process is today largely complete, although it was arguably incomplete in the 1960s and 1970s.

Dialectics, or Historical Materialism, in Marxist Class

Marx saw class categories as defined by continuing historical processes. Classes, in Marxism, are not static entities, but are regenerated daily through the productive process. Marxism views classes as human social relationships which change over time, with historical commonality created through shared productive processes. A 17th century farm labourer who worked for day wages shares a similar relationship to production as an average office worker of the 21st century. In this example, it is the shared structure of wage labour that makes both of these individuals "working class."

Objective and Subjective Factors in Class in Marxism

Marxism has a rather heavily defined dialectic between objective factors (i.e., material conditions, the social structure) and subjective factors (i.e. the conscious organization of class members). While most Marxism analyses people's class based on objective factors (class structure), major Marxist trends have made greater use of subjective factors in understanding the history of the working class. E.P. Thompson's *The Making of the English Working Class* is a definitive example of this "subjective" Marxist trend.

Thompson analyses the English working class as a group of people with shared material conditions coming to a positive self-consciousness of their social position. This feature of social class is commonly termed class consciousness in Marxism, a concept which became famous with Georg Lukács' *History and Class Consciousness* (1923). It is seen as the process of a "class in itself" moving in the direction of a "class for itself," a collective agent that changes history rather than simply being a victim of the historical process. In Lukács' words, the proletariat was the "subject-object of history", and the first class which could separate false consciousness (inherent to the bourgeois's consciousness), which reified economic laws as universal (whereas they are only a consequence of historic capitalism).

Max Weber

The seminal sociological interpretation of class was advanced by Max Weber. Weber formulated a three-component theory of stratification, with class, status and party (or politics) as subordinate to the ownership of the means of production, but for Weber how they interact is a contingent question and one that will vary from society to society. Weber is also known for his six "American Dream" Values which are: 1) Hard work, 2) Universalism, 3) Individualism, 4) Wealth, 5) Activism, and 6) Rationality.

ACADEMIC MODELS

Schools of sociology differ in how they conceptualize class. A distinction can be drawn between *analytical* concepts of social class, such as the Marxian and Weberian traditions, and the more *empirical* traditions such as socio-economic status approach, which notes the correlation of income, education and wealth with social outcomes without necessarily implying a particular theory of social structure. The Warnerian approach can be considered *empirical* in the sense that it is more descriptive than analytical.

The traditional 'pigeon-holing' mainstay of much of the advertising industry used to be that of social class. Recently, however, as affluence has become more widespread, the process has become much less clear. It is now argued that the new 'opinion leaders' come from within the same social class. The class groupings that were traditionally used by advertising agencies (for example in the NRS social grade schema were: AB - Managerial and professional, C1 -Supervisory and clerical, C2- Skilled manual, DE-Unskilled manual and unemployed.) have been reported to be of decreasing value in recent decades, especially in the distinction between clerical workers and manual workers in education and disposable income.

Whereas some four decades ago, when these groupings were first widely used, the numbers in each of the main categories (C, D and E) were reasonably well balanced, today the C group in total (although now usually split to give C1 and C2) forms such a large sector that it dominates the whole classification system and offers less in terms of usable concentration of marketing effort.

WILLIAM LLOYD WARNER

An early example of a stratum class model was developed by the sociologist William Lloyd Warner in his 1949 book, *Social Class in America*. For many decades, the Warnerian theory was dominant in U.S. sociological theory.

Based on social anthropology, Warner divided Americans into three classes (upper, middle, and lower), then further subdivided each of these into an "upper" and "lower" segment, with the following postulates:

- Upper upper class. "Old money." People who have been born into and raised with wealth; mostly consists of old "noble" or prestigious families (e.g., Earl of Shrewsbury, Vanderbilt, Rockefeller).
- Lower upper class. "New money." Individuals who have become rich within their own lifetimes (e.g., entrepreneurs, movie stars, top athletes, as well as some prominent professionals).
- Upper middle class. Professionals with a college education, and more often with postgraduate degrees like MBAs, Ph.D.s, MDs, JDs, MSs, etc. (e.g., doctors, engineers, dentists, lawyers, bankers, corporate executives, head teachers, university professors, scientists, pharmacists, airline pilots, ship captains, actuaries, high level civil servants, politicians, and military officers, architects, artists, writers, poets, and musicians).
- Lower middle class. Lower-paid white collar workers, but not manual labourers. Often hold Associates or Bachelor degrees. (e.g., police officers, fire fighters, primary and high school teachers, accountants, nurses, municipal office workers and low to mid-level civil servants, sales representatives, non-management office workers, clergy, technicians, small business owners).
- Upper lower class. Blue-collar workers and manual labourers. Also known as the "working class."
- Lower lower class. The homeless and permanently unemployed, as well as the "working poor."

To Warner, American social class was based more on attitudes than on the actual amount of money an individual made. For example, the richest people in America would belong to the "lower upper class" since many of them created their own fortunes; one can only be born into the highest class. Nonetheless, members of the wealthy upper-upper class tend to be more powerful, as a simple survey of U.S. presidents may demonstrate (i.e., the Roosevelts; Kennedys; Bushes).

Another observation: members of the upper lower class might make more money than members of the lower middle class (i.e., a well-salaried factory worker vs. a secretarial worker), but the class difference is based on the type of work they perform.

In his research findings, Warner observed that American social class was largely based on these shared attitudes. For example, he noted that the lower middle class tended to be the most conservative group of all, since very little separated them from the working class. The upper-middle class, while a relatively small section of the population, usually "set the standard" for proper American behavior, as reflected in the mass media.

Professionals with salaries and educational attainment higher than those found near the middle of the income strata (e.g. bottom rung professors, managerial office workers, architects) may also be considered as being true middle class.

Coleman and Rainwater

In 1978 sociologists Coleman and Rainwater conceived the "Metropolitan Class Structure" consisting of three social classes, each with a number sub-classes.

- Upper Americans
  - o Upper-upper class; (ca. 1%) Old money stemming from inherited wealth. Persons in this class typically have an "Ivy league college degree." Their household income in 1978 was over $500,000 ($1,673,215 in 2005 dollars)
  - o Lower-upper class; (ca. 1%) This is the "Success elite" consisting of "Top professionals [and] senior corporate executives." People in this class have degrees from "Good colleges." Their household income was also commonly in excess of $77,000 ($251,000 in 2005 dollars).*Nouveau riche* (French for "new rich"), or new money, refers to a person who

has acquired considerable wealth within his or her generation. This term is generally used to emphasize that the individual was previously part of a lower socioeconomic rank, and that such wealth has provided the means for the acquisition of goods or luxuries that were previously unobtainable.

- o Upper-middle class; (ca. 19%) Also called the "Professional and Managerial" class, it consists of "Middle professionals and managers" with a college and often graduate degrees. Household incomes for this group lay between $35,000 ($114,000 in 2005 dollars) and $60,000 ($183,000 in 2005 dollars)

- Middle Americans
  - o Middle class; (ca. 31%) This class consists of "Lower-level managers; small-business owners; lower-status professionals (accountants, teachers); sales and clerical" workers. Middle class persons had a high school and some college education. Their household incomes commonly ranged between $10,000 and $20,000 ($30,000 - $60,000 in 2005 dollars)
  - o Working class; (ca. 35%) This class consists of "Higher blue collar (craftsman, truck drivers); lowest-paid sales and clerical" workers. Younger individuals in 1978 who were members of this class had a high school education. Their household income lay in between $7,500 and $15,000 ($23,000 - $45,000 in 2005 dollars)
- Lower Americans (ca. 13%)
  - o Semipoor; This class had high school education and consisted of "labour and service" workers with household incomes ranging from $4,500 to $6,000 ($14,000 - $18,000 in 2005 dollars)
  - o The bottom; Those who are "Often unemployed" or rely on welfare payments.Household incomes of less than $4,500 ($14,000 in 2005 dollars)

Thompson & Hickey

In their 2005 sociology textbook, *Society in Focus*, sociologists William Thompson and Joseph Hickey present a five class model in which the middle class is divided into two sections and the term working class is applied to clerical and pink collar workers. Their class system goes as follows:

- Upper class, (ca. 1%-5%) individuals with considerable power over the nation's economic and political institutions. This group owns a disproportionate share of the nation's resources. The top 1% had incomes exceeding $250,000 with the top 5% having household incomes exceeding $140,000. This group features strong group solidarity and is largely constituted by the heirs to multi-generational fortunes. Prominent government officials, CEOs and successful entrepreneurs are among the upper class even if not of elite background.
- Upper middle class, (ca. 15%) white collar professionals with advanced post-secondary education such as physicians, professors, lawyers, corporate executives, and other management. While households commonly have six figure incomes in this group, the majority of income earners do not. Only 6% of persons had six figure incomes while 15% were upper middle class. While high educational attainment commonly serves as the staple mark of this group, entrepreneurs and business owners may also be upper middle class even if lacking advanced educational attainment.
- Lower middle class, (ca. 33%) individuals who worked their way through college and commonly have a Bachelor's degree or some college education. School teachers, sales-employees and lower to mid level supervisors rank among those in this particular group. Household income is generally in the range of $30,000 to $75,000. Workers in this group are mostly white collar but have less autonomy in their work than do upper middle class professionals. Members of this class often attempt to emulate those in the two higher classes and have recently become overly indebted by their desire to have a comfortable lifestyle.
- Working class, (ca. 30%) individuals who occupy both blue and white collar occupations. Pink collar workers in predominantly female clerical positions are common in this class. Job security tends to be low for this group

and unemployment as well as losing health insurance remain potent economic threats. Household incomes typically range from $16,000 to $30,000.

- Lower class, repeated cycles of unemployment, working multiple low-level part-time jobs are common among this group. Many families fall below the poverty line from time to time when employment opportunities are scarce.

Gilbert & Kahl

In *The American Class Structure, 6th edition* (Wadsworth 2002) as well the preceding 5th edition, Dennis Gilbert lays out an even more precise breakdown of American social classes. Dennis Gilbert stresses that "there is really no way to establish that a particular model is 'true' and another 'false.'" He furthermore states that his "model emphasizes *sources of income*" and that household income, being very dependent on the number of income earners, varies greatly within each social class. The class descriptions in quotes below are lifted from the 5th edition, pages 284 and 285.

- Capitalist class; (ca. 1%) *"Subdivided into nationals and locals, whose income is derived largely from return on assets."* However, the top 1.5% of households made $250,000 or more with only 146,000, 0.01% of households having incomes of $1,600,000 or more.
- Upper middle class; (ca. 14%) *"...college trained professionals and managers (a few of whom ascend to such heights of bureaucratic dominance or accumulated wealth that they become part of the capitalist class)."* Educational attainment is the main feature of this class. They enjoy great job autonomy and economic security. Household incomes vary greatly depending of the number of income earners." Considering US Census Bureau According to the 2005 Economic Survey, the top 15% of income earners made $62,500 or more with the top 15% of households having six figure incomes.
- Middle class; (ca. 30%) *"...members have significant skills and perform varied tasks at work, under loose supervision. They earn enough to afford a comfortable, mainstream lifestyle. Most wear white collars, but some wear blue."*

In 2005 incomes for this group would have ranged from $50,000 to $90,000 for households and $27,500 to $52,500 for individuals.

- Working class; (ca. 30%) *"People who are less skilled than members of the middle class and work at highly routinized, closely supervised manual and clerical jobs. Their work provides them with a relatively stable income sufficient to maintain a living standard just below the mainstream."* Incomes in 2005 would have ranged from $10,000 to $27,500 for individuals and $20,000 to $50,000 for households.
- Working poor; (ca. 13%) *"...people employed in low-skill jobs, often at marginal firms. The members of this class are typically labourers, service workers, or low-paid operators. Their incomes leave them well below mainstream living standards. Moreover, they cannot depend on steady employment."* In 2004 the bottom 12.2% of households made less than $12,500.
- Underclass (ca. 12%) *"...members have limited participation in the labour force and do not have wealth to fall back on. Many depend on government transfers."* The average household income is $12,000 a year, and the class makes up 12% of the population.

Chinese Model

In the Structure and Evolution of Chinese Social Stratification, sociologist Li Yi lays out a detailed model of Chinese social stratification after 1949. In China today, there is a peasant class, a working class (urban state worker and urban collective worker, urban non-state worker, and peasant worker), a capitalist class (about 15 million), and a class of cadre (about 40 million) and quasi-cadre (about 27 million).

IRANIAN MODEL

Farhad Nomani and Sohrab Behdad in their book *Class and Labour in Iran; Did the Revolution Matter?* (Syracuse University Press, 2006) define and quantify social classes in Iran and examine the changes in the configuration of social classes in the post-revolutionary Iran. Nomani and Behdad base their analysis (à la Erik Olin Wright) on three dimensions of (1) property ownership, (2) possession of scarce skills/credentials, and (3) organizational assets/authority. They recognize four distinct class categories and the ambiguous category of political functionaries of the state:

1. Capitalists: Owners of physical and financial means of economic activities, who employ workers. Capitalists are divided into modern and traditional occupational categories.
2. Petty bourgeoisie: Self-employed persons who do not hire any paid worker but may rely on unpaid family labour. They, too, consist of modern and traditional categories.
3. The middle class: Employees of the state or the private sector, in administrative-managerial and professional-technical positions. They exercise some authority and enjoy relative autonomy. In this category are those who are employed in economic activities and social services of the state. Those employed in the administrative or managerial position in the political apparatus of the state are not included here.
4. The working class: Workers who do not own the means of economic activity and do not benefit from the authority and autonomy of those in the middle class. They are employees of the state or the private sector, excluding those in the lower ranks of the political apparatus of the state.

Those employed in the political apparatus of the state, engaged in political administration, national defense and domestic surveillance, constitute the ambiguous class category of political functionaries. This category includes higher rank of state administrators, managers, and military and para-military officers, the rank file of the political apparatus, and the lower rank members of the coercive forces (including the military draftees).

The post 1979 revolutionary turmoil had notable impacts on the class reconfiguration of Iran. The disruption of the accumulation process in the first revolutionary decade (Khomeini period) retarded the capitalist relations of production (structural involution). This condition gave rise to deproletarianization of labour and peasantization of agriculture, and a general expansion in petty-commodity activities and a rise of the petty bourgeoisie, alongside a huge expansion of state activities. In the post-Khomeini period, the effort toward reconstitution of capitalist relations of production via an economic liberalization policy (deinvolutionary process) reversed some of the previous trends. In the second post-revolutionary period an increase in proletarianization of labour and de-peasantization of agriculture is observed. The first (involutionary [2]) period promoted traditional capitalists and the petty bourgeoisie, whereas in the second (deinvolutionary) period the number of modern capitalists, modern petty bourgeoisie, and the middle class (especially those employed by the private sector) increased significantly.

MIDDLE CLASS

In about the 1770s, when the term "social class" first entered the English lexicon, the concept of a "middle class" within that structure was also becoming important. The Industrial Revolution was allowing a much greater portion of the population to have time for the kind of education and cultural pursuits once restricted to the European feudal division of aristocracy, bourgeoisie, and peasantry which in that period would have included what later became the industrial proletarians of the towns and cities.

Today, concepts of social class assume three general categories: an upper class of proprietors and senior managers; a middle class of people who may not exert power over others, but may earn a significant proportion of their income through commerce, land ownership, or professional employment; and a lower class, who rely on wages for their livelihood.

It is important, however, to highlight the distinction of such a class model from that of the British concept of class in which the terms upper, middle and working-class have different definitions. The chief difference relates to the association of inherited wealth and landed property as a defining characteristic of the upper class. This distinguishes its members from those of the middle class whose membership is more fluid and more reliant upon employment status and its income. This is a broad generalization as there are classes within the middle class, such as the upper middle class whose interest in culture, and whose manners and mores distinguish them from other ranks in the middle strata, but is nonetheless a useful marker by which to distinguish the British concept of class from that of the new world.

In the United States, the term "middle class" is applied very broadly and includes people who would elsewhere be considered working class. As the vast majority of Americans identify themselves as being middle class, there are multiple theories as to what constitutes the American middle class. The term has been used to describe people from all walks of life, from janitors to attorneys. The definition of middle class is also relevant to the perspective of the individual. Due to the high standard of living in wealthy countries such as the U.S., the term middle class is also relevant to the standard of living of the majority of people in the world.

From this perspective, the term middle class becomes more inclusive. As a result, the US middle class is often sub-divided into two or three groups. While one set of theories claim that the middle class is composed of those in the middle of the social strata, other theories maintain that professionals and managers who have a college degree make up most of the middle class. In 2005 roughly 35% of Americans worked in the professional/ professional support or managerial field and 27% had a college degree. Sociologists such as Dennis Gilbert or Joseph J. Hickey argue that the middle class is divided into two sub-groups. The upper middle class consists of white collar professionals with advanced educations and constitutes roughly 15% of the population. In 2005 the top 15% of income earners (age 25+) had incomes exceeding $62,500. The lower middle class (or middle-middle class for those who divide the middle class into three segments) consists of other mostly white collar employees with less autonomy in their work, lower educational attainment, lower personal income and less prestige than those of the upper middle class.

Sociologists such as Gilbert, Hickey, James Henslin, and William Thompson have brought forth class models in which the middle class is divided into two sections which combine to represent 47% to 49% of the population. Economist Michael Zweig defines class as power relationships among the members of a society, rather than as a lifestyle or by income. Zweig says that the middle class is only about 34% of the U.S. population, typically employed as managers, supervisors, small business owners and other professional people.

CLASS STRUCTURE IN VARIOUS SOCIETIES

Although class can be discerned in any society, some cultures have published specific guidelines to rank. In some cases, the ideologies presented in these rankings may not concur with the mainstream power dialectic of social class as it is understood in modern English use.

PRE-CAPITALIST CLASS STRUCTURES

Ancient Rome

Social class in ancient Rome played a major role in the lives of Romans. Ancient Roman society was hierarchical. Free-born adult male Roman citizens were divided into several classes, both by ancestry and by property. There were also several classes of non-citizens with different legal rights, along with married women, children, and slaves, who had no rights, and could be legally killed, ejected, or sold by the head of their household.

Renaissance Europe

The Mantegna Tarocchi, sets of cards made as an educational aid in Ferrara in the late 15th century, used the following hierarchy for the "Conditions of Man", largely ignoring the rural population:

- Beggar
- Servant (Famiglio)
- Craftsman (Artigiano)
- Merchant (Mercante) - presumably living mostly off income as a landlord
- Gentleman (gentiluomo)
- Knight (cavaliere)
- Doge (doge)- i.e. a local ruler
- King (Re)
- Emperor (Imperatore)
- Pope (Papa).

AZTEC

Aztec society traditionally was divided into classes. The highest class were the *pîpiltin* or nobility. Originally this status was not hereditary, although the sons of *pillis* had access to better resources and education, so it was easier for them to become *pillis*. Later the class system took on hereditary aspects. The second class were the *mâcehualtin* (people), originally peasants. Eduardo Noguera estimates that in later stages only 20% of the population was dedicated to agriculture and food production. The other 80% of society were warriors, artisans and traders.

Slaves or *tlacotin* also constituted an important class. Aztecs could become slaves because of debts, as a criminal punishment or as war captives. A slave could have possessions and even own other slaves. Traveling merchants called *pochtecah* were a small, but important class as they not only facilitated commerce, but also communicated vital information across the empire and beyond its borders. They were often employed as spies.

Chinese

Confucian doctrine later minimized the importance of the nobles (except the emperor), abolished great men and scholars as noble classes, and further divided commoner workers based on the perceived usefulness of their work. Scholars (now not exclusively nobles) ranked the highest because the opportunity to conceive clear ideas in a state of leisure would lead them to wise laws (an idea that has much in common with Plato's ideal of a philosopher king). The scholars were mainly from the gentry, who owned land, and may be educated and wealthy but had no aristocratic titles. Under them were the farmers, who produced necessary food, and the artisans who produced useful objects. Merchants ranked at the bottom because they did not actually produce anything, while soldiers were sometimes ranked even lower because of their perceived expendability. The Confucian model is notably different from the modern European view of social class, since merchants could attain great wealth without reaching the social status accorded to a poor farmer. In practice, a rich merchant might purchase land to reach farmer status, or even buy a good education for his heirs in the hopes that they would attain scholar status and go into the imperial civil service. The Chinese model was widely disseminated throughout east Asia.

Pre-revolutionary French

France was an monarchy with a king and other princes at the top of the class structure. The French States-General, established in 1302 was an assembly whose members were ranked according to hereditary class. The First Estate was the clergy, all Roman Catholic, and by this time with the bishops and higher roles dominated by sons of the nobility.

The Second Estate consisted of lay members of the nobility, who constituted approximately two percent of the total population. The Third Estate consisted, technically, of everyone else, but was represented by representatives elected by a complicated system, in practice dominated by the bourgeois lawyers who held offices in the various regional Parlements. The peasantry had no official status in this system.

This may be contrasted with the ideologically high status of farmers in Confucian China. The rigidity of the French hereditary system has been suggested as a major cause of the French Revolution.

INCA

The society of the Inca Empire was centered in what is now Peru, from 1438 BC to 1533 AD. Over that period, the Inca used conquest and peaceful assimilation to incorporate in their empire a large portion of western South America, centered on the Andean mountain ranges. The Inca empire proved short-lived: by AD 1533, Atahualpa, the last Inca emperor, called Sapa Inca, was killed on the orders of the conquistador Francisco Pizarro, marking the beginning of Spanish rule.

Population

We don't know the exact number of people inhabiting Tawantinsuyu at its peak. There are estimates ranging from as few as 4 million people to more than 37 million. The reason for these various estimates is that in spite of the fact that the Inca kept excellent census records using their quipu, knowledge of how to read them has been lost and almost all of them had been destroyed by the Spaniards in the course of their conquest.

Social Structure

The most powerful figure in the empire was the Sapa Inca ('the unique Inca'), who was the Inca king, and the *coya*, who was the queen. When a new ruler was chosen, his subjects would build his family a new royal dwelling. The former royal dwelling would remain the dwelling of the former Inca's family. Only descendants of the original Inca tribe ever ascended to the level of Sapa Inca. Most young members of the Inca's family attended Yachayhuasis (houses of wisdom) to obtain their education.

Part of the reason the Inca empire expanded so much over a short period of time is because of a unique belief. This belief states that a Sapa Inca continues to rule over his lands, even after he has died. Any one ruler only becomes rich and powerful if he owns his lands. This means that in order to obtain lands that were his alone, each new ruler must conquer more peoples and spread his territory further. Hence, with each new emperor, the empire expands.

The Tahuantinsuyu was a federalist system which consisted of a central government with the Inca at its head and four provinces: Chinchaysuyu (NW), Antisuyu (NE), Qontisuyu (SW), and Qollasuyu (SE). The four corners of these provinces met at the center, Cuzco. Each province had a governor who oversaw local officials, who in turn supervised agriculturally-productive river valleys, cities and mines. There were separate chains of command for both the military and religious institutions, which created a system of partial checks and balances on power. The local officials were responsible for settling disputes and keeping track of each family's contribution to the mita (mandatory public service).

Childhood

Inca childhood was harsh by today's standards. When a child was born, the Inca would wash the baby in cold water and wrap it in a quilt. Later, the baby was put in a pit in the ground as a simple playground. By around age one, the baby could expect to receive very severe discipline.

At age fourteen, boys earned a loincloth in a ceremony to mark their manhood. Boys from noble families were subjected to many different procedures of endurance and knowledge.

After the test, they received earplugs and a weapon, the colour of which represented rank in society.

Women

Women were an essential part of Inca society. Their principal role in society was to care for their children, cook, weave, make *chicha* beer and work at the fields; however, they had many other household duties to make their lives after marriage very strenuous.

Marriage

Incan women were typically married at the age of sixteen. In Inca society, due to economic regulations, men of lower rank could only have one wife. The aristocracy, starting with the curaca, were allowed to engage in polygamy. Trial marriages were typical within Inca culture. In this type of marriage, the man and woman would agree to try out being married to one another for a few years. At the end of this time, the woman could go home to her parents if she wished, and her husband could also send her home if he did not think it would work out. However, once the marriage was made final, they could only divorce if the woman was childless.

Women would almost always marry men in the same social class as them. However, while it was very rare for them to marry a man with a higher social ranking, it was still possible for some young women. The only way for a young woman to alter her social ranking would be if a man of higher ranking took notice of her. In the Inca society, a wedding was not a joyous celebration. Instead, it was looked at more as a business-like agreement. Therefore, for the Inca, marriage was an economic agreement between two families. Once a woman was married, she was expected to collect food and cook, watch over the animals and the children. A woman's household obligations would not change after she became pregnant. When she did find out she was pregnant she prayed and made offerings to an Inca god, Kanopa.

Arts

The Inca were a conquering society, and their expansionist assimilation of other cultures is evident in their artistic style. The artistic style of the Inca utilized the vocabulary of many regions and cultures, but incorporated these themes into a standardized imperial style that could easily be replicated and spread throughout the empire. The simple abstract geometric forms and highly stylized animal representation in ceramics, wood carvings, textiles and metalwork were all part of the Inca culture. The motifs were not as revivalist as previous empires. No motifs of other societies were directly used with the exception of Huari and Tiwanaku arts.

Architecture

Architecture was by far the most important of the Inca arts, with pottery and textiles reflecting motifs that were at their height in architecture. The stone temples constructed by the Inca used a mortarless construction process first used on a large scale by the Tiwanaku. The Inca imported the stoneworkers of the Tiwanaku region to Cusco when they conquered the lands south of Lake Titicaca. The rocks used in construction were sculpted to fit together exactly by repeatedly lowering a rock onto another and carving away any sections on the lower rock where the dust was compressed. The rocks fit together so well that a knife blade could not be slipped between them. Their forts were made of huge stone so perfectly cut that no tar or plaster was needed. The tight fit and the concavity on the lower rocks made them extraordinarily stable in the frequent earthquakes that strike the area. The Inca used straight walls except on important religious sites and constructed whole towns at once.

The Inca also sculpted the natural surroundings themselves. One could easily think that a rock along an Inca trail is completely natural, except if one sees it at the right time of year when the sun casts a shadow, betraying its synthetic form. The Inca rope bridges were also used to transport messages and materials by Chasqui running messengers. The Inca also adopted the terraced agriculture that the previous Huari civilization had popularized. But they did not use the terraces solely for food production. At the Inca *tambo*, or inn, at Ollantaytambo there is evidence that the terraces were planted with flowers. The terraces of Moray are just one example of Incan terracing. It is possible that they were used to develop new strains of crops as large temperature differentials between the top and bottom terraces have not been observed, or they may have been purely decorative.

The Inca provincial thrones were often carved into natural outcroppings, and there were over 360 natural springs in the areas surrounding Cusco, such as the one at Tambo Machay. At Tambo Machay the natural rock was sculpted and stonework was added, creating alcoves and directing the water into fountains. These pseudo-natural carvings functioned to show both the Incas' respect for nature and their command over it.

Shipbuilding

For fishing, trade, construction, transport and military purposes, the Inca built seagoing vessels called balsas by weaving together totora reeds. The largest of these vessels were 20 to 30 meters long, making them comparable in length to Spanish Caravels. This method of constructing ships from woven reeds is an ancient Peruvian tradition which long predates the Inca. There are depictions of such vessels in Moche pottery dating back to 100 A.D.

Clothing

Inca officials wore stylized tunics that indicated their status. It contains an amalgamation of motifs used in the tunics of particular officeholders. For instance, the black and white checkerboard pattern topped with a red triangle is believed to have been worn by soldiers of the Inca army. Some of the motifs make reference to earlier cultures, such as the stepped diamonds of the Huari and the three step stairstep motif of the Moche.

Cloth was divided into three classes. *Awaska* was used for household use, having an approximate thread count of about 120 threads per inch, and usually made from llama wool. Finer cloth, *qunpi*, was divided into two classes: The first, woven by male *qunpikamayuq* (keepers of fine cloth) from alpaca wool, was collected as tribute from throughout the country and was used for trade, to adorn rulers and to be given as gifts to political allies and subjects to cement loyalty. The other class of *qunpi* ranked highest. It was woven in the Acllawasi (acllahuasi) by "aclla" (female virgins of the sun god temple) from vicuña wool and used solely for royal and religious use. These had thread counts of 600 or more per inch, unsurpassed anywhere in the world, until the Industrial Revolution of the 19th century. Aside from the tunic, a person of importance wore a *llawt'u*, a series of cords wrapped around the head. To establish his importance, the Inca Atahualpa commissioned a *llawt'u* woven from vampire bat hair. The leader of each ayllu, or extended family, had its own headdress.

In conquered regions, traditional clothing continued to be worn, but the finest weavers, such as those of Chan Chan, were transferred to Cusco and kept there to weave *qunpi*. (The Chimú had previously transferred these same weavers to Chan Chan from Sican.)

The Incan government controlled all clothing of their society. One would receive two outfits of clothing, one formal and one casual pair, and they would then proceed to wear those same outfits until they could literally be worn no longer. Since the government was in such strict control on their clothing, the Incans could not alter their clothing without the permission of the government.

Hairstyles

Discoveries have been made about the Incan hairstyles through studying their ancient mummies. It is believed that women of this culture had very long hair that they would most typically braid. Men on the other hand, would still have relatively long hair, yet would occasionally cut it with a certain type of knife. It has been thought that certain hairstyles may distinguish one class from another.

Jewelry

The wearing of jewelry was not uniform throughout the empire. Chimú artisans, for example, continued to wear earrings after their integration into the empire, but in many other regions, only local leaders wore them.

Ceramics and Metalwork

Ceramics were for the most part utilitarian in nature, but also incorporated the imperialist style that was prevalent in the Inca textiles and metalwork. In addition, the Inca played drums and on woodwind instruments including flutes, pan-pipes and trumpets made of shell and ceramics.

The Inca made beautiful objects of gold, silver, copper, bronze and tumbago. But precious metals were in shorter supply than in earlier Peruvian cultures. The Inca metalworking style draws much of its inspiration from Chimú art and in fact the best metal workers of Chan Chan were transferred to Cusco when the Kingdom of Chimor was incorporated into the empire. Unlike the Chimú, the Inca do not seem to have regarded metals to be as precious as fine cloth. Nonetheless, the metalworks of the Incas were perhaps the most advanced in America. When the Spanish first encountered the Inca they were offered gifts of *qunpi* cloth. Incan ceramics are usually very distinct and easy to recognize. The shapes of the vessels are highly standardized. The most typical Incan pottery would have a spherical body with a cone shaped base. This spherical body usually includes two vertical side handles with a tall neck and flaring rim. The Incans often would place animal heads on their pottery as well usually near the top of the vessel. There were also several other popular styles for Incan ceramics which included a shallow dish with a single bird head and handle, a pedestal beaker, and a single or double handled bottle.

Incans often decorated their ceramics with a multitude of images and colors. They usually decorated their pottery with bright colors of red, yellow, orange, black and white. Much like all other forms of Incan art, the pottery was often decorated with geometric shapes. The Incans would put diamonds, squares, checkers, triangles, circles and dots on almost all of their ceramic work. Other common themes were animals and insects like llamas, birds, jaguars, alpacas, bees, butterflies as well as block-like humans.

As part of a tax obligation to the commoners, mining was required in all the provinces. Even though the Inca Empire contained a lot of precious metals, the Incans did not value their metal as much as fine cloth. The Incans adopted much of their metal-working characteristics from the metalwork of Chimu. Because of their expertise in metalworking, after the fall of Chimu many metalworkers were taken back to the capital city of Cuzco to continue their metalworking for the emperor. Copper, tin, gold, and silver were all obtained from mines or washed from the river gravels. These metals would then be handed over to metallurgists. Because the Inca had a system that emphasized political and religious organization, there were many specialized artisans like metallurgists. There were also specialized weavers, cloth makers, pottery makers, and many more. Both copper and bronze would be used for basic farming tools or weapons. Some of the common bronze and copper pieces found in the Incan empire included sharp sticks for digging, club-heads, knives with curved blades, axes, chisels, needles and pins. All of these items would be forged by a metallurgist and then spread throughout the empire.

The Incans reserved their more precious metals for ornaments and decorations. Gold and silver were common themes throughout the palaces of Incan emperors. It was said that the walls and thrones were covered with gold and that the emperor dined on gold and silver service. These golden plated services would often be inlaid with llamas, butterflies or other creatures. Even beyond the gold and decoration of the emperor's palace were the ornaments that decorated all of the temples throughout the empire. The temples of the Incans were strewn with sacred and highly precious objects. Headdresses, crowns, ceremonial knives, cups, and a lot of ceremonial clothing were all inlaid with gold or silver.

Many historians believe that the choice of gold was to distinguish the more "sacred" or "holy" pieces from others. The commonality of gold has much to do with the Incan religion surrounding the sun. Because of the beautiful reflection that gold casts, it gave the appearance of containing the sun, making the precious metal even more valued in a sun-obsessed society. Gold was reserved for the highest class of Incan society which consisted of priests, lords and of course the Sapa Inca or emperor.

Education

The Inca used quipu or bunches of knotted strings, for accounting and census purposes. Much of the information on the surviving quipus has been shown to be numeric data; some numbers seem to have been used as mnemonic labels, and the color, spacing, and structure of the quipu carried information as well. Since it isn't known how to interpret the coded or non-numeric data, some scholars still hope to find that the quipu recorded language. The Inca depended largely on oral transmission as a means of maintaining the preservation of their culture. Inca education was divided into two distinct categories: vocational education for common people of Inca and highly formalized training for the nobility.

Medicine

The Inca made many discoveries in medicine. They performed successful skull surgery, which involved cutting holes in the skull to release pressure from head wounds. Coca leaves were used to lessen hunger and pain, as they still are in the Andes. The Chasqui (messengers) chewed coca leaves for extra energy to carry on their tasks as runners delivering messages throughout the empire.

Recent research by Erasmus University and Medical Center workers Sewbalak and Van Der Wijk showed that, contrary to popular belief, the Inca people were not addicted to coca. Another remedy was to cover boiled bark from a pepper tree and place it over a wound while still warm.

The Inca also used guinea pigs not only for food but for a so-called well-working medicine.

Burial Practices

The Inca believed in reincarnation. Those who obeyed the Incan moral code — *ama suwa, ama llulla, ama quella* (do not steal, do not lie, do not be lazy) — went to live in the Sun's warmth. Others spent their eternal days in the cold earth.

The Inca also believed in mummifying personages. The mummies would be provided with an assortment of objects which were to be taken into the pacarina. The mallquis were also used in various rituals or celebrations. The deceased were generally buried in a sitting position. One such example was the 500-year-old mummy "Juanita the Ice Maiden", a girl very well-preserved in ice that was discovered at 20,000 feet, near the summit of Mt. Ampato in Southern Peru. Her burial included many items left as offerings to the Inca gods.

Religion

The belief system of the Incas was polytheistic. Inti, the Sun God, was the most important god, which the Incas believed was the direct ancestor of the Sapa Inca, the title of the hereditary rulers of the empire.

Other Practices

The Inca practiced cranial deformation. They achieved this by wrapping tight cloth straps around the heads of newborns in order to alter the shape of their still-soft skulls. These deformations did not result in brain damage. Researchers at the Field Museum believe that the practice was used to mark different ethnicities across the Inca Empire.

Food and Farming

It is estimated that the Inca cultivated around seventy crop species. The main crops were potatoes, sweet potatoes, maize, chili peppers, cotton, tomatoes, peanuts, an edible root called oca, and the pseudograins quinoa and amaranth. The crops developed by the Inca and preceding cultures makes South America one of the historic centers of crop diversity (along with the Middle East, India, Mesoamerica, Ethiopia, and the Far East). Many of these crops were widely distributed by the Spanish and are now important crops worldwide. Salsa was originated by the Inca people using tomatoes, chili peppers, and other spices.

The Inca cultivated food crops on dry Pacific coastlines, high on the slopes of the Andes, and in the lowland Amazon rainforest. In mountainous Andean environments, they made extensive use of terraced fields which not only allowed them to put to use the mineral-rich mountain soil which other peoples left fallow, but also took advantage of micro-climates conducive to a variety of crops being cultivated throughout the year. Agricultural tools consisted mostly of simple digging sticks.

The Inca also raised llamas and alpacas for their wool, meat, and to use them as pack animals and captured wild vicuñas for their fine hair.

The Inca road system was key to farming success as it allowed distribution of foodstuffs over long distances. The Inca also constructed vast storehouses, which allowed them to live through El Niño years while some neighboring civilizations suffered.

Inca leaders kept records of what each *ayllu* in the empire produced, but did not tax them on their production. They instead used the *mita* for the support of the empire.

The Inca diet consisted primarily of fish and vegetables, supplemented less frequently with the meat of cuyes (guinea pigs) and camelids. In addition, they hunted various animals for meat, skins and feathers. Maize was malted and used to make chicha, a fermented alcoholic beverage.

Economy

According to Ferreira and Chamot: *"The social system of the Incas had an ancient Andean origin based on the ayllu, an extended family group with a common ancestor. The economic system was also based on ancient social structures and can be explained through several principles, namely reciprocity, redistribution, and vertical control."*

These authors also add: *"Redistribution, a practice employed by the state, ensured that all agricultural goods not exchanged by reciprocity were to be distributed in the different areas of the empire in the case of bad crops."* In essence, the government of the Inca functioned as a safeguard against mass starvation.

INDIAN

Traditionally, the Indian caste system was one of the oldest and most important systems of social class. It differs from Varnashrama Dharma found in Hinduism, which allowed people born into a certain Varna to move upward or downwards depending on their qualification. It divided society based on skill and qualifications. Briefly, the Brahmin varna was idealized as a leisurely priest class devoted to religious ceremonies, while the Kshatriya defended them as military princes. The modern concept of the middle class was represented by the Vaishya varna artisans, farmers, and merchants, and the lower varna were the Shudra labourers. Within this basic framework were arranged a huge number of jatis, or subcastes. It should be recognised not as a religious system (as Varnashrama Dharma prescribed in Hinduism), but a social system, which evolved from Varnashrama Dharma. After, the end of British occupation in 1947, the Constitution of India introduced various affirmative action plans to abolish the caste system. The people outside of the main Varnas were called Untouchables, because they were to not be touched by the "Twice Borns", or the higher three Varnas.

IRANIAN

Under the Qajar dynasty of Iran, the class structure was set up as follows:

- the permanent hereditary class of Qajar princes
- an upper class of "nobles and notables"
- religious leaders and students of theology
- merchants (note the difference from east Asian models)
- agricultural landowners
- master artisans and shopkeepers

As in many official class structures, the labourers who made up the majority of the population but owned no land and relied on wages were not even considered part of the structure at all.

JAPANESE

The Japanese class structure, while influenced by the Chinese, was based on a much more feudal environment. The Emperor was not claimed to be a deity until pre-World War II military government did so but still was unquestionably at the pinnacle of the Japanese class structure (and still is, although no longer officially considered a god). However, for much of Japanese history the emperor was not allowed outside the palace grounds and his will was "interpreted" by a shogun, or military dictator. Beneath the shogun, daimyos or regional lords, administered the provinces through their samurai lieutenants. Perhaps through Chinese influence, and perhaps springing from a lack of arable land, the Japanese class structure also ranked farmers above merchants and other bourgeois. Classes changed after the Golden Age.

FOUR DIVISIONS OF SOCIETY

The four divisions of society refers to the model of society in ancient China and was a meritocratic social class system in China, and other subsequently influenced Confucian societies. The four castes—gentry, farmers, artisans and merchants—are combined to form the term Shìnónggôngshâng. The concept was first brought up in the Confucian classic Spring and Autumn Annals, and was influential in countries with Confucian influence.

The ranking of the divisions was influenced by confucianist thinking: The wise ruler was at the top, followed by the farmer who produces the wealth of the society. The artisan only reuses the wealth created, while the merchant only distributes the goods. The physiocratic school of François Quesnay, a Confucianist, influenced the French Ancien Régime.

The Four Divisions

The four divisions are usually given in the following order: gentry, farmers, artisans, merchants; but this does not necessarily imply hierarchy. Different sources have cited the divisions in different order.

Gentry

This means different things in different countries. In China, Korea, and Vietnam, this meant that the Confucian scholar gentry that would- for the most part- make up most of the bureaucracy. This caste would contain both the more-or-less hereditary aristocracy as well as the meritocratic scholars that rise through the rank by public service and, later, by imperial exams.

In Japan, this caste essentially equates to the samurai class. In Edo period, with the creation of the Domains (*han*) under the rule of Toyotomi Hideyoshi, all land was confiscated and reissued as fiefdoms to the daimyo. The small lords, the samurai, were ordered to either give up their swords and rights and remain on their lands as peasants, or move to the castle cities to become paid retainers of the daimyo. Only a few samurai were allowed to remain in the countryside; the landed samurai. Some 5% of the population were samurai. Only the samurai could have proper surnames, which after the Meiji Restoration became compulsory to all inhabitants.

Farmers

In a largely agrarian society, the farmers occupy a high position in Chinese, Japanese, Korean, and Vietnamese society, at least in theory. Some sources, such as Xunzi, list them before the gentry, based on the Confucian view that they directly contributed to the welfare of the state. In China, the farmer lifestyle is also closely linked with the ideals of Confucian gentlemen, and aging scholars and bureaucrats often retire to a life of farming—again, at least in theory.

Artisans

The artisans were ranked below farmers, for they only create products from other products. In Japan, artisans typically lived within larger towns, thus, below the castles towns were divided into four parts: the samurai quarter, the merchant quarter, the artisans quarter, and the *hanamachi*, where theaters, brothels and gambling dens were located. In the towns, different ways of life developed, with the *chônindô* of the artisans and merchants and the *bushidô* of the samurai.

Merchants

The merchants were ranked the lowest due to the fact that they do not produce anything, only profit from others' creations. Ironically, the merchant class were often the wealthiest group and held influence above and beyond their supposed social standing. As early as Spring and Autumn period in China, wealthy merchants have influenced state politics and, in the case of Lü Buwei.

In Japan's Edo period, the peasants, around 80% to 90% of the population, had to carry the burden of the economy. Taxes were paid in rice, 40% to 50% of the harvest, collected from the village as a community.

Others

The imperial household and the highest hereditary nobility are typically considered separate from the four divisions, whether they held ultimate power, as in much of imperial China, or were mere ceremonial figureheads as in feudal Japan. In Japan, there are groups that does not even rank amongst the castes. The *Burakumin* were effectively outcasts, because their occupations were taboo under Buddhism and Shinto. They were the undertakers, the slaughterers and the tanners. The *hinin*, literally "Non-people" were the second group: travelling minstrels and convicted criminals.

KOREAN

The Korean ruling class, or Korean power elite, is the relatively small number of Korean people who through similar schools, education, family clans, upbringing, or corporate chaebol wealth and urban power control decision making and policy within either of the partitioned Koreas. This group is placed within the historical tradition of Confucianism and yangban scholars whose creation can be dated towards the end of the Goryeo dynasty; and that continues through the republican post-1945 and contemporary period; and which is represented by a controlling benevolent stewardship of the politics and economy of Korea by seniors or the older urban-dwelling elements of the population which crosses class, religious, party, and political lines.

CAPITALIST CLASS STRUCTURES

The social structure of the United Kingdom continues to be built on notions of social class. Though definitions of social class vary, most are linked to factors such as occupation, level of education and wealth. Until recently even the Parliament of the United Kingdom was organised on a class basis, with the House of Lords representing the hereditary upper class, and the House of Commons representing everyone else — technically the "commoners". The Queen maintains her status at the top of the social class structure.

Since the 1980s there have been a number of social changes — the reform of the House of Lords, the expansion of home-ownership and higher education — which have altered the social landscape. Some have gone so far as to proclaim a classless society, although such claims have been met with scepticism.

Heraldry and Social Class

An English subject with arms registered in the College of Arms, or a Scotsman in the Lyon Court, can be referred to as armigerous. Any British subject can apply for arms from their respective authority but only those of sufficient social standing would be granted arms. Arms in and of themselves are imperfectly aligned with social status, in that many of high status will have no right to arms whilst, on the other hand, those entitled to arms by descent can include branches of families which have fallen far down the social scale. Nevertheless, a right to bear arms under the Law of Arms is, by definition, linked either to the personal acquisition of social status, inspiring application for a personal grant of arms, or to descent from a person who did so in the past. Rightly or wrongly, therefore, the use of a coat of arms is linked to social prestige. In the early twentieth century, it was argued by heraldic writers such as Arthur Charles Fox-Davies that only those with a right to a coat of arms could correctly be described (if men) as gentlemen and of noble status; however, even at the time this argument was controversial, and it was rejected by other writers such as Oswald Barron and Horace Round. In the Order of Malta, where proof of technical nobility is a requirement of certain grades of membership, British members must still base their proof upon an ancestral right to a coat of arms.

Class Structure

Below is a description of the various social classes.

Upper Classes

The upper class in Britain is statistically very small and consists of the peerage, gentry, and landowners. These people were traditionally the wealthiest in the land having inherited money and position. Typically they would speak with Received Pronunciation accent and have been educated at public schools.

In the United Kingdom, entry to the upper class is still considered difficult, if not impossible, to attain unless one is born into it. Marriage into upper-class families rarely results in complete integration, since many factors (to be outlined below) raise a challenging barrier between the upper, upper middle, and middle classes.

Titles, while often considered central to the upper class, are not always strictly so. Both Captain Mark Phillips and Vice Admiral Timothy Laurence, the respective first and second husbands of HRH The Princess Anne lacked any rank of peerage, yet could scarcely be considered to be anything other than upper class. The same is true of Francis Fulford, who memorably featured in Channel 4's documentary *The F***ing Fulfords* and whose family has owned estates in Devon for over 800 years. In fact the Fulfords represent the group that makes up the largest component of the upper class: the landed gentry.

That being said, those in possession of a hereditary (as opposed, importantly, to a conferred) peerage – for example a Dukedom, a Marquessate, an Earldom, a Viscounty or a Barony (though any of these may be conferred) – will, almost invariably, be members of the upper class, though a Life Peerage is that of the rank of Baron, most Life Peers are not Upper Class.

Where one was educated is often considered to be more important than the level of education attained. Traditionally, upper class children will be brought up — at home — by a Nanny for the first few years of life, until old enough to attend a well-established prep school or pre-preparatory school. Moving into secondary education, it is still commonplace for upper-class children to attend one of Britain's prestigious public schools, typically Ampleforth College, Eton College, Harrow School, Marlborough College, Rugby School, Westminster School and Winchester College, although it is not unheard of for certain families to send their children to grammar schools.

Insofar as continuing education goes, this can vary from family to family; it may, in part, be based on the educational history of the family. In the past, both the British Army and Clergy have been the institutions of choice, but the same can equally apply to the Royal Navy, or work in the Diplomatic Corps. HRH Prince Harry of Wales, for instance, has recently completed his training at the Royal Military Academy Sandhurst in preparation for entry into the Army. Otherwise, Oxbridge,the London School of Economics, Imperial College and other 'traditional' universities (such as Durham University, the University of Edinburgh, and St Andrews University) are the most popular sources of higher education for the upper class, although a high academic standard is required and social class does not as readily secure entry as it once did.

Sports — particularly those involving the outdoors — are a popular pastime, and are usually taken up from a school age or before, and improved upon throughout the educational years. Traditionally, at school, rugby union is much more popular than football: indeed, the two sports are often taken to represent the two extremes of social classes 'at play', although paradoxically rugby is not played at Winchester. Other frequented sports include lawn tennis (which has a broad appeal and could hardly be considered to be dominated by any one class), croquet (quite the opposite), cricket and golf.

Equestrian activities are also popular — with both sexes. There is a long-standing tradition of the upper class having close links to horses; indeed, one of the foremost example of three-day eventing prowess is Zara Philips, daughter of Princess Anne and recently-crowned *Sunday Times* Sportswoman of the Year. Men who ride will more often participate in polo, as is the case with both HRH Prince Charles and his sons, Their Royal Highnesses Prince William and Prince Harry.

Hunting and shooting, too, are favoured pastimes. Some upper class families with large estates will run their own shoots (typically they would need 1,000 acres (4 km^2), or more, though some shoots do operate on about half that), but many will know someone who keeps pheasants, or other game, and may instead shoot with them. Much as with horses, there is a particular affinity for dogs (especially Labradors and spaniels) amongst the upper class — and, equally, sporting pursuits that involve them. It should, however, be noted that none of the aforementioned sports are, of course, exclusively upper class.

Language, pronunciation and writing style have been, consistently, one of the most reliable indicators of class. (Upper and otherwise.) The variations between the language employed by the upper classes and those not of the upper classes has, perhaps, been best documented by linguistic Professor Alan Ross's 1954 article on U and non-U English usage. The discussion was furthered in *Noblesse Oblige* - and featured contributions from, among others, Nancy Mitford. The debate was revisited in the mid-1970s, in a publication by Debrett's called 'U and Non-U revisited'. Ross contributed to this volume too, and it is remarkable to notice how little the language (amongst other factors) changed in the passing of a quarter of a century.

The choice of house ('home', to a non-U-speaker), too, is an important feature of the upper class. While it is true that there are fewer upper class families that are able to maintain both the well-staffed town house and country house than in the past, there are still many families that have a hereditary 'seat' somewhere in the country that they have managed to retain: Woburn Abbey, for example, has been in the family of the Duke of Bedford for centuries. Many upper class country houses are now open to the public, or have been placed in the care of the National Trust to aid with the funding of much-needed repairs. (In some cases, both are true).

The inside of a house, however grand the façade, is equally indicative of class. An upper class house (if privately owned, and not staffed) tends to be a comparatively untidy composite of grand furniture — having been inherited — which may have become frayed and threadbare over time and vast piles of ancient books, papers and other old reading material for which there is now no home.

Many upper class families will be in possession of works of art by old masters, valuable sculpture or period furniture, having had said pieces handed down through several generations. Indeed, inheriting the vast majority of one's possessions is the traditional form in upper class families. On that point, there is a well-known derisive quotation from Conservative politician Michael Jopling, who referred to cabinet colleague Michael Heseltine as the kind of person who 'bought his own furniture' (in the Alan Clark Diaries). (The former was then put down himself by a Baron as "the kind of person who bought his own castle".)

So too is the organisation (or lack thereof) of the garden an important upper class trait. Bedding plants, rockeries, hanging baskets and goldfish ponds will be nowhere evident; instead we find avenues of limes or sequoia, box hedges, shrub roses, herbaceous borders and stone pathways. Upper class gardens will look more natural and unconstructed than artificially preened (although as with houses, this is not always true where staff are employed).

Money and material possessions are often thought of as a less important factor for the United Kingdom's upper class than for the upper classes of other countries; although this allows for an upper class family to be impoverished, an upper class family is likely to have had wealth at some point in its history.

Vast financial prosperity (only slightly dependent on how it is earned) is the subject of derision and contempt — the nickname "fat cat," suggesting mercenariness, is not one often levelled at members of the upper class. According to anthropologist Kate Fox, the main difference between the English and American social system is that in the latter, the rich and powerful believe they deserve their wealth and power and are more complacent. In the former, they tend to have a greater sense of social responsibility and compassion for those less privileged than themselves. However, Fox's thesis is undercut by the fact that America has a vibrant culture of civic engagement, especially in the form of volunteerism. Additionally, Americans donate more money, as a percentage of GDP, to charity than the British do. It is, of course, also significant that the British government has more extensive social welfare programs than the US government, and that private charity is therefore less of a necessity in Britain: GNI numbers, then, as opposed to GDP numbers, suggest different conclusions regarding the respective generosity of each nation.

THE MIDDLE CLASS

The upper middle class in Britain typically consists of professionals with tertiary education, speaking Received Pronunciation. The higher upper middle class are traditionally educated at more prestigious Public Schools. The lower section of the upper middle class tend to occupy less prestigious public schools.

Traditional careers would include barristers, doctors, Army officers, academics, art dealers, senior civil servants, the clergy and working within the City of London in high managerial positions. A typical Mosaic geodemographic type for this group would be cultural leadership.

This is a very specific class in England and is, in many respects, peculiar to England as its characteristics do not fit easily within the social gradations of the other constituent nations of the United Kingdom. Frequently its members are members of professions (traditionally the law, the military and the clergy, more recently extending to medicine, academia and finance), although merchants too were able to penetrate its ranks. However, being a member of a profession does not automatically elevate a person to this class, and it is quite common for an upper middle class person not to work in a traditional profession.

Higher-end upper middle class families may also have previous ancestry that often directly relates to the upper classes. Although not necessarily of the landowning classes - as a result, perhaps, of lack of a male heir - many families' titles/styles have not been inherited and therefore many families' past status became dissolved. An English subject with arms registered in the College of Arms, or a Scotsman in the Lyon Court, can be referred to as armigerous (armiger). Any British subject can apply for arms from their respective authority but only those of sufficient social standing would be granted arms. Arms in and of themselves are imperfectly aligned with social status, in that many of high status will have no right to arms whilst, on the other hand, those entitled to arms by descent can include branches of families which have fallen far down the social scale. Nevertheless, a right to bear arms under the Law of Arms is, by definition, linked either to the personal acquisition of social status, inspiring application for a personal grant of arms, or to descent from a person who did so in the past. Rightly or wrongly, therefore, the use of a coat of arms is linked to social prestige.

In the early twentieth century, it was argued by heraldic writers such as Arthur Charles Fox-Davies that only those with a right to a coat of arms could correctly be described (if men) as gentlemen and of noble status; however, even at the time this argument was controversial, and it was rejected by other writers such as Oswald Barron and Horace Round. In the Order of Malta, where proof of technical nobility is a requirement of certain grades of membership, British members must still base their proof upon an ancestral right to a coat of arms.

Popular modern day examples of the upper middle class include David Cameron (British Prime Minister), Hugh Grant (British Hollywood actor), Matthew Pinsent (British Olympian and TV personality) and Christopher Cazenove.

Middle Middle Class

Middle middle class in Britain typically consists of bourgeois with degrees from the less prestigious universities, or possibly no tertiary education. They would speak in accents which are provincial as well as Estuary English and received pronunciation. They would be engaged in owning and running local businesses; working for larger corporations as junior and middle management; teaching,social work and engineering, accountancy, information technology, nursing and other skilled jobs. Displays of conspicuous consumption are considered vulgar by them; instead they prefer to channel excess income into investments, including property. They are highly politically and socially engaged and might be regular churchgoers, sit on local committees and governing boards or stand for political office. Education is greatly valued by the middle classes: they will make every effort to ensure their children get a university education; although they are often unable to afford private schooling, they will go to great lengths to get their children into "good" state schools, such as moving house into the catchment area. They also value culture and make up a significant proportion of the book-buying and theatre -going public. They prefer TV documentaries and dramas over reality shows, BBC radio 4 over pop stations and broadsheet newspapers over tabloids. Typical Mosaic geodemographic types would include Provincial Privilege. The comedy character Margo Leadbetter is a satirical stereotype for this group, as is Jilly Cooper's Howard Weybridge.

Nouveau Riche

Nouveau riche are people from poorer backgrounds who have made money themselves, primarily in business, middle-class professions, or entertainment. They may retain the mannerisms of their original social group or may imitate the behaviour of the traditional upper class by, for instance, sending their children to public school or taking elocution lessons, but often in a way that is seen as gauche by the real upper class and middle classes (satirised as Mr Nouveau Richards by Jilly Cooper). This group is characterised by ostentatious displays of conspicuous consumption. Premier League Footballers are typical of this group.

Spiralist Meritocracy

This group was identified by Jilly Cooper in her book *Class* as people from working class or lower middle class backgrounds who gained an education at grammar school and university and have subsequently obtained professional or managerial jobs within companies or government. Jilly Cooper stated that these people are more likely to move geographically than the more local bourgeois *middle middle class*. These people are less socially secure than the traditional upper middle class, and would speak in a mixture of accents depending on their origin. A typical Mosaic Geodemographic type for this group would be Corporate Chieftains

Mondeo Man

Mondeo Man was described by Kate Fox as a person employed in the private sector in a salesman or entry level management position who drives a company car such as a Ford Mondeo. These people would have had limited education and cultural aspirations, but are keen to "move up in the world" and are seen by politicians and marketers as representing Middle England. An example of a person from this social group in UK popular culture is Gareth Cheeseman. Motorway man is considered by polling organisations to be the current equivalet of Mondeo Man.

Lower Middle Class

The lower middle class in Britain consists of people in white collar jobs living in less prosperous suburbs. They would typically not have had a university education, at least before the 1980s expansion in higher education. These people would speak in local accents, although relatively mild. A shibboleth for people from this group is the use of the word *pardon* rather than *sorry* or *say again* when they have not been able to hear the other speaker (referred to as *Pardonia* by Kate Fox). Typical Mosaic Geodemographic types for this group would include Sprawling Subtopia or for Successful British Asians Asian Enterprise. The Comedy character Hyacinth Bucket is a satirical stereotype for this social group. Votes in this area are split and minority parties will have a stronger proportion.

THE WORKING CLASS

These people would be in skilled blue collar jobs, traditionally in industry but in recent decades showing entrepreneurial development as the stereotypical white van man, or self employed contractors. These people would speak in local accents and have craft apprenticeships rather than university education. Typical Mosaic types for this group include White Van Culture or Affluent Blue Collar. More likely to vote conservative than the unskilled working class. The lifestyle they aspire to is that of nouveau-riche celebrities rather than the traditional upper and middle classes. Fictional examples of working-class entrepreneurs include Phil and Grant Mitchell in Eastenders, who are involved in a number of business enterprises, and Del

Boy Trotter, for all that he is aspirational rather than successful. The Coogan's Run character Ernest Moss represents the traditional skilled workman.

Unskilled Working Class

Traditionally, these people would work in blue collar jobs with low incomes. They would typically have left school as soon as legally permissible and not value education. Examples of Mosaic geodemographic groups for these people would be Coronation Street or Rustbelt Resilience. Fictional stereotypes include Andy Capp and Albert Steptoe, who is not only unaspirational himself but crushes the aspirations of his son Harold. They are the mainstay of the Labour party vote, but there are also working class conservatives, as exemplified by Alf Garnett.

It has been argued that with the decline in manufacturing and increase in the service sector, lower-paid white collar jobs are effectively working class. Call centres in particular, have sprung up in former centres of industry.

THE UNDERCLASS

Identified as emerging in the 1990s, this group consists of the long-term unemployed, single-parent families and elderly pensioners, dependent on state benefits. Many would be in public housing or council estates. Typical Mosaic Geodemographic types for these people are Tower Block Living or Sharing a stair case.

Language as a class indicator

- U and non-U English - Social Vocabulary from the 1950s compiled by Nancy Mitford. U represented Upper & Upper middle class vocabulary of the time and Non-U represented lower middle class vocabulary.
- Received Pronunciation, England's prestige accent used by Upper Class and Upper Middle class people. (A Scottish equivalent can be found in Morningside, Edinburgh, which has the highest concentration of millionaires in the UK outside of London)
- Estuary English - Traditionally a lower middle class accent from Southeast England now more widely used and influencing RP

- Cockney - Traditionally the working class accent of London
- Mockney - A deliberate affectation of the working-class London (Cockney) accent by Middle class people to gain "street credibility"

UK Social Stereotypes

- Toff - upper class, aristocratic
- Rah - Upper to upper middle class
- Sloane Ranger - Upper to upper middle class
- Worcester woman - Lower middle to middle middle class
- Essex Man - Skilled working class, materialistic
- White van man - Working class, entrepreneurial, aggressive driver
- Chav, charver (North-East England and Yorkshire), scallie (North West England) or Ned (Scotland) - anti-social working, or underclass

The Parliament of the United Kingdom still contains a vestige of the pre-capitalist European class structure. The Queen maintains her status at the top of the social class structure, with the House of Lords up until very recently still representing the hereditary upper class, however due to the Life Peerage the vast majority of Lords in the House of Lords are of common birth and are not classified as Upper Class as they were not born into it, and the House of Commons technically representing everyone else. The House of Commons until the early 20th century represented the industrialist and landed classes. In the Victorian era of the United Kingdom, social class became a national obsession, with nouveau riche industrialists in the House of Commons trying to attain the status of House of Lords landowners through culture, marriage, title, and the construction of follies.

From a sociological point of view the class system in Britain changed substantially during the 'Thatcher Era'. Home ownership (on mortgage) was extended throughout the middle classes and below. With the loss of the majority of traditional working class industrial jobs from the market, a new 'underclass', below working class emerged. The 'underclass', defined as unemployed relying on state benefits, is the new bottom of the British class system. In Britain people considered of lower social standing can earn high incomes, but an individual's social class is still largely assessed by their parent's mannerisms, education and the status.

LATIN AMERICAN

In colonial Latin America access to positions of power and wealth were delineated by race. Accordingly, Peninsulars (Spaniards born in Spain and Portuguese born in Portugal) held the top ranks- including titles such as Viceroy, Captain General, etc. They were followed by Criollos (Those directly descended from Spaniards but born in America), who held considerable power and class but were barred from the highest decision-making posts. After these there was a system of castes, listed in order of rank, there were around a hundred castes, one of these were:

- Mestizo (Mixed Amerindian and Spaniard);
- Mulatto (Mixed Spaniard and African)
- Amerindian
- Zambo (Mixed Amerindian and African)
- Negro.

It is to be noted that even today there is a strong correlation between class and ethnicity.

New Zealand

Class in New Zealand is a product of both Mâori and Western social structures. New Zealand was traditionally supposed to be a 'classless society' but this claim is problematic in a number of ways, and has been clearly untrue since at least the 1980s.

MÂORI HIERARCHIES

Mâori society has traditionally been one based on rank, which derived from ancestry (whakapapa). Chiefs were invariably descended from other chiefs, although chieftainship was not the exclusive right of the first born son of the previous chief. If he did not show signs of leadership ability he would be passed over in favour of a brother or other relative. In some tribes women could take on leadership roles, although this was not usual. Women, lowly born men, and even people from other tribes were able to achieve positions of considerable influence. Such people have included Princess Te Puea Herangi and 'kingmaker' Wiremu Tamihana. Until the advent of Christianity it was normal for prisoners of war to be enslaved. Slaves had no rights and could be killed at the will of their master. However their children were free members of the tribe.

Present-day Mâori society is far less hierarchical than it traditionally was, although it is still stratified by European standards. A disproportionate number of Mâori MPs come from chiefly families, for example. However, a number of lowly-born Mâori have achieved positions of considerable mana within their communities by virtue of their achievements or learning.

The 'Classless Society'

Until about the 1980s it was often claimed that New Zealand was a 'classless society'. Historian Keith Sinclair wrote in 1969 that although New Zealand was not a classless society, "it must be more nearly classless... than any advanced society in the world". From the nineteenth century many visitors also made this claim, for example British socialists Sidney and Beatrice Webb. The evidence for this was the relatively small range of wealth (that is, the wealthiest did not earn hugely more than the poorest earners), lack of deference to authority figures, high levels of class mobility, a high standard of working class living compared to Britain, progressive labour laws which protected workers and encouraged unionism, and a welfare state which was developed in New Zealand before most other countries.

Recently James Belich has argued that most of this is not evidence of an absence of class but rather of the relatively high status and standard of living of the working class in the nineteenth and early twentieth centuries. Unlike in Britain at this time, New Zealand working class people could regularly eat meat, own their own homes, and own horses (and later cars), while still being working class. Until the advent of compulsory secondary education in the 1930s, class mobility was limited, although much less so than in Britain.

It has also been argued that in New Zealand race takes the place of class, with Mâori and other Polynesians earning less, having a lower standard of living and less education, and working in lower status jobs than people of European descent. They also face prejudice akin to that facing working class people in many

European countries. Some argue that New Zealand only became a (white) 'workingman's paradise' because of the marginalisation of Mâori and in particular the appropriation of Mâori land.

New Zealanders' egalitarianism has been criticised as discouraging and denigrating ambition and individual achievement and success. New Zealanders tend to value modesty and distrust those who talk about their own merits. They especially dislike anyone who seems to consider themselves better than others even if the person in question is demonstrably more talented or successful than others. It is partly for this reason that mountaineer Sir Edmund Hillary is so admired in New Zealand; despite being the first person to climb Mount Everest he was always very modest. Extreme humility was arguably partly responsible for the early death of Prime Minister Norman Kirk, who may have survived his various health problems had he used his status to get preferential treatment from the public health system, or used private healthcare. This attitude can manifest itself in the tall poppy syndrome, which describes the 'cutting down' of anyone thought to have risen above the general mass of people.

New Zealand's claims to be a classless society were dealt a fatal blow in the 1980s and 1990s by the economic reforms of the fourth Labour government and its successor, the fourth National government. The reforms (sometimes called *Rogernomics*) made by these governments severely weakened the power of unions, removed a lot of protection from workers, cut social welfare benefits and made state housing less affordable. Over the period of these reforms, the gap between rich and poor New Zealanders has increased dramatically, with the incomes of the richest 10% of New Zealanders advancing while the other 90% stayed largely static. In addition the number of New Zealanders living in poverty is much higher than in the 1970s.. In an article entitled "Countries with the Biggest Gaps Between Rich and Poor", BusinessWeek ranked New Zealand at 6th in the world:

"The U.N. Development Program recently came out with a report looking, among other things, at income inequality worldwide... According to the OECD, New Zealand had the biggest rise in inequality among member nations in the two decades starting in the mid-1980s."

However although wealth is much more unevenly distributed than previously, New Zealand still lacks most of the overt signals of class which mark countries such as Britain. Most people do not care what others' parents do for a living, who a person is descended from, or where they went to school, and New Zealanders almost invariably have more respect for those who have earned their money through hard work than those who have inherited it or made it through investment.

The trend of greater social disparity has also seen a change in attitudes. Younger New Zealanders increasingly accept inequality as an unavoidable social reality, and egalitarian concerns are less popular.

Measures of Social Class

In 1972 Elley and Irving published *Socioeconomic Status in New Zealand*, which became one of the most cited papers in New Zealand social sciences. They outlined a socioeconomic index, now known as 'Elley-Irving (E-I)', based on 1966 Census data. E-I proposed six social strata based upon education and income, and grouped by occupation.

"The publication of the scale was welcomed by many researchers but regarded with suspicion by a number of lay critics who presumably clung to the belief that New Zealand was still a classless society. One newspaper headlined the production of a "snobbery scale". Such characterizations, and the numerous critics who misinterpreted its intentions, no doubt added to the frequency of its citing, but it is true that many researchers have made appropriate use of it for its original purpose. It is cited often because it is a useful tool. "—Warwick B. Elley, describing the impact of his paper

In the 1990s, P. Davis et al. published *New Zealand Socioeconomic Index of Occupational Status*, known as NZSEI. It was based on a 'returns to human capital' model of the stratification process and originally used data from the 1991 New Zealand Census (n=1,051,926) to generate scores for 97 occupational groups. It was later updated using 2006 Census data. NZSEI is a linear scale of ranked occupation, produced using an algorithm involving age, income and education, and aggregated to six discrete groupings (called *Socio-economic Status*, SES) to enable comparison with E-I and ISEI.

The NZSEI is derived from Census data of employed people, but it can be extended to most of the population using previous occupation (if retired or currently unemployed), or the occupation of the household's main income earner.

In contrast, the *NZDep2006 Index of Deprivation* is an index of geographic deprivation based upon 9 variables—telephone, benefit, unemployment,household income, car access, single parent family, no qualifications, home ownership, overcrowding.

Circa 2007, Caldwell & Brown published a popular book, which identified eight "hidden tribes" in New Zealand, labelling them after various towns or suburbs: North Shore, Grey Lynn, Balclutha, Remuera, Otara, Raglan, Cuba Street, Papatoetoe.

United States

Social class certainly exists in the United States, though it remains a controversial concept with many competing definitions. Many Americans believe in a simple three-class model that includes the "rich", the "middle class", and the "poor". More complex models that have been proposed describe as many as a dozen class levels; while still others deny the very existence, in the strict sense, of "social class" in American society. Most definitions of class structure group people according to wealth, income, education, type of occupation, and membership in a specific subculture or social network.

Dennis Gilbert, William Thompson, Joseph Hickey, and James Henslin have proposed class systems with six distinct social classes. These class models feature an upper or capitalist class consisting of the rich and powerful, an upper middle class consisting of highly-educated and wealthy professionals, a middle class consisting of college-educated individuals employed in white collar industries, a lower middle class, a working class constituted by clerical and blue collar workers whose work is highly routinized, and a lower class divided between the working poor and the unemployed underclass.

A Classless Society?

Some academics consider American society sociologically and economically fragmented in such a manner that no clear class distinctions can be made. This means that there are no pronounced breaks in socioeconomic strata, which makes class division highly subjective and disputable. Others, such as sociologist Dennis Gilbert, dispute the concept of a well-mixed society, and claim that distinct social networks can be identified for each class. W. Lloyd Warner also asserts the existence of class markers:

"We are proud of those facts of American life that fit the pattern we are taught but somehow we are often ashamed of those equally important social facts which demonstrate the presence of social class. Consequently, we tend to deny them, or worse, denounce them and by doing so we tend to deny their existence and magically make them disappear from consciousness." —W. Lloyd Warner, *What Social Class Is In America*.

Warner asserts that social class is as old as civilization itself and has been present in nearly every society from before the Roman Empire, through medieval times, and to the modern-day United States. He believes that complex societies such as the United States need an equally complex social hierarchy.

Markers

Some definitions of class look only at numerical measures such as wealth or income. Others take into account qualitative factors, such as education, culture, and social status. There is no consensus on which of these variables is essential and which are merely common correlates. It is also disputed whether sharp lines can be drawn; one point of view in the debate:

"A stratified society is one marked by inequality, by differences among people that are regarded as being higher or lower...it is logically possible for a society to be stratified in a continuous gradation between high and low without any sharp lines...in reality...there is only a limited number of types of occupations... People in similar positions...grow similar in their thinking and lifestyle...they form a pattern, and this pattern creates social class." *—Dennis Gilbert, The American Class Structure, 1998*

Social Status

"It is impossible to understand people's behavior...without the concept of social stratification, because class position has a pervasive influence on almost everything...the clothes we wear...the television shows we watch...the colors we paint our homes in and the names we give our pets... Our position in the social hierarchy affects our health, happiness, and even how long we will live." —*William Thompson, Joseph Hickey, Society in Focus, 2005*

Social class is sometimes presented as a description of how members of the society have sorted themselves along a continuum of positions varying in importance, influence, prestige, and compensation. In these models, certain occupations are considered to be desirable and influential, while others are considered to be menial, repetitive, and unpleasant. (In some cases, non-occupational roles such as a parent or volunteer mentor, are also considered.) Generally, the higher the ranking on such a scale, the higher the skill and education levels required to perform it.

Some sociologists consider the higher income and prestige of higher ranked jobs to simply be incentives to encourage members of society to obtain the skills necessary to perform important work. This is an important mechanism in the economic theory of capitalism, and is compatible with the notion that class is mutable and determined by a combination of choices and opportunities.

In other cases, class or status is inherited. For example, being the son or daughter of a wealthy individual, may carry a higher status and different cultural connotations than being a member of nouveau riche ("new money"). Those taking the functionalist approach to sociology and economics view social classes as components essential for the survival of complex societies such as American society.

Income

Income in the United States is most commonly measured by U.S. Census Bureau in terms of either household or individual and remains one of the most prominent indicators of class status. As 42% of all households, 76% of those in the top quintiles, had two income earners the discrepancy between household and personal income is quite considerable. In 2005 the top 15% of income earners made $62,500 or more, while 18% of households had incomes over $100,000. Personal income is largely the result of scarcity. As individuals who hold higher status positions tend to possess rare skills or assume positions society deems very essential, have higher incomes. Overall the median household income was $46,326 in 2005 while the median personal income (including only those above the age of 25) was $32,140.

Per capita household income, the income a household is able to allocate to each member of the household is also an important variable in determining a given household's standard of living. A high household income may be offset by a large household size; thus, resulting in a low per capita household income. In 2005, the median household income per capita was $24,672.

"It should be stressed...that a position does not bring power and prestige *because* it draws a high income. Rather, it draws a high income because it is functionally important and the available personnel are for one reason or another scarce. It is therefore superficial and erroneous to regard high income as the cause of a man's power and prestige, just as it is erroneous to think that a man's fever is the cause of his disease... The economic source of power and prestige is not income primarily, but the ownership of capital goods (including patents, good will, and professional reputation). Such ownership should be distinguished from the possession of consumers' goods, which is an index rather than a cause of social standing." *—Kingsley Davis and Wilbert E. Moore, Principles of Stratification*

As mentioned above, income is one of the most prominent features of social class; it is not one of its causes. In other words, income does not determine the status of an individual or household but rather reflects on that status. Some say that income and prestige are the incentives provided by society in order to fill needed positions with the most qualified and motivated personnel possible. However such a conclusion is contrary to the widespread observation that upper management at many companies is less knowledgeable and competent than many of their underlings, and that their positions are largely the result of fortuitous birth situations and networking. This situation is lampooned in the popular social commentary comic strip "Dilbert".

The New York Times has used income quintiles to define class. It has assigned the quintiles from lowest to highest as lower class, lower middle class, middle class, upper middle class, and upper class. These definitions equate class with income, permitting people to move from class to class as their income changes.

Dual Income Controversy

Income is one of the most commonly used attributes of a household to determine its class status. The relationship between income, which mostly arises from the scarcity of a certain skill, may however, prove to be more complex than initially perceived. While the idea is that income reflects status, household income may just be the product of two or more incomes.

In 2005, 42% of American households had two income earners. The vast majority (77%) of households in the top quintile had two or more income earners. This means that the majority of household income in the top quintile are the result of two income earners pooling their resources, establishing a close link between perceived affluence and the number of income earners in a given household. This raises the question of whether or not the combination of incomes results in higher social status. Of course, there is no definite answer as class is a vague sociological concept.

"The parade of income earners with height representing income suggest that the relationship between the distribution of income and the class structure is... blurred in the middle... we saw dual-income working class marchers looking down on single-income upper-middle class marchers. In sum, the class structure as we have defined it... does not exactly match the distribution of household income." *—Dennis Gilbert, The American Class Structure, 1998*

Sociologist Dennis Gilbert states that it is possible for households to out-earn other households over higher class standing through increasing their number of income earners. He furthermore states that household size also played an essential role, as the standard of living for two persons living off one upper middle class personal income may very well be higher than that of a household with four members living off two working class personal incomes. The combination of two or more incomes, allow for households to increase their income substantially without moving higher on the occupational ladder or attaining higher educational degrees. Thus it is important to remember that the favorable economic position of households in the top two quintiles is in some cases the result of combined income, rather than demand for a single worker.

Education

Tertiary education (or "higher education") is required for many middle-class professions, depending on how the term middle class is to be defined.

Tertiary education is rarely free, but the costs vary widely: tuition at elite private colleges often exceeds $200,000 for a four-year program. On the other hand, public colleges and universities typically charge much less (for state residents), and many, such as the University of California system, rival the elite private schools in reputation and quality.Also, scholarships offered by universities and government do exist, and low-interest loans are available. Still, the average cost of education, by all accounts, is increasing.

The attainment of post-secondary and graduate degrees is the perhaps most important feature of a middle and upper middle class person with the university being regarded as the most essential institution and gatekeeper of the professional middle class. Educational attainment is also directly linked to income.

In 2005, the vast majority of those with doctorate and professional degrees were among the nation's top 15% of income earners. Those with bachelor degrees had incomes considerably above the national median while the median income for those with some college education remained near the national median. According to U.S. Census Bureau, 9% of persons aged 25 or older had a graduate degree, 27.9% had a Bachelor's degree or more with 53% having attended college.

With 85% of the population having graduated high school, it becomes apparent that the average American does not have a college degree, but is likely to have attended college for some time and has graduated high school. Overall, educational attainment serves as the perhaps most essential class feature of most Americans, being directly linked to income and occupation.

Culture

Social classes feature their own sub-cultures and have therefore developed slightly different manners of socializing their offspring. Due to class mobility individuals may also assimilate to the culture of another class when ascending or descending in the social order. However, one does need to remember that all social classes in the United States, except the upper class, consist of tens of millions of people. Thus social classes form social groups so large that they feature considerable diversity within and any statement regarding a given social class' culture needs to be seen as a broad generalization.

Since 1970, sociologists such as Paula LeMasters and Melvin Kohl have set out repeatedly to research class based cultures. Class culture has been shown to have a strong influence on the mundane lives of people, affecting everything from the manner in which they raise their children, initiation and maintenance of romantic relationship to the color in which they paint their houses. The strongest cultural differences seem to run along the professional middle class-working class divide. A recent increase in residential class segregation and the overall tendency of individual to associate mostly with those of equal standing as themselves has further strengthened class differences.

Parental views are the perhaps most essential factor in determining the socialization process which shapes new members of society. The values and standards used in child rearing are commonly closely related to the parent's occupational status. Parents from the professional class tend to raise their children to become curious independent thinkers, while working class parents raise their children to have a more communal perspective with a strong respect for authority. Middle class parents tend to emphasize internal standards and values while working class parents emphasize external values.

Sociologist Dennis Gilbert uses a list of values identified by Melvin Kohn to be typical of the professional middle and working class. Middle class parents values for their children and themselves included: "Consideration of Others, Self-Control, Curiosity, Happiness, Honesty, Tolerance of Nonconformity, Open to Innovation... Self-Direction." This contrasted with surveyed working class individuals, who reported: "Manners,

Obedience... Neatness, Cleanliness, Strong Punishment of Deviant Behavior, Stock to Old Ways, People not Trustworthy... Strict Leadership" as values for themselves and their children. There is a strong correlation between these values and the occupational activities of the respondents. The job characteristics of middle class respondents included: *"Work Independently, Varied Tasks, Work with People or Data,"* versus working class parents of reported *"Close Supervision and Repetitive Work..."*

"Not once in a professional middle-class home did I see a young boy shake his father's hand in a well-taught *manly* gesture... Not once did I hear a middle-class parent scornfully-or even sympathetically-call a crying boy a sissy or in any way reprimand him for his tears... even as young as six or seven, the working class boys seemed more emotionally controlled-more like miniature men-than those in the middle-class families." *—Sociologist Lillian Rubin in Gilbert, 1998*

Gender roles are also viewed differently by those in the higher and lower social classes. Middle class individuals, who were more open towards "nonconformity" and emphasized individual self-direction as well as critical thinking, were also less stringent in their application of gender roles. Working class individuals, on the other hand, emphasized gender roles. While working class people have more and more assimilated to middle class culture regarding their view and application of gender roles, differences remain. Professional class people are more likely to have an egalitarian distribution of work in their household with both spouses being equals in heterosexual marriages. According to Dennis Gilbert, "College life, generally a prologue to upper-middle class careers, delays marriage and encourages informal, relatively egalitarian association between men and women."

Upper Class

This term is applied to a wide array of elite groups existing in the United States of America. The term commonly includes the so-called "blue bloods" (multi-generational wealth combined with leadership of high society) such as the Astor or Roosevelt families. There is disagreement over whether the "nouveau riche" should be included as members of the upper class or whether this term should exclusively be used for established families. Twentieth century sociologist W. Lloyd Warner divided the upper class into two sections: the "upper-upper class" (or bourgeoise) and "lower-upper class" (or yuppies). The former includes established upper-class families while the latter includes those with great wealth. As there is no defined lower threshold for the upper class it is difficult, if not outright impossible, to determine the exact number or percentage of American households that could be identified as being members of the upper-class(es).

Income and wealth statistics may serve as a helpful guideline as they can be measured in a more objective manner. In 2005, approximately one and half percent (1.5%) of households in the United States had incomes exceeding $250,000 with the top 5% having incomes exceeding $157,000. Furthermore only 2.6% of household held assets (excluding home equity) of more than one-million dollars. One could therefore fall under the assumption that less than five percent of American society are members of rich households. The richest 1% of the American population owns as much as the combined wealth of the bottom 90%, or perhaps even more.

Members of the upper class control and own significant portions of the corporate America and may exercise indirect power through the investment of capital. The high salaries and the potential for amassing great wealth through stock options have greatly increased for the power and visibility of the "corporate elite". Many sociologists and commentators, however, make a distinction between the upper class (in the sense of those in the families of inherited wealth) and the corporate elite. By implication, the upper class is held in lower regard (as inheritors of idle wealth) than the self-made millionaires in prestigious occupations.

Yet another important feature of the upper class is that of inherited privilege. While most Americans, including those in the upper-middle class need to actively maintain their status, upper class persons do not need to work in order to maintain their status. Status tends to be passed on from generation to generation without each generation having to re-certify its status. Overall, the upper class is the financially best compensated and one of the most influential socio-economic classes in American society.

Corporate Elite

The high salaries and, especially, the potential wealth through stock options, has supported the term *corporate elite*. Top executives, including Chief Executive Officers, are among the financially best compensated occupations in the United States. The median annual earnings for a CEO in the United States were $140,350 (exceeding the income of more than 90% of U.S. households). *The Wall Street Journal* reports the median compensation for CEOs of 350 major corporations was $6,000,000 in 2005 with most of the money coming from stock options.

In New York City in 2005, the median income (including bonuses) of a corporate "chief operating officer" (the #2 job) was $377,000. The total compensation for a "top IT officer" in charge of information technology in New York City was $218,000. Thus even below the CEO level of top corporations, financial compensation will usually be sufficient to propel a households with a mere one income earner in the top 1%. In 2005 only 1.5% of American households had incomes above $250,000 with many reaching this level only through having two income earners.

"Top executives are among the highest paid workers in the U.S. economy. However, salary levels vary substantially depending on the level of managerial responsibility; length of service; and type, size, and location of the firm. For example, a top manager in a very large corporation can earn significantly more than a counterpart in a small firm.

Median annual earnings of general and operations managers in May 2004 were $77,420. The middle 50% earned between $52,420 and $118,310. Because the specific responsibilities of general and operations managers vary significantly within industries, earnings also tend to vary considerably...the Median annual earnings of chief executives in May 2004 were $140,350; although chief executives in some industries earned considerably more...the median income of chief executive officers in the nonprofit sector was $88,006 in 2005, but some of the highest paid made more than $700,000." —*U.S. Department of Labour,*

Many politically powerful people make money before coming to office, but in general the political power elite have official incomes in the $150,000 to $185,000 range; members of Congress are paid $165,000, and are effectively required to have a residence in their district as well as one in Washington.

Upper Middle

The upper middle class consists of highly-educated salaried professionals whose work is largely self-directed. Many have advanced graduate degrees and household incomes commonly exceed the high five-figure range. Members of this class commonly value higher education - most holding advanced academic degrees - and are often involved with personal and professional networks including professional organizations. The upper middle class tends to have great influence over the course of society.

Occupations which require high educational attainment, are well-compensated and are held in high public esteem such as physicians, lawyers, scientists and professors are largely considered to be upper middle class. The very well-educated are seen as trend setters with movements such as the anti-smoking movement, pro-fitness movement, organic food movement, and environmentalism being largely indigenous to this particular socio-economic grouping. Education serves as perhaps the most important value and also the most dominant entry barrier of the upper middle class.

Sociologists such as Dennis Gilbert, Willam Thompson, and Joseph Hickey estimate the upper middle class to constitute roughly 15% of the population (or roughly three in every twenty persons). The main hallmark and most distinguishing feature of this class is its high educational attainment.

Middle Class

The middle class is perhaps the mostly vaguely defined of the social classes. The term can be used either to describe a relative elite of professionals and managers – also called the upper middle class -- or it can be used to describe those in-between the extremes of wealth, disregarding considerable differences in income, culture, educational attainment, influence, and occupation.

As with all social classes in the U.S., there are no definite answers as to what is and what is not middle class. Sociologists such as Dennis Gilbert, James Henslin, William Thompson, and

Joseph Hickey have brought forth class models in which the middle class is divided into two sections that combined constitute 47% to 49% of the population.

The upper middle or professional class constitutes the upper end of the middle class which consists of highly educated, well-paid professionals with considerable work autonomy. The lower end of the middle class – called either lower middle class or just middle class – consists of semi-professionals, craftsmen,office staff, and sales employees who often have college degrees and are very loosely supervised.

Jerry Carrier in "The Making of the Slave Class" asserts that American's perception of a middle class country is a myth. He asserts that about two-thirds of American's are working class and their incomes and class status are severely limited because of culture. He contends that no real class mobility exists in America.

"Everyone wants to believe they are middle class. For people on the bottom and the top of the wage scale the phrase connotes a certain Regular Joe cachet. But this eagerness to be part of the group has led the definition to be stretched like a bungee cord." —*Dante Chinni, the Christian Science Monitor,*

Although income thresholds cannot be determined since social classes lack distinct boundaries and tend to overlap, sociologists and economist have put forward certain income figures they find indicative of middle class households. Sociologist Leonard Beeghley identifies a husband making roughly $57,000 and a wife making roughly $40,000 with a household income of roughly $97,000 as a typical middle class family.

Sociologists William Thompson and Joseph Hickey identify household incomes between $35,000 and $75,000 as typical for the lower middle and $100,000 or more as typical for the upper middle class. Though it needs to be noted that household income distribution neither reflects standard of living nor class status with complete accuracy.

Traditional Middle Class

Those households more or less at the center of society may be referred to as being part of the American middle or middle-middle class in vernacular language use. In the academic models featured in this article, however, the middle class does not constitute a strong majority of the population. Those in the middle of the socio-economic strata—the proverbial Average Joe—are commonly in the area where the working and lower middle class overlap.

The most prominent academic models split the middle class into two sections. Yet, it remains common for the term middle class to be applied for anyone in between either extreme of the socio-economic strata. The middle class is then often sub-divided into an upper-middle, middle-middle, and lower-middle class. In colloquial descriptions of the class system the middle-middle class may described as consisting of those in the middle of the social strata. Politicians and television personalities such as Lou Dobbs can be seen using the term middle class in this manner, especially when discussing the middle class squeeze. The wide discrepancy between the academic models and public opinions that lump highly educated professionals together in the same class with secretaries, may lead to the conclusion that public opinion on the subject has become largely ambiguous.

Lower Middle Class

The lower middle class is, as the name implies, generally defined as those less privileged than the middle class. People in this class commonly work in supporting occupations. Although they seldom hold advanced academic degrees, a college degree (usually a bachelor's degree) is almost always required for entry into the lower middle class.

Sociologists Dennis Gilbert, William Thompson, and Joseph Hickey, however, only divide the middle class into two groups. In their class modes the middle class only consists of an upper and lower middle class. The upper middle class, as described above, constitutes roughly 15% of the population with highly educated white collar professionals who commonly have salaries in the high 5-figure range and household incomes in the low six figure range. Semi-professionals with Bachelor's degrees and some college degrees constitute the lower middle class. Their class models show the lower middle class positioned slightly above the middle of the socio-economic strata. Those in blue and pink collar as well as clerical occupations are referred to as working class in these class models.

Working Class

The term working class is applies to those that work at this tier in the social hierarchy. Definitions of this term vary greatly. While Lloyd Warner found the vast majority of the American population to be in either the upper-lower class or lower-lower class in 1949, modern-day experts such as Michael Zweig, an economist for SUNY–Stony Brook, argue that the working class constitutes most of the population.

Dennis Gilbert places 13% of households among the "working poor" with 12% being in the "underclass". Thompson & Hickey place roughly 17% to 20% of households in the lower classes. The lower classes constituting roughly a fifth to a quarter of American society consists mainly of low-rung retail and service workers as well as the frequently unemployed and those not able to work. Overall, 13% of the population fall below the poverty threshold. Hunger and food insecurity were present in the lives of 3.9% of American households, while roughly twenty-five million Americans (ca. 9%) participated in the food stamp program.

AGRICULTURE

Before industrialization, "yeoman farmers"—self-sufficient, politically independent landowners—made up a large portion of the country's population. Jeffersonian democracy and Jacksonian democracy successfully expanded the political rights of the yeomen, and the geographical extent of the nation to provide them farms. This culminated in the Homestead Act of 1862 which provided hundreds of thousands of free farms. Before 1865 large southern plantations used slaves. After emancipation, a system of sharecropping and tenant farming for both whites and blacks in the South provided a semi-independent status for farmers who did not own their land. In contemporary times, migrant agricultural workers—mostly Mexicans—perform field and packing work.

Farmers

Only 0.7% of the population of the United States is employed in the agricultural sector. Most are proprietors of independent farms. Once the dominant American social class, this group diminished in overall numbers during the 20th century, as farm holdings grew more consolidated, farming operations became more mechanized, and most of the population migrated to urban areas.

Today, the agricultural sector has essentially taken on the characteristics of business and industry generally. In contemporary usage, a "farmer" is someone who owns and operates a farm, which more often than not will be a sizable business enterprise; "agricultural workers" or "farm workers", who perform the actual work associated with farming, typically come out of the lower classes; indeed, they are often near-destitute immigrants or migrant farm workers. In this respect, farming mirrors big business: like any enterprise, a farm has owners (who may be a family or a corporation), salaried managers, supervisors, foremen and workers.

With the number of farms steadily diminishing, the stereotypical humble homestead is increasingly the exception, for viable farming now means agribusiness; the large amounts of capital required to operate a competitive farm require large-scale organization. The large landowners in California's Central Valley, Coachella Valley and Imperial Valley fall squarely within the upper class. Among farmers, "income" in the conventional sense is not an accurate standard of wealth measurement, because farmers typically keep their official income low by placing their assets into farming corporations rather than drawing the money directly. The stereotypical poor, marginal farmer "eking out a living" from the soil, an image deeply ingrained in most Americans' minds by folklore, films, and even history texts, has now been largely displaced by agribusiness, which has bought them out and consolidated their holdings.

CLASS MOBILITY

Class ascendancy—namely that each successive generation will have a higher standard of living than its predecessor—is a central theme in American literature and culture and plays a key role in the American dream. While social class in the United States is thought to be largely based on achievement, climbing the social ladder is more difficult for those born into less advantageous positions.

Occupation (perhaps the most important class component), educational attainment, and income can be increased through a lifetime. However, factors such as wealth inheritance and local education system—which often provides lower quality education to those in poor school districts —may make rising out of poverty a challenge. Class mobility in the United States decreased between the 1970s and the 1990s. Recently a number of works have denied the existence of upward mobility. The New York Times in 2005, in a series of articles called "Class Matters" shed doubt on upward mobility and in 2010 Jerry Carrier in his book *The Making of the Slave Class* stated flatly there is no upward mobility in America and that the reason for this is culture which limits opportunity and income.

CLASS AND POLITICS

Income remains one of the main indicators of class, as it commonly reflects high educational attainment as well as a prestigious occupation. Today there remains a strong correlation, if not causation, between political activism as well as political representation and household income. Furthermore, a discrepancy in the political attitudes can be found among individuals residing in households with differing incomes.

During the 2000 election, voter turnout among those in the top 26% with household incomes exceeding $75,000 was 27% higher than the average. Some rather controversial issues such as race were impacted by household income. With higher voter turnout and affiliation with professional organizations and other popular political lobbies such as the AARP or NAACP, those with higher incomes were more likely to be represented in the political process with the government being more attuned to their needs.

Education also has an effect on voting record. Generally, the more educated a person is, the more likely he or she is to vote with those having graduate degrees being more likely to vote Democrat. While a rise in income generally increases the likelihood of a person voting Republican, many upper middle class professionals with post-graduate degrees are more likely to vote Democrat.

The presence of upper middle class liberals as households with incomes exceeding $100,000 and those with graduate degrees were the only demographics where Ralph Nader won 1% of the vote. Even though those with post-graduate degrees only constituted 8.9% of the general population, they constituted 16% of all voters. This means that the most highly educated 16% of voters were expected to vote Democrat even though most of their similarly high paid but lesser educated counterparts did not.

Class and Health

Income also had a significant impact on health as those with higher incomes had better access to health care facilities, higher life expectancy, lower infant mortality rate and increased health consciousness. While the United States lacks socialized medicine similar to that found in many other post-industrialized developed nations across Europe and Asia, 85% of the U.S. population were insured in 2005. Yet, discrepancies seem to remain beyond the difference between insured and uninsured. In 2006, Harvard researchers divided the U.S. into "eight Americas."

Life expectancy ranges from 84.9 years for the 10,400,000 Asian Americans who had an average per capita income of $21,566. Urban African Americans with an average per capita income of a $14,800 had a life expectancy of merely 71.1 years.

Furthermore, the United States like other post-industrial nations saw increased health consciousness among persons of higher social status. Persons of higher status are less likely to smoke, more likely to exercise regularly and be more conscious of their diet. Additionally, poor Americans are more likely to consume lower quality, processed foods. One can therefore conclude that low socio-economic status contributes to a person's likelihood of being obese.

CURRENT ISSUES

There have been fierce debates in the area of sociology about whether or not social class has become relevant in terms of shaping identity. The arguments suggesting that it is no longer relevant are brought forward by supporters of postmodernism. One argument for class being unimportant follows:

Arguments against relevance of class:

- French sociologist Mattei Dogan has argued in his "From Social Class and Religious Identity to Status Incongruence in Post-Industrial Societies" (*Comparative Sociology*,

2004) that the relevance of social class has declined, giving way to a different form of social identification that is largely cultural and religious, and which raises identity conflicts called status incongruence. This can be observed, in particular, in the developing countries, but even in many post-industrial societies.

Arguments for Relevance of Class

Major areas of social science still rely on class based explanations of personal identity, for instance, the history from below school of Marxist history. Outside of Marxist influenced thought, there is still much evidence suggesting that class affects everyone. Some ideas from different sociologists follow:

- Jordan suggested that those in poverty had the same attitudes on work and family as those in other classes, this being backed up with surveys expressing that the poor/working class/lower class feel almost shame about their position in society.
- MacIntosh and Mooney noted that there was still an upper-class which seems to isolate itself from other classes. It is almost impossible to get into the upper-class. They (upper-class) kept their activities (marriage, education, peer groups) as a closed system.
- Marshall et al. noted that many manual class workers are still aware of many class issues. They believed in a possible conflict of interest, and saw themselves as working class. This counters the postmodern claims that it is consumption which defines an individual.
- Andrew Adonis and Stephen Pollard (1998) discovered a new super class, which consisted of elite professionals and managers, which held high salaries and share ownership.
- Chapman noted there was still an existence of a self-recruiting upper-class identity.
- Dennis Gilbert argues that class is bound to exist in any complex society as not all occupations are equal and that households do form pattern of interaction that give rise to social classes.

5

Religion and the Law

There are laws and statutes that make reference to religion. This has led to claims from some scholars that religious freedom is literally impossible to uphold. Also, the Western legal principle of separation of church and state tends to engender a new, more inclusive civil religion.

Religion and Science

Religious knowledge, according to religious practitioners, may be gained from religious leaders, sacred texts (scriptures), and/or personal revelation. Some religions view such knowledge as unlimited in scope and suitable to answer any question; others see religious knowledge as playing a more restricted role, often as a complement to knowledge gained through physical observation. Some religious people maintain that religious knowledge obtained in this way is absolute and infallible (religious cosmology).

The scientific method gains knowledge by testing hypotheses to develop theories through elucidation of facts or evaluation by experiments and thus only answers cosmological questions about the physical universe. It develops theories of the world which best fit physically observed evidence. All scientific knowledge is subject to later refinement in the face of additional evidence. Scientific theories that have an overwhelming preponderance of favorable evidence are often treated as facts (such as the theories of gravity or evolution).

Many scientists have held strong religious beliefs and have worked to harmonize science and religion. Isaac Newton, for example, believed that gravity caused the planets to revolve about the Sun, and credited God with the design. In the concluding General Scholium to the Philosophiae Naturalis Principia Mathematica, he wrote: "This most beautiful System of the Sun, Planets and Comets, could only proceed from the counsel and dominion of an intelligent and powerful being." Nevertheless, conflict has repeatedly arisen between religious organizations and individuals who propagated scientific theories that were deemed unacceptable by the organizations. The Roman Catholic Church, for example, has in the past reserved to itself the right to decide which scientific theories were acceptable and which were unacceptable. In the 17th century, Galileo was tried and forced to recant the heliocentric theory based on the church's stance that the Greek Hellenistic system of astronomy was the correct one.

Today, religious belief among scientists is less prevalent than it is in the general public. Surveys on the subject give varying results. The Pew Research Center found in 2009 that 33% of American scientists and 83% of the general public believe in God, another 18% of scientists and 12% of the public believe more generally in a higher power, and 41% of scientists and 4% of the public believe in neither. A mailed survey to members of the National Academy of Sciences found that 7% of respondents to believed in a personal God. Elaine Howard Ecklund found that about two-thirds of scientists at elite research universities believed in God and that nearly 50 percent of them were religious.

The philosophical theory of pragmatism (first propounded by William James) has been used to reconcile scientific with religious knowledge. Pragmatism holds that the truth of a set of beliefs is indicated by its usefulness in helping people cope with a particular context of life. Thus, the fact that scientific beliefs are useful in predicting observations in the physical world can indicate a certain truth for scientific theories and the fact that religious beliefs can be useful in helping people cope with difficult emotions or moral decisions can indicate a certain truth for those beliefs.

The Catholic Church has always concurred with Augustine of Hippo who explicitly opposed a literal interpretation of the Bible whenever the Bible conflicted with science. The literal way to read the sacred texts became especially prevalent after the rise of the Protestant reformation, with its emphasis on the Bible as the only authoritative source concerning the ultimate reality. This view is often shunned by both religious leaders (who regard literally believing it as petty and look for greater meaning instead) and scientists who regard it as an impossibility.

Some Christians have disagreed with the validity of Keplerian astronomy, the theory of evolution, the scientific account of the creation of the universe and the origins of life. However, Stanley Jaki has suggested that the Christian worldview was a crucial in the emergence of modern science. Historians are moving away from the view that Christianity was always in conflict with science—the so-called conflict thesis. Gary Ferngren in his historical volume about science and religion states: "While some historians had always regarded the conflict thesis as oversimplifying and distorting a complex relationship, in the late 20th century it underwent a more systematic reevaluation. The result is the growing recognition among historians of science that the relationship of religion and science has been much more positive than is sometimes thought. Although popular images of controversy continue to exemplify the supposed hostility of Christianity to new scientific theories, studies have shown that Christianity has often nurtured and encouraged scientific endeavour, while at other times the two have co-existed without either tension or attempts at harmonization. If Galileo and the Scopes trial come to mind as examples of conflict, they were the exceptions rather than the rule."

In the Bahá'í Faith, the harmony of science and religion is a central tenet. The principle states that that truth is one, and therefore true science and true religion must be in harmony, thus rejecting the view that science and religion are in conflict. 'Abdu'l-Bahá, the son of the founder of the religion, asserted that science and religion cannot be opposed because they are aspects of the same truth; he also affirmed that reasoning powers are required to understand the truths of religion and that religious teachings which are at variance with science should not be accepted; he explained that religion has to be reasonable since God endowed humankind with reason so that they can discover truth. Shoghi Effendi, the Guardian of the Bahá'í Faith, described science and religion as "the two most potent forces in human life." Proponents of Hinduism claim that it is not afraid of scientific explorations, nor of the technological progress of mankind. According to them, there is a comprehensive scope and opportunity for Hinduism to mold itself according to the demands and aspirations of the modern world; it has the ability to align itself with both science and spiritualism. This religion uses some modern examples to explain its ancient theories and reinforce its own beliefs. For example, some Hindu thinkers have used the terminology of quantum physics to explain some basic concepts of Hinduism such as Maya or the illusory and impermanent nature of our existence.

Evolutionary Theory and Religion

At one time, evolutionists explained religion as something that conferred a biological advantages to its adherents. More recently, Richard Dawkins has explained it in terms of the evolution of self-replicating ideas, or memes as he calls them, distinct from any resulting biological advantages they might bestow. Susan Blackmore regards religions as particularly tenacious memes. Chris Hedges regards meme theory as a misleading imposition of genetics onto psychology.

RELIGION AS A CHRISTIAN CONCEPT

In recent years, some academic writers have described religion according to the theory of social constructionism, which considers how ideas and social phenomena develop in a social context. Among the main proponents of this theory of religion are Timothy Fitzgerald, Daniel Dubuisson and Talad Assad. The social constructionists argue that religion is a modern concept that developed from Christianity and was then applied inappropriately to non-Western cultures. Dubuisson, a French anthropologist, says that the idea of religion has changed a lot over time and that one cannot fully understand its development by relying on etymology, which "tends to minimize or cancel out the role of history". "What the West and the history of religions in its wake have objectified under the name 'religion'", he says, " is... something quite unique, which could be appropriate only to itself and its own history."

He notes that St. Augustine's definition of *religio* differed from the way we used the modern word "religion". Dubuisson prefers the term "cosmographic formation" to religion. Dubuisson says that, with the emergence of religion as a category separate from culture and society, there arose religious studies. The initial purpose of religious studies was to demonstrate the superiority of the "living" or "universal" European world view to the "dead" or "ethnic" religions scattered throughout the rest of the world, expanding the teleological project of Schleiermacher and Tiele to a worldwide ideal religiousness. Due to shifting theological currents, this was eventually supplanted by a liberal-ecumenical interest in searching for Western-style universal truths in every cultural tradition. Clifford Geertz's definition of religion as a "cultural system" was dominant for most of the 20th century and continues to be widely accepted today.

According to Fitzgerald, the history of other cultures' interaction with the religious category is not about a universal constant, but rather concerns a particular idea that first developed in Europe under the influence of Christianity. Fitzgerald argues that from about the 4th century CE Western Europe and the rest of the world diverged. As Christianity became commonplace, the charismatic authority identified by Augustine, a quality we might today call "religiousness", exerted a commanding influence at the local level. This system persisted in the eastern Byzantine Empire following the East-West Schism, but Western Europe regulated unpredictable expressions of charisma through the Roman Catholic Church. As the Church lost its dominance during the Protestant Reformation and Christianity became closely tied to political structures, religion was recast as the basis of national sovereignty, and religious identity gradually became a less universal sense of spirituality and more divisive, locally defined, and tied to nationality. It was at this point that "religion" was dissociated with universal beliefs and moved closer to dogma in both meaning and practice. However there was not yet the idea of dogma as personal choice, only of established churches. With the Enlightenment religion lost its attachment to nationality, says Fitzgerald, but rather than becoming a universal social attitude, it now became a personal feeling or emotion.

Friedrich Schleiermacher in the late 18th century defined religion as *das schlechthinnige Abhängigkeitsgefühl*, commonly translated as "a feeling of absolute dependence". His contemporary Hegel disagreed thoroughly, defining religion as "the Divine Spirit becoming conscious of Himself through the finite spirit." William James is an especially notable 19th century subscriber to the theory of religion as feeling.

Asad argues that before the word "religion" came into common usage, Christianity was a *disciplina*, a "rule" just like that of the Roman Empire. This idea can be found in the writings of St. Augustine (354–430). Christianity was then a power structure opposing and superseding human institutions, a literal Kingdom of Heaven. It was the discipline taught by one's family, school, church, and city authorities, rather than something calling one to self-discipline through symbols.

These ideas are developed by N. Balagangadhara. In the Age of Enlightenment, Balagangadhara says that the idea of Christianity as the purest expression of spirituality was supplanted by the concept of "religion" as a worldwide practice. This caused such ideas as religious freedom, a reexamination of classical philosophy as an alternative to Christian thought, and more radically Deism among intellectuals such as Voltaire.

Much like Christianity, the idea of "religious freedom" was exported around the world as a civilizing technique, even to regions such as India that had never treated spirituality as a matter of political identity. In Japan, where Buddhism was still seen as a philosophy of natural law, the concept of "religion" and "religious freedom" as separate from other power structures was unnecessary until Christian missionaries demanded free access to conversion, and when Japanese Christians refused to engage in patriotic events.

Other Writers

Similar views have been put forward by writers who are not social constructionists. George Lindbeck, a Lutheran and a postliberal theologian, says that religion does not refer to belief in "God" or a transcendent Absolute, but rather to "a kind of cultural and/or linguistic framework or medium that shapes the entirety of life and thought... it is similar to an idiom that makes possible the description of realities, the formulation of beliefs, and the experiencing of inner attitudes, feelings, and sentiments." Nicholas de Lange, Professor of Hebrew and Jewish Studies at Cambridge University, says that "The comparative study of religions is an academic discipline which has been developed within Christian theology faculties, and it has a tendency to force widely differing phenomena into a kind of strait-jacket cut to a Christian pattern. The problem is not only that other 'religions' may have little or nothing to say about questions which are of burning importance for Christianity, but that they may not even see themselves as religions in precisely the same way in which Christianity sees itself as a religion."

Political Religion

The theory of political religion concerns governmental ideologies whose cultural and political backing is so strong that they are said to attain power equivalent to those of a state religion, to which they often exhibit significant similarities in both theory and practice. Such political religions generally vie with existing transcendent religions, and try, if possible, to replace or eradicate them. The term was first proposed by the religious scholar Hans Maier. The term is sometimes treated as synonymous with civil religion, but although some scholars use the terms as equivalent, others see a useful distinction, using "civil religion" as something weaker, which functions more as a socially unifying and essentially conservative force, where a political religion is radically transformational, even apocalyptic.

The term is sometimes used outside academia, often with meanings tangential to or opposite to the sociological usage (for example, applying it to a church), with the use intended as a derogatory description of excessive adherence to something political or ideological. Even when used correctly, supporters of an ideology will generally reject the application of the term "political religion".

The term *political religion* is a sociological one, drawing on the sociological aspects of religion which can be often be found in certain secular ideologies. A political religion occupies much the same psychological and sociological space as a theistic religion, and as a result it often displaces or co-opts existing religious organizations and beliefs; this is described as a "sacralisation" of politics. However, although a political religion may co-opt existing religious structures or symbolism, it does not itself have any independent spiritual or theocratic elements - it is essentially secular, using religion only for political purposes, if it does not reject religious faith outright. The first scholars to use the concept of political religion (or occasionally-used synonyms such as "secular religion" and "lay religion") were Protestant and Catholic intellectuals and theologians, such as Luigi Sturzo, Adolf Keller, Paul Tillich, Gerhard Leibholz, Waldemar Gurian and Eric Voegelin.

These linked the concept to modernity, mass society and the rise of the bureaucratic state, and seeing in political religions "the climax of the rebellion against the religion of God", also described them as 'pseudo-religions', 'substitute religions', 'surrogate religions', 'religions manipulated by man' and 'anti-religions'. Yale political scientist, Juan Linz and others have noted that secularization of the twentieth century had created a void which could be filled by a total ideology, making the political religions of totalitarianism possible.

Aspects of Political Religions

Key qualities often (not all are always strongly present) shared by religion (particularly cults) and political religion include

- Structural
  - o differentiation between self and *other*, and demonisation of *other* (in theistic religion, the differentiation usually depends on adherence to certain dogmas and social behaviours; in political religion, differentiation may be on grounds such as nationality, social attitudes, or membership in "enemy" political parties, instead)
  - o a charismatic figurehead, with messianic tendencies; if figurehead is deceased, powerful successors;
  - o strong, hierarchical organisational structures
  - o a desire to control education, in order to ensure the security of the system
- Belief
  - o a coherent belief system for imposing symbolic meaning on the external world, with an emphasis on security through purity;
  - o an intolerance of other ideologies of the same type
  - o a degree of utopianism

- o the belief that the ideology is in some way natural or obvious, so that (at least for certain groups of people) those who reject it are in some way "blind"
- o a genuine desire on the part of individuals to convert others to the cause
- o a willingness to place ends over means - in particular, a willingness to use violence and fraud
- o fatalism - a belief that the ideology will inevitably triumph in the end.

Not all of these aspects are present in any one *political religion*; this is only a list of some common aspects.

Suppression of Religious Beliefs

Political religions vie with existing religions, and try, if possible, to replace or eradicate them. Loyalty to other entities, such as a church or a deity are often seen to interfere with loyalty to the political religion. The authority of potential religious leaders also presents a threat to the authority of the political religion.

As a result, some or all religious sects are either suppressed or banned. An existing sect may be converted into a state religion, but dogma and personnel may be modified to suit the needs of the party or state. Where there is suppression of religious institutions and beliefs, this might be explicitly accompanied by atheistic doctrine as in state atheism.

Juan Linz has posited the friendly form of separation of church and state as the counterpole of political religion but describes the hostile form of separation of church and state as moving toward political religion as found in totalitarianism.

Absolute Loyalty

Loyalty to the state or political party and acceptance of the government/party ideology is paramount. Dissenters may be expelled, ostracized, discriminated against, imprisoned, "re-educated", or killed. Loyalty oaths or membership in a dominant (or sole) political party may be required for employment, government services, or simply as routine. Criticism of the government may be a serious crime. Enforcements range from ostracism from one's neighbours to execution.

Fear

The political religion often helps maintain its power base by instilling fear of some kind in the population. For example, North Korea holds frequent air raid drills to emphasize the possibility of imminent invasion. In China, the government emphasizes the danger of instability. The Stalinists maintained a state of panic by claiming that Trotskyist conspirators were sabotaging the Soviet Union. In Germany, the Reichstag fire, blamed on Communist terrorism, provided an opportunity for Adolf Hitler to declare a state of emergency. In the United States, the fear of Communism or Terrorism (as evidenced in the Red Scare and the War on Terror) have been used similarly.

Domestic displays of military power may be frequent. Citizens may obey harsh state mandates out of fear of being reported by fellow citizens or caught by the secret police.

When the political religion lacks complete control of the state, it may instead emphasize the threat posed to society by some otherwise-recognized or hypothetical threat or whichever rival party or group it deems to be the most "demonic".

Externalization of Blame

A common tactic of political religions is to pin blame for the nation's problems on a particular entity or group. North Korea blames its economic problems on the Western world. In Nazi Germany, Jews and other minority groups were the target.

Cult of Personality

A political religion often elevates its leaders to near-godlike status. Displays of leaders in the form of posters or statues may be mandated in public areas and even private homes. Children may be required to learn the state's version of the leaders' biographies in school.

Propaganda

Political gatherings may supplement or replace religious ceremonies to help reinforce loyalty. The state usually controls the mass media for similar reasons, filling it with propaganda. Political religions that do not have such a level of mandated control may, instead, use commercial means to influence editorial and programming decisions. Certain leisure or cultural activities may also be mandated to reinforce some aspect of loyalty or the state ideology.

HISTORICAL CASES

According to Emilio Gentile, "Fascism was the first and prime instance of a modern political religion." "This religion sacralized the state and assigned it the primary educational task of transforming the mentality, the character, and the customs of Italians. The aim was to create a 'new man,' a believer in and an observing member of the cult of Fascism." "The argument [that fascism was a 'political religion'] tends to involve three main claims: i) that fascism was characterized by a religious form, particularly in terms of language and ritual; ii) that fascism was a sacralized form of totalitarianism, which legitimized violence in defence of the nation and regeneration of a fascist 'new man'; and iii) that fascism took on many of the functions of religion for a broad swathe of society."

Nazism

"Among committed [Nazi] believers, a mythic world of eternally strong heroes, demons, fire and sword - in a word, the fantasy world of the nursery - displaced reality." Heinrich Himmler was fascinated by the occult, and sought to turn the SS into the basis of an official state cult.

Stalinism

Stalinism refers to the policies and governmental philosophy of Joseph Stalin, leader of the Soviet Union from 1922–1953. The term came into prominence during the mid-1930s, when Lazar Kaganovich, a Soviet politician and associate of Stalin, reportedly declared, "Let's replace Long Live Leninism with Long Live Stalinism!"

Stalin initially met this usage with hesitancy, dismissing it as excessively praiseful and contributing to a cult of personality. In the Cold War-era United States, Stalinism took on a decidedly more negative meaning, akin to what the New York Times dubbed "red fascism."

Stalinism, when used in its broadest sense, refers to socialist states akin to the Stalin-era Soviet Union, i.e. that are characterized by a totalitarian figure head, secret police, propaganda, and especially brutal tactics of political cohersion.

According to Encyclopedia Britannica, "Stalinism is associated with a regime of terror and totalitarian rule."

Stalinist Policies

Stalinism usually defines the style of a government rather than an ideology. The ideology was "Marxist–Leninist theory", reflecting that Stalin himself was not a theoretician, in contrast to Marx and Lenin, and prided himself on maintaining the legacy of Lenin as a founding father for the Soviet Union and the future Communist world. Stalinism is an interpretation of their ideas, and a certain political regime claiming to apply those ideas in ways fitting the changing needs of society, as with the transition from "socialism at a snail's pace" in the mid-twenties to the rapid industrialisation of the Five-Year Plans. Sometimes, although rarely, the compound terms "Marxism–Leninism–Stalinism" (used by the Brazilian MR-8), or *teachings of Marx / Engels / Lenin / Stalin*, are used to show the alleged heritage and succession.

Simultaneously, however, many people who profess Marxism or Leninism view Stalinism as a perversion of their ideas; Trotskyists, in particular, are virulently anti-Stalinist, considering Stalinism a counter-revolutionary policy using vague Marxist-sounding rhetoric to achieve power.

From 1917 to 1924, Lenin, Trotsky, and Stalin often appeared united, but their ideological differences never disappeared. In his dispute with Trotsky, Stalin de-emphasised the role of workers in advanced capitalist countries (for example, he considered the U.S. working class as bourgeoisified labour aristocracy). Also, Stalin polemicised against Trotsky on the role of peasants, as in China, whereas Trotsky's position was in favor of urban insurrection over peasant-based guerrilla warfare.

The main contributions of Stalin to communist theory were:

- The groundwork for the Soviet policy concerning nationalities, laid in Stalin's 1913 work *Marxism and the National Question*, praised by Lenin.
- 'Socialism in One Country'
- The theory of aggravation of the class struggle along with the development of socialism, a theoretical base

supporting the repression of political opponents as necessary.

Stalinism has been described as being synonymous with totalitarianism, or a tyrannical regime. The term has been used to describe regimes that fight political dissent through violence, imprisonment, and killings. However given that fascist, theocratic, and otherwise anti-communist governments have used these methods to curb dissent just as much as pro-communist governments have, the term "Stalinism" may only really be accurate when describing a government that is pro-Stalin or that proclaims itself to be a socialist state while taking the above measures. Personality cults are also common to all Stalinist regimes. Nicolae Ceausescu, Mao Zedong, Kim Il-Sung and Stalin himself all constructed cults of personality that use propaganda to identify the current regime as heroic or benevolent.

STALINIST ECONOMIC POLICY

At the start of the 1930s Stalin launched a wave of radical economic policies, which completely overhauled the industrial and agricultural face of the Soviet Union. This came to be known as the 'Great Turn' as Russia turned away from the near-capitalist New Economic Policy. The NEP had been implemented by Lenin in order to ensure the survival of the Communist state following seven years of war (1914–1921, World War I from 1914 to 1917, and the subsequent Civil War) and had rebuilt Soviet production to its 1913 levels. However, Russia still lagged far behind the West, and the NEP was felt by Stalin and the majority of the Communist party, not only to be compromising Communist ideals, but also not delivering sufficient economic performance, as well as not creating the envisaged Socialist society. It was therefore felt necessary to increase the pace of industrialisation in order to catch up with the West.

Fredric Jameson has said that "Stalinism was [...] a success and fulfilled its historic mission, socially as well as economically" given that it "modernised the Soviet Union, transforming a peasant society into an industrial state with a literate population and a remarkable scientific superstructure." Robert Conquest disputed such a conclusion and noted that "Russia had already been fourth to fifth among industrial economies before World War I" and that Russian industrial advances could have been achieved without collectivisation, famine or terror. The industrial successes were far less than claimed, and the Soviet-style industrialisation was "an anti-innovative dead-end", according to him. According to several Western historians, Stalinist agricultural policies were a key factor in causing the Soviet famine of 1932–1933, which the Ukrainian government now calls *the Holodomor*, recognizing it as an act of genocide. However, there is still considerable debate in other countries as to whether or not the famine can be recognized as genocide.

MAOISM

Maoism, also known as Mao Zedong Thought, is a variant of Marxism, which is itself a form of communism, derived from the teachings of the Chinese political leader Mao Zedong (1894-1976). Developed during the 1950s and 1960s, it is widely applied as the political and military guiding ideology in the Communist Party of China (CPC) from Mao's ascendancy to its leadership until the party was taken over by Deng Xiaoping, who implemented Deng Xiaoping Theory and Chinese economic reforms in 1978. Nonetheless, although not fully adhered to by the government of the People's Republic of China anymore due to the reforms, Maoist parties and groups exist throughout the world, most notably in Peru, India, and Nepal, in the latter of which, the Maoist party won the elections in 2008.

Marxist Origins

Mao drew information from the writings of Marx, Engels and Lenin in elaborating his theory. Philosophically, his most important reflections emerge on the concept of "contradiction" (*maodun*). These are contained in two major essays: "On contradiction" and "On the correct handling of contradictions among the people". He adopts therein the positivist-empiricist idea (shared by Engels) that contradiction is present in matter itself (and thus, also in the ideas of the brain). Matter always develops through a dialectical contradiction: "The interdependence of the contradictory aspects present in all things and the struggle between these aspects determine the life of things and push their development forward. There is nothing that does not contain contradiction; without contradiction nothing would exist". Thanks to this development or unfolding, something that was subordinated in the past may become dominant in the present and the future. This should be directly read in the light of the principle of class struggle, Mao said. Furthermore, each contradiction ("class struggle", then: the contradiction holding between relations of production and the concrete development of forces of production) expresses itself in a series of other contradictions, some dominant, others not. "There are many contradictions in the process of development of a complex thing, and one of them is necessarily the principal contradiction whose existence and development determine or influence the existence and development of the other contradictions". Thus, the principal contradiction should be tackled with priority when trying to make the basic contradiction "solidify".

His basic stand on contradiction is founded on Marxist epistemology. The two essays just quoted contain reflections on this issue, but the theme is elaborated further in the essay "On practice. On the relation between knowledge and practice, between knowing and doing". "Practice" connects "contradiction" with "class struggle" in the following way: Inside a mode of production, there are 3 realms where practice functions: economic production, scientific experimentation (which also takes place in economic production and should not be radically disconnected from the former) and finally, class struggle. These may be considered the proper objects of economy, scientific knowledge, and politics. The three of them deal with matter in its various forms, socially mediated. As a result, they are the only realms where knowledge may arise (since truth and knowledge only make sense in relation to matter, according to Marxist epistemology). Mao emphasizes—like Marx in trying to confront the "bourgeoisie idealism" of his time—that knowledge must be based on empirical evidence. Knowledge result from hypotheses verified in the contrast with a real object; this real object, despite being mediated by the subject's theoretical frame, retains its materiality and will offer resistance to those ideas that do not conform to its truth. Thus, in each of these realms (economic, scientific and political practice), contradictions (principle and secondary) must be identified, explored and put to function to achieve the communist goal. This involves the need to know, "scientifically", how the masses produce (how they live, think, and work), to obtain knowledge of how class struggle (the main contradiction that articulates a mode of production, in its various realms) expresses itself.

Maoism's political orientation emphasizes the "revolutionary struggle of the vast majority of people against the exploiting classes and their state structures", which Mao termed a "People's War". Usually involving peasants, its military strategies have involved guerrilla war tactics focused on surrounding the cities from the countryside, with a heavy emphasis on political transformation through mass involvement of the lower classes of society.

Maoism departs from conventional European-inspired Marxism in that its focus is on the agrarian countryside, rather than the industrial urban forces. This is known as Agrarian socialism. Notably, Maoist parties in Peru, Nepal and Philippines have adopted equal stresses on urban and rural areas, depending on the country's focus of economic activity. Maoism broke with the state capitalist framework of the Soviet Union under Nikita Khrushchev and dismisses it as modern revisionism, a traditional pejorative term among communists referring to those who fight for capitalism in the name of socialism.

In its post-revolutionary period, Mao Zedong Thought is defined in the CPC's Constitution as "Marxism-Leninism applied in a Chinese context", synthesized by Mao Zedong and China's "first-generation leaders". It asserts that class struggle continues even if the proletariat has already overthrown the bourgeoisie, and there are capitalist restorationist elements within the Communist Party itself. Maoism provided the CCP's first comprehensive theoretical guideline with regards to how to continue socialist revolution, the creation of a socialist society, socialist military construction, and highlights various contradictions in society to be addressed by what is termed "socialist construction". While it continues to be lauded to be the major force that defeated "imperialism and feudalism" and created a "New China" by the Communist Party of China, the ideology survives only in name on the Communist Party's Constitution; Deng Xiaoping abolished most Maoist practices in 1978, advancing a guiding ideology called "Socialism with Chinese characteristics.

Leninism

Klaus-Georg Riegel, in his article "Marxism-Leninism as a political religion", said "Lenin's utopian design of a revolutionary community of virtuosi as a typical political religion of an intelligentsia longing for an inner-worldly salvation, a socialist paradise without exploitation and alienation, to be implanted in the Russian backward society at the outskirts of the industrialised and modernised Western Europe."

Modern Examples

The North Korean government has promulgated Juche as a political alternative to traditional religion. The doctrine advocates a strong nationalist propaganda basis and is fundamentally opposed to Christianity and Buddhism, the two largest religions on the Korean peninsula. Juche theoreticians have, however, incorporated religious ideas into the state ideology. According to government figures, Juche is the largest political religion in North Korea. The public practice of all other religions is overseen and subject to heavy surveillance by the state.

Turkmenistan

During the long rule of president Saparmurat Niyazov large pictures and statues of him could be seen in public places in Turkmenistan. In an interview with the television news program "60 Minutes", Niyazov said the people of Turkmenistan placed them there voluntarily because they love him so much, and that he did not originally want them there. In addition, he granted himself the title "Türkmenbaºy", meaning "Leader of all Ethnic Turkmens" in the Turkmen language. A book purportedly authored by Niyazov, *Ruhnama* ("Book of the Soul") was required reading in educational institutions and was often displayed and treated with the same respect as the Qur'an. The study of Ruhnama in the academic system was scaled down but to some extent continued after Niyazov's death (in 2006), as of 2008.

6

Family Planning Attitude and Practice

For a country like India, adoption of small family size norm is very essential and in this regard, family planning programme initiated by the Government of India as early as in 1952 play a vital role. There exist wide differences in the levels of knowledge, attitudes and practice of contraception in the community and much variations are found to be significantly varying across various regions in the country. The present study also concurs with the earlier studies in the case of level of knowledge of family planning programme. Except 4 per cent of the respondents, almost all of them have heard of family planning programme. With regard to their attitude towards the programme, and overwhelming proportion of them (81.8%), without much variation across the less and more developed areas, have appreciated the programme. However, the actual practice level among them is reported to be significantly vary across the two contrasting areas.

For instance, while the proportion of those who have ever used any method of family planning is reported to be 54.3 per cent among the more developed areas, their proportion has come down to 25.5 per cent in the case of the less developed areas. Such a wide variations across the areas clearly reflects on the existing variations in the health infrastructural facilities, level of development and other factors, besides the socioeconomic, demographic, health and cultural background of the community members. In the case of post adoption services also, the data reveal that the health personnel's involvement is very low

(19.3%) among the women of the less developed areas as compared to 21.1 per cent of them reported from the more developed areas. This confirms that relatively better follow up services for the adopters of contraception prevailing in more developed areas as against that in the less developed areas might be a factor for the better performance of family planning adoption in the former areas.

UTILIZATION OF HEALTH SERVICES

Utilization of health services plays an important role in improving the population coverage for Reproductive Health Programme. In this regard, the type of health centre the community member visiting during their ill health, the level of satisfaction about health service facilities are some of the major issues which helps in assessing their acceptability of various health services.

The utilization of various health centres like government hospitals, primary health centres, sub centres located in the area are more by the women from the more developed areas (30.4%) as against only 7 per cent in the case of those from the less developed areas. In contrast, the utilization of only primary health centre is mostly (53.1%) by the women from the less developed areas when compared to 21.6 per cent of them from the more developed areas. The utilization of sub centre which is a local level health unit, is significantly higher among those from the more developed areas which reveals the acceptability and accessibility of the local level sub centre in these areas when compared to only 16.9 per cent of them in the less developed areas.

The data on the level of satisfaction with the utilization of health service facilities indicate that an overwhelming proportion (84.6%) of the women from the more developed areas when compared one third (37.4%) from those of the less developed areas are fully satisfied with the existing health services. An attempt is also made in the study to assess the health service acceptability of the respondents in terms of various facilities viz, location of the clinic, cleanliness and orderliness of the clinic, comfortableness of waiting room, waiting time before seeing the doctor, time spent by the doctor with the patient, facilities existing around the clinic, and satisfaction with referral facilities.

The data on all the indicators of service acceptability show that the respondents level of satisfaction with respect to these indicators are relatively higher in the less developed areas when compared to their counterparts in the more developed areas. The findings indicate that in view of the higher level of utilization of these facilities and also of the availability of alternative health system like, private hospital and other health centres, the respondents belonging to the more developed areas have stated a greater level of satisfaction with the facilities available at the government health centres. On the contrary, in the absence of other alternative health systems and also of utilizing the locally available indigenous systems, women from the less developed areas have expressed their greater satisfaction with the facilities available at the government health centres. The dissatisfaction of the clients would incline them only not to attach importance to the advice of the health personnel working at these government health centres.

Therefore, increasing the credibility of the service personnel and also to increase the influence of these persons among the clients for motivating them to accept and utilize various Reproductive Health Programmes, better amenities may have to be urgently provided at these centres.

Conclusions and Recommendations

A vast country, like India, with very wide disparities in various sectors of development among different states, uniform strategies for the country as a whole will not yield the desired results. As the reproductive health programme is a source of strength to all other schemes of socioeconomic development, effective measures have to be initiated to improve its performance among all states. Therefore, there is a necessity for formulating policies and programmes on realistic estimates and parameters and more meaningfully in a decentralized manner for effective promotion of the programme in all regions. Identification of regions and broad cultural groups within each region on the basis of their performance in health programme has to be initiated. It would provide clues to the health personnel to channelize their effects on a realistic and differential basis among the regions and cultural groups, wherever performance of health programme varies.

In conclusion, it is observed that the number and types of variables and their extent of influence on reproductive health programmes across different cultural and regional groups significantly vary. Further, there are certain common specific factors that influence reproductive health status of the people belonging to different in the cultures and regions. Hence, these findings raise a number of issues for formulating policies in the field of reproductive health, not uniformly for the country as a whole, but differentially for sub-regions in various parts of the country.

Similarly, the pattern of various in-puts for developing the reproductive health programme may also have to be suitably modified in view of the diversity of the factors and their influence on health care programmes across different cultures and ecological regions. Thus, the findings are unique in many aspects and should have far-reaching, theoretical, methodological, policy and programme implications in the reproductive health care programmes. Some of the most important implications of the present study are given below:

1. The findings of this research would suggest the need for a change in methodology for studies on Reproductive Health Programmes. As differences exist in the performance in health programmes in different regions and cultural groups, it is essential to study the various determinants by stratifying the population according to regions, communities and other stratification variables. This would be a methodological achievement for improving explanatory efforts to understand better, the determinants of reproductive health status of women among different regions and groups.
2. Identification of areas and broad cultural groups within each area on the basis of their performance in RCH programme would provide clues to the health personnel to channalise their efforts on a realistic and differential basis among the regions and cultural groups, wherever performance in various health programmes varies.
3. Lack of proper infrastructural health facilities in the less developed, areas rightly indicates the urgency of increasing infrastructural and health services and doctor-patient ratio in these areas. Hence differential financial

and other inputs may have to be provided for different areas on the basis of their requirements and the existing performance in various health programmes in general and reproductive health programmes in particular.

CHILD MORTALITY IN INDIA

A large number of studies from many developing countries have shown a strong negative association between mother's educational level and child mortality. Nevertheless, there is still considerable uncertainty about how strong the total impact of education actually is, let alone the underlying mechanisms and the variations between different settings. One important reason for the uncertainty, as pointed out by many authors (*e.g.* Hobcraft 1993), is that a woman's education is determined by her parents' resources and attitudes and various other factors that may also have a bearing on mortality, and that are often unavailable or inadequately measured in the data that are used.

However, this is not the only measurement issue that deserves attention. One should also be concerned about the possibility that an individual-level perspective may fail to reveal the entire impact of education. Perhaps there is a beneficial effect of the education of other women in the community, above and beyond that of the mother's own education? In that case, an expansion of education would reduce mortality not only because more women enter into an educational category associated with lower mortality, but also because everyone, including those who themselves remain uneducated, take advantage of the generally higher level of education in the community.

Such a community-level contribution was seen in recent analyses of fertility from Africa (Kravdal 2002) and India (McNay, Cassen and Arokiasamy 2003). It has also been reported in some studies of health and mortality in developed countries that education and other socioeconomic resources in the community are influential (*e.g.* Pickett and Pearl 2001), but the possible importance of community education has been ignored in the literature on child mortality in developing countries.

The otherwise excellent paper by Desai and Alva (1998) may serve as an interesting illustration of the lack of attention to the community education effect. Their goal was to show that the effect of mother's education may be severely biased in the simple models that are often estimated. They first included a rural/urban indicator and various individual variables linked with (although not necessarily determinants of) education, and found that the effect was substantially weakened. Realizing that also a number of unobserved factors at the community level might be linked with both education and mortality, their next step was to include village fixedeffects instead of the rural/urban indicator, which further reduced the education effect. This would be very smart, if it were not for the possibility that one particular community factor, namely other people's education, might influence mortality. In this fixed-effects approach it is essentially thrown out with all other community factors (but it was implicitly touched in the concluding discussion).

The objective of this study is to find out whether the education of other women in the community is substantially important for child mortality in India, taking various possible determinants of education into account. There are still as many as 68 per 1000 of the Indian children who die before their first birthday and 95 per 1000 who die before their fifth, as a national average for 1994-1999 (International Institute for Population Sciences and OCR Macro 2000). Moreover, the general educational level is rather low. For example, 57% of the women of reproductive age in the late 1990s had less than three years of education, and only 14% had ten or more years. In this situation, a better assessment of the health benefits of school investments should be welcome.

The main focus is on the deaths to children less than five years old, but models for health and health care variables that are presumably important for mortality are also estimated. Indicators of women's autonomy are included as potentially mediating or confounding factors. Women's lack of autonomy, which is particularly pronounced in South Asia, has been suggested by many authors as an important reason for high child mortality.

However, there is still not much solid statistical evidence for such effects, and little is known about the role women's autonomy plays in the education-mortality relationship. Besides, the importance of two other possible mediators, women's health knowledge and reproductive behaviour, is checked. The analysis is based on data from the National Family Health Survey of 1998-1999. This survey has a very large, clustered sample of about 90 000 respondents and includes more questions on women's autonomy than most other Demographic and Health Surveys.

THEORETICAL CONSIDERATIONS

Why Should We Expect Community Education to be Important for Mortality? While it is widely recognized that a child's mortality is influenced by its mother's education, little explicit attention has been paid to the possibility that also the education of other women in the community may be of importance. Three main causal channels are relevant: social learning, social influence, and indirect mechanisms. Social learning means that knowledge and attitudes are transmitted directly from others by communication and observation, whereas social influence refers to a more passive imitation of behaviour, driven by a desire to gain other people's approval or avoid sanctions. The indirect mechanism is that others' ideas, resources, or behaviour can influence society and social institutions and thereby individual behaviour or events.

More specifically, women who live in communities where many others have some education may have more knowledge about good health behaviour and be more generally well-informed and less fatalistic than women at the same educational level elsewhere. This may lead to better nutrition of the children, higher prevalence of vaccination, a more hygienic environment, and more appropriate home care in case of disease, and it may make it easier to get professional help and communicate with health workers.

Whereas this particular mechanism perhaps seems most plausible for women who themselves have little education, it is not necessarily irrelevant for the better-educated, who may benefit from having a larger group of women with whom they can discuss ideas that they have been exposed to at school or through reading. Another possible effect is that a rise in women's education may contribute to undermine old ideas about women's rights and obligations compared to men. An improvement of women's autonomy as a contextual phenomenon, and the concomitant changes in women's individual position, may influence child mortality for a number of reasons. These mechanisms, as well as the possibly reverse effect from women's autonomy to education, are dealt with in more detail below. Moreover, broader economic transformations may take place as a result of a better-educated work force. In particular, the community may become wealthier and thus have better opportunities to establish, for example, good sanitation systems and health care facilities.

Also a change in political attitudes may follow from a higher general level of education in the community and foster a growth in such public services. As further discussed below, however, the causal effects may also run in the opposite direction, for example from wealth to education, or there may be a spurious relationship between the general educational level and the existence of health care facilities. For similar reasons, women who live in areas where the average educational level is relatively high may have lower fertility than others (Kravdal 2002). This may be favourable from a child health perspective. In particular, short spacing has repeatedly been reported to increase mortality. In spite of their strong effects, the reproductive factors appear to be responsible for only a very small part of the association between child mortality and the mother's own education, but a larger contribution might be seen when the community level also is considered.

A quite different mechanism is that a higher proportion of educated women in the community will contribute to making other children less sick, which will reduce the chance of seeing the child die from a contagious disease.

On the other hand, education may also contribute to increase child mortality. Many investigations have shown that educated women tend to breastfeed for a shorter period than others (*e.g.* United Nations 1995), which may have serious implications for the child's health. A similar relationship can perhaps be found at the community level. When many other women in the community are educated, attitudes toward women's work may have become more liberal and jobs in the modern sector that are attractive to and suitable for women, and where they cannot bring their children with them, may have been created. This may have consequences both for breastfeeding and child care more generally. In addition, a generally high educational level may produce negative attitudes to breastfeeding regardless of any labour market transformations.

Also the educational level among men in the community may influence child mortality. For example, a woman who is surrounded by many educated men, and for that reason perhaps also has an educated husband herself, may have more knowledge than others about the advantages of seeking help from the modern health sector. Some of the other arguments above may also be relevant. Because of the possible effect of men's general educational level and its close correlation with that of women, it should be included in statistical models intended to shed light on the implications of specific efforts to stimulate girls' schooling.

Many of the possible effects of community education discussed above may depend on the child's sex or age. For example, the mother's education or literacy have often been found to be less important for infants than older children, and a similar pattern might be seen for community education. However, these issues are largely ignored in this study.

LEVEL OF AGGREGATION

In principle, the influential "other women" may be close neighbours, other women in the village, or even women in other parts of the country, and they may have the same or a different age. In this study, it is the education of other women of reproductive age in the same village or in an area of a similar size that is in focus. Whereas each woman certainly does not interact directly with all other women within such an area, she may interact with a sub-group that can be considered randomly selected. Besides, those with whom she interacts directly may themselves be part of interaction chains that in total include the entire female population. Because there are also indirect mechanisms, it is theoretically reasonable to include indicators of the overall situation, such as the average length of education among all women in the area, as community variables in statistical models.

DETERMINANTS OF EDUCATION

As mentioned above, the relationships between education and various other factors are causally ambiguous. For example, economic strength is not only a result of education, but also a determinant. Moreover, the statistical association between community education and access to health care facilities may reflect both a causal and a spurious effect. As an example of the latter, the political attitudes and the efficiency of the administrative authorities may be key factors behind both education, the existence of health care facilities in the village, and the quality of these facilities. In this study, it is only the proximity of the facilities that is included, not their quality, and it is considered an indicator of factors that are also important for education.

Urbanization is largely a determinant of education (although education may fuel urbanization in the long run, and a woman's own education may be one factor behind her move from a rural to an urban area). Having a large population in a small area facilitates educational expansion, and a modern, non-agricultural sector calls for an educated labour force. On the whole, urbanization also tends to reduce mortality because of, for example, better developed preventive and curative health services and water and sewage systems.

Also the religious attitudes in the community may be important for the willingness to invest in schools, in addition to influencing mortality for other reasons. The reverse causality, from education to religion, seems less plausible. Besides, the percentage of people in scheduled castes or tribes may be a determinant of education.

THE IMPORTANCE OF WOMEN'S AUTONOMY

Women's autonomy is another factor that is thought to be closely linked with education, one way or the other, and that may have a substantial impact on child mortality. Using Jejeebhoy's (1995) terminology, women's "decision-making autonomy" (opportunity to take part and be heard in discussions with parents, husbands, or in-laws) and "physical autonomy" (freedom of movement) are probably particularly important for mortality. These factors might, for example, operate through such factors as the use of preventive health services, as shown by Bloom, Wypij and Das Gupta (2001), the child's nutrition, as suggested by Miles-Doan and Bisharat (1990), or the treatment of sick children, as suggested by *e.g.* Caldwell (1986) and Das Gupta (1990). The "economic autonomy" has been considered another aspect of women's autonomy, and refers to their ability to fend for themselves economically, which depends on their skills, their rights to land and inheritance, their access to credit, whether they are allowed to keep the money they earn, and other political and sociocultural factors.

Some authors have argued that economic autonomy may be important for fertility (*e.g.* Mason 1987, 1997). In that case, it may also have a bearing on mortality. Besides, the possibility of a more direct effect cannot be excluded. These three aspects of women's autonomy are, of course, difficult to separate. They affect each other mutually and definitions will necessarily be blurred. In addition, Jejeebhoy (1995) has suggested another closely related dimension, "emotional autonomy", which refers to the closeness between husband and wife. This also may have a bearing on child mortality (Jejeebhoy 1998). Indicators of all these four dimensions of women's autonomy are included in this study.

The Reciprocal Link Between Women's Education and their Autonomy Community norms and institutional structures are strong determinants of the individual woman's autonomy, but there are also individual variations caused by such factors as the woman's own age, education, economic resources, religion, and position in the life cycle.

However, there is no unambiguously positive relationship between women's education and autonomy (*e.g.* Basu 1996). For example, some studies have shown that better-educated women may have no more freedom of movement than others, and perhaps even less (*e.g.* Balk 1997). It has also been argued that the influence of education and other individual characteristics on women's autonomy is highly context-dependent. For example, Jejeebhoy and Sathar (2001) found that education was an unimportant determinant in the north of India, but that it had significant impact in the south.

In addition to the possible impact of a woman's schooling on her individual autonomy, there may be corresponding effects at the community level: As already mentioned, an expansion of education may tend to reduce men's dominance more generally. Moreover, the inverse relationship is indeed plausible: Poor parents would see little need to educate their daughters if they reckon that community norms about women's position would not allow them to make use of it for paid work anyway, and that their in-laws perhaps will put their hands on any income they might earn. In fact, women's expectedly poor productivity because of low autonomy is also an argument for many families, along with the kinship and (still informally existing) dowry system and the need for sons to perform religious acts, for not wanting to have many daughters at all.

Data and Methods

Data: The analysis is based on data from the National Family Health Survey of 1998-1999 (NFHS II), in which about 90000 ever-married women aged 15-49 were interviewed. The restriction to ever-married women is unproblematic because of the low out-of wedlock fertility in India. There is supposed to be little underreporting of deaths (International Institute for Population Sciences and OCR Macro 2000). Besides, the age heaping at multiples of six months should be no concern in this study that is focused on educational differentials and mortality over a five-year period.

The survey has a clustered sample. Within each state, a number of census enumeration areas ("primary sampling units"; PSUs) were selected on the basis of certain criteria. In total, there were 3215 such areas in the survey, each typically spanning one or a few villages, or part of a town or city. On average, about 30 households in each area were randomly chosen, and all women of reproductive age in these households were selected for interview. Weights specific to a small group of PSUs were defined to make the survey nationally representative.

In this study, averages of educational level and various other variables are calculated for these approximately 30 women (or, for the autonomy indicators, those who are married). These averages can be considered proxies for the corresponding PSU averages. For education, the measurement error introduced by using such a proxy was shown in a simulation experiment by Kravdal (2002) to be unimportant. Further evidence of the appropriateness of basing the community-level variables on so small sub-samples is provided below. Exclusion of the woman in focus before calculating the averages does not influence the effect estimates, of course. In addition to the individual data, the survey includes characteristics of each village within the rural PSUs. The information on distance to health care facilities is used in this study.

Models: Discrete-time hazard models for mortality of children born within the five years before interview are estimated in the aML software (Lillard and Panis 2000). Each child contributes a series of six-month observation intervals up to a maximum of five years. Tests showed this to be sufficiently short intervals. Twins are excluded. The sample includes 3996 child deaths.

Besides, logistic models for 15 health and health care indicators are estimated for children who were less than three years old and still alive at interview and who had no more than one younger sibling. The women were only interviewed about the health and health care of the two youngest children below about age three (born after 1 January 1995 in states where the fieldwork started in 1998 and after 1 January 1996 in states where it started in 1999), and most of the questions were further restricted to the survivors. Besides, some children are left out of the analysis because of missing information on the dependent variable in focus. More specifically, models for the following probabilities are estimated:

- whether the mother had moderate or severe anemia (Hb < 10g/dl)
- whether the mother had received antenatal care from a health worker (physician, nurse, midwife, other health professional, or home health worker)
- whether the mother had received at least one tetanus injection before birth
- whether the child had been fully vaccinated (restricted to children who were 12-23 months old at interview, because the children should be fully vaccinated at the time of their first birthday, according to international and Indian guidelines)
- whether the child had ever received vitamin A supplementation (restricted to children older than 12 months, because the current Programme on Prevention of Blindness prescribes doses every six months starting at the age of nine months)

- whether the child had suffered from diarrhoea the last two weeks before interview
- whether the child had suffered from cough accompanied by fast breathing (symptoms of acute respiratory infection) the last two weeks
- whether a child with diarrhoea had been taken to a health facility or provider for advice or treatment.
- whether a child with diarrhoea had been given oral rehydration
- whether a child with cough and fast breathing had been taken to a health facility or provider for advice or treatment.
- whether a child younger than four months received only breast milk, *i.e.* no solid food, no plain water, and no other liquid (in accordance with recommendations, which have been criticized by Anandaiah and Choe (2000))
- whether a child aged 6-11 months was given both breastmilk and solid or semi-solid food (as recommended)
- whether the child had moderate or severe anemia (Hb < 10g/dl)
- whether the child was stunted (height less than two standard deviations below the median for the international reference population at that age, which indicates chronic undernutrition)
- whether the child was wasted (weight less than two standard deviations below the reference median for that height, which indicates acute undernutrition)

Individuals in the same PSU may share some unobserved characteristics. Generally, failure to account for such factors gives too small standard errors of the community-effect estimates. In this study, a random term at the PSU level is included in all models, but has no importance for the conclusions.

(It would also have been relevant, although even less important substantially, to include random terms at lower levels. Some variables are measured for a household, from which there may be more than one woman in the sample, and many women have had more than one child during the five-year period.)

Various Methodological Problems

It is the characteristics of the PSU in which the woman lived at interview that are included in the models, which is not ideal. The child mortality experienced by a woman early in the five-year period is influenced by the situation in the community at that time, which may be different, and community education is determined by the situation even further back in time. Besides, many women have not even lived in the area throughout the five-year period. Fortunately, excluding children whose mothers had moved to the area after the child was born turned out to give very similar results.

There are similar problems at the individual level. For example, the household wealth at the time of interview cannot itself have contributed to determine the mother's education, but may be considered an indication of the economic standard of her family of origin. In principle, it is also problematic that her education and other characteristics may be a result of mortality or health events during the five years before interview. However, this cannot be a major concern. Few women take education after having become mothers, regardless of the children's health and survival, and the autonomy indices and most of the other individual variables are probably also largely unaffected by such factors.

Many variables that may influence the educational level are included, but the estimates may, of course, nevertheless be biased. As an illustration, let us compare an uneducated woman who lives in an area with a generally high educational level and another uneducated woman who lives in an area where the average educational level is much lower, but where other observed community characteristics are the same.

These women may differ in many ways, for example in general wealth or gender norms that are not captured by the included variables, or in factors that are not considered at all in this study. In addition to these differences between the communities in which the two women live, there may be unobserved differences between the women themselves.

For example, if one of the two areas is economically better developed than the other, the woman who lives in that area may also herself be richer than the other woman. If there had been two or more surveys in the same PSUs, one might have pooled the samples and included fixed-effects at the PSU level, which would have picked up at least the persistent unobserved community-level factors. However, different PSUs were used in the NFHS-2 and NFHS-1 surveys, so this approach could not be used.

Another methodological problem lies in the modelling of health and health care among children below age three who are still alive at interview. There may be correlated unobserved factors behind survival up to interview and the health and health care reported at that time. To check the size of this selection bias, probit models were estimated jointly for (i) health or health care and (ii) the probability of being alive and having non-missing data for the corresponding variable, with individual error terms that were allowed to be correlated. This was done for five different health or health care variables, and the education effects were always similar to those obtained in the corresponding separate models. Some of the variables are fairly strongly correlated, so one might perhaps suspect a multicollinearity problem.

However, the standard errors in the most complex models are not much larger than in simple models that were estimated at a preliminary stage. Besides, the estimates in all models are very robust toward exclusion of observations. For example, when 15% of the respondents were taken out at random, either initially or only when calculating averages, very small changes in the estimates were seen. This is also an additional argument for the appropriateness of basing the analysis on averages from such small sub-samples.

DEFINITION OF INDEPENDENT VARIABLES

The definition of the independent variables should be sufficiently clear from the short labels in the tables, but a few words about wealth and autonomy may be needed. A wealth index is constructed by summing ownership of the following consumer goods: radio, television, bicycle, motorcycle, and car. According to Bollen, Glanville and Stecklov (2002), this should be a fairly good proxy for economic status. Electricity in the household is included as an additional indicator of wealth and modernization. A simple index of women's physical autonomy is constructed by summing over the following two 0/1 variables: whether the woman needs permission to go to the market, and whether she needs permission to visit relatives or friends.

Similarly, an index of decision-making autonomy is formed on the basis of information about whether the woman takes decisions herself, or at least jointly with her husband or others, on the following: what to cook, whether to obtain health care for herself, whether to purchase jewellery or other major household items, and whether to stay with her parents or siblings.

Two variables that cannot be summed up to an index are chosen as main indicators of economic autonomy. One of them is whether the woman is allowed to have some money set aside that she can use as she wishes. The other is whether she participates in the decisions on how the money she earns will be used, provided that she earns cash at all. A cash-earning variable is also included in the models, but not considered an autonomy indicator on par with the others. When forming a community variable for women's access to the money they earn, a missing value indicator is set to 1 for the areas where no women in the interviewed households earned cash (which included 7% of the women), and is otherwise 0.

An index of emotional autonomy is defined as the sum of responses to questions about whether, generally, a husband is justified in beating his wife in three different situations: if her family does not give him or his family the expected amount of money, if she goes out without telling him, or if she neglects the house or the children. Because this does not refer to the woman's own situation, it is included only as a community-level variable. A 0/1 dummy for whether the woman wants more sons than daughters and a corresponding community-level variable are included as additional autonomy indicators.

Because much of the data on decision-making is relevant primarily for those who are married at interview, the analysis of the importance of women's autonomy is restricted to that group. The knowledge index is defined as the sum of three 0/1 indicators of whether the woman had heard of oral rehydration therapy, whether she had heard about AIDS, and whether she knew at least one important way to prevent HIV infection.

India Host Family Planning

India Host Family Planning Meeting: India had hosted the Expert Group Meeting on Family Planning, Health and Family Well-Being in Bangalore in October 1992. The meeting, one of six expert group meetings preceding the International Conference on Population and Development, of 1994, had brought together renowned experts in family planning, policy-makers, representatives of both inter-governmental and non governmental organizations, and United Nations officials.

Despite the success of a number of family planning programmes in developing regions of the world, implementation problems continue to hinder progress in some countries. The meeting attempted to address these problems. Changes in the social, economic and demographic conditions of the world are such that even when programmes are successful, there is no room for complacency. Programmes should be continually evaluated and reviewed. The considerable increase in the number of couples who will need access to family planning services and information by the year 2000 will be a major consideration in shaping family planning programmes in the years ahead.

Family planning is not just a demographic issue. It is also an issue related to individual rights, socioeconomic development, preservation of the environment, and the health and well-being of women, couples, families and society at large. The participants will examine the issues in this light, and will place special emphasis on both operational and financial questions.

The general objectives of the meeting are how to improve the efficiency and effectiveness of existing family planning programmes and services; how to reach larger segments of the population; how to devise innovative approaches to new or existing problems; and how to obtain the funding needed for the ever-increasing demand for family planning services.

The Expert Group Meeting encompasses seven sessions. The session on "Society and Family Planning" will examine societal aspects of family planning programmes in developing countries, in particular, the political, economic and socio-cultural context in which programmes operate, with special emphasis on the role and status of women. The session on "Family Planning Programmes: Lessons Learned" will discuss the impact of family planning programmes around the globe and attempt to draw lessons from those experiences. "Programme Implementation" will address important operational aspects of family planning programmes, including their organization and management; quality of services; human resource development; unreached populations; adolescent fertility; information, education and communication activities; community-based delivery systems; social marketing of contraceptives; and future contraceptive requirements and logistics management needs.

Nowadays, family planning programmes are seen not only as programmes to reduce fertility, but as programmes which promote the welfare of the entire family. The session devoted to "Family Planning and Health" will discuss safe motherhood and child survival, and sexually-transmitted diseases, including AIDS. "Family Planning and Family Well-Being" will review changes in the size and structure of the family and consider the implications of these changes for family well-being and child development.

An emerging issue which will be addressed is that of people's involvement in family planning programmes. Direct community involvement helps ensure that services are provided in accordance with community preferences, and are thus more likely to be accepted. Another question which participants will consider is the cost of contraception for individual couples, which in some circumstances may still be an important barrier to contraceptive practice. How much can users around the world afford to pay, and how much will Governments need to spend to make family planning information, supplies and services fully available? The future role of NGOs and the private sector in family planning service delivery will also be raised, in view of the expected rise in the number of users and the cost of providing high quality services. The final session of the expert Group Meeting will be devoted to the discussion and adoption of a set of recommendations to be presented to the Preparatory Committee of the International Conference on Population and Development, 1994.

Family Planning Improves

Child Survival and Health: Babies who survive and children who enjoy good health are universal humanitarian goals. Strategies to advance these goals in developing countries include both direct investments in health and nutrition programmes and the increased availability of family planning services. These two strategies complement each other, and should be viewed together. Especially in times of fiscal austerity and reduced international assistance, they should not be pitted against each other in competition for scarce funds.

The basic conditions necessary for newborns to survive and for children to flourish are no secret. The ideal would be for all babies to be born to mothers who are in good health, who have obtained adequate prenatal care and who have access to the health facilities necessary for a safe delivery. Also needed are sufficient breastfeeding, good nutrition after weaning, hygienic living conditions-especially clean water and modern sanitation-and medical care that includes immunization against childhood diseases.

But two other, related factors also contribute to improved child health and survival in developing countries. These are smaller families and the use of methods of contraception that allow couples to plan their families. When women can plan when and how many children to have, the number of "high-risk" pregnancies and births is reduced, and infant and child health and survival improve.

Because the conditions that enhance babies' health and chances of survival can be found in most of the developed world, the high infant mortality rates of the past have largely disappeared in the West. In France, Japan and the United States, for example, fewer than 10 babies die for every 1,000 live births. Thus, for most Americans, the death of a baby is a rare event. Yet some older Americans can remember when infant deaths were as common in the United States as they are currently in many parts of the developing world (Chart A). In 1920, the U.S. infant mortality rate was as high as Nigeria's is today (87 infant deaths for every 1,000 live births. In 1965, it still equalled the current rate of 25 deaths per 1,000 in Sri Lanka, and in inner-city communities particularly, the rate remains close to that level.

We have known for some time that better timing and spacing of pregnancies improves child health and survival.

Large-scale studies in Western Europe and North America, published in the late 1970s and early 1980s, confirmed the beneficial effects that planned and timely childbearing have on child survival. More recent evidence from developing countries also compellingly links improved child survival with smaller family size and well-timed pregnancies.

This Issues in Brief will show how family planning can lead to significant improvements in the survival of newborns and the health of small children. Because women who use contraceptive methods can choose when to become pregnant, they are better prepared than women whose pregnancies are unexpected to seek care for themselves during pregnancy, and able to time their pregnancies to achieve the best situation for the infant.

HIGH-RISK PREGNANCIES

Pregnancies may have a high risk of a poor or tragic outcome if they occur shortly after a birth, are among very young mothers or women past their childbearing prime, or are among women who have already had many births. In addition, high-risk pregnancies increase the mother's risk of dying in childbirth, and when the mother dies, her newborn's risk of dying during its first year of life is also increased.

The ways in which ill-timed pregnancies raise the mortality risks for babies are not fully understood. Most experts agree that the causes are primarily biological, even though social factors also play a role. A mother's age, the number of births she has already had and the spacing of those births all affect her health and her ability to carry a subsequent pregnancy safely to term. Many high-risk pregnancies end in the birth of premature or very low birth weight babies, and such infants often fail to thrive, or lack the resilience needed to overcome the many threats to survival they may face during the first days and months of life. The early weaning that occurs if a mother quickly becomes pregnant again exposes the still-fragile infant to a number of infectious organisms through its intake of water and food rather than breastmilk.

In some instances, newborns face more than one risk-enhancing situation: Some older women giving birth have already had several children; some women with large families have had many pregnancies in rapid succession; and some adolescent mothers not only are physically immature, but are giving birth for the second or third time.

In addition, many women in the developing world whose pregnancies are high-risk for biological reasons also are at risk for social and economic reasons. They often are impoverished, and many live in unsanitary housing, are malnourished and have little education. And many women receive little or no medical care during pregnancy or when they give birth. For these reasons, disentangling the complex web of biological, social, economic and demographic factors that influence rates of child survival is difficult.

CLOSELY SPACED BIRTHS

Babies born less than two years apart are much more likely to die than those born after a longer interval, as Chart B shows. This is a serious problem in developing countries where a substantial minority of births occur within less than 24 months of a previous one. That closely spaced births account for one in five of all births in Pakistan; one in six in the Dominican Republic, Madagascar, Niger, Tunisia, and Trinidad and Tobago; one in seven in Ecuador, Kenya, Mexico, the Philippines, Rwanda and Sri Lanka; and around one in 10 in another 16 of the 45 developing countries listed.

Closely spaced births present a risk to the health of all three family members involved: the mother herself, who does not have sufficient time to regain her strength after delivery; the initial child, who often has to be weaned early; and the baby born subsequently, who is likely to be premature or low-birth-weight. If all births occurring within less than two years of each other could be more widely spaced, one in four infant deaths in developing countries might be prevented.

Some traditional childbearing practices have helped to ensure lengthy intervals between births. In a number of societies, for example, women have breastfed for long durations. At the same time, cultural taboos often require a lactating woman to abstain from sexual relations. Both sexual abstinence and the lengthy duration of breastfeeding have served to lengthen the interval between successive pregnancies. But as these practices become less common than in the past, the incidence of closely spaced births is likely to increase.

As populations everywhere become more urbanized, as commercial infant formulas become more accessible and as women of childbearing age work away from the home in increasing numbers, both the average length of time babies are breastfed and the once common practice of sexual abstinence after a recent birth are declining in many countries. If women who stop breastfeeding and resume sexual relations do not immediately start to practice some form of contraception, they will soon be at risk of becoming pregnant again.

AGE OF MOTHERS

Throughout the developing world, babies born to women younger than 20 are, on average, one-third more likely to die than infants born to women in their 20s and 30s. This is mostly because babies born to very young mothers are more likely to be premature, to be low-birth-weight and to suffer from complications at the time of delivery. And many adolescents do not know how to obtain or cannot afford good prenatal and delivery care. In addition, teenage births are likely to be first births, and first births always carry a higher risk than subsequent births.

The link between early childbearing and lower rates of infant survival in developing countries has serious implications. One in five women aged 20-24 report having had their first child before their 18th birthday, and two out of five report doing so before they were 20.[5] This high incidence of teenage childbearing is partly because even when adolescents want to prevent pregnancy, they often face special problems in obtaining the contraceptive products or services that would enable them to do so.

In addition, babies born to women older than 40 are at somewhat greater risk of dying in infancy than those whose mothers are in their 20s and 30s. To compound the problem, older women often have several children already, and babies born after the mother has already had a number of children are also more likely to die in infancy than babies whose mother has had only one or two previous births. Further, in the developing world, many older women with large families are in poor health: They often suffer from such problems as anemia, poor nutrition, cardiovascular disease or uterine prolapse.

For these reasons, helping older women avoid unwanted pregnancy improves child survival. Indeed, high levels of contraceptive sterilization in Latin America (mostly among women in their 30s or older who have had all the children they want) is likely to be one reason for the overall lower infant death rates in Latin America compared with those of Asia and Sub-Saharan Africa.

UNPLANNED PREGNANCIES

Many women in developing countries acknowledge-even after a new baby is born and part of the family-that they did not plan to have that child. The proportion of births that are reported as unplanned ranges from one-quarter to one-half in most countries. This is troubling because there is some evidence-although it is mostly based on the experience of developed countries-of a link between whether parents wanted a child and its survival and well-being.

In developed countries, women who plan to become pregnant and want a child tend to recognize that they are pregnant soon after conception. Partly because of this earlier awareness, they visit a doctor sooner and generally take better care of themselves during pregnancy than women with unwanted pregnancies. Women with wanted pregnancies are also likely to receive more consideration, support and care from family members. A review by the U.S. Institute of Medicine of the research on this topic concluded that "the child of an unwanted conception is at greater risk of weighing less than 2,500 grams at birth, of dying in its first year of life, of being abused, and of not receiving sufficient resources for healthy development."

In developing countries, there is less evidence that a baby's safe delivery and healthy growth is linked to whether the pregnancy was a wanted one. In addition, prenatal, maternal and child health services are often not widely available or are of poor quality, and poverty sharply limits how well a family can take care of infants and children who are in poor health.

Yet there is little reason to believe that the degree to which a baby is wanted would not have some effect on women's care of themselves during pregnancy and of their newborns subsequently. One study on Indonesia, Korea and the Philippines demonstrates that even after factors such as the parents' education and economic level and the availability of health clinics are taken into consideration, babies are more likely to suffer from acute respiratory infections and severe diarrhea if the pregnancy was unwanted than if it was wanted.

UNDERSTANDING THE DANGER

Most women understand the dangers of having children at closely spaced intervals, of having large numbers of children and of having children late in their reproductive years-the three major biological factors associated with high-risk pregnancies. When married women in developing countries who already have four children are asked if they would like to have more, about eight out of 10 say no; so do half of women with fewer children.

Even among women who say they want another child, the vast majority want to delay their next pregnancy. Their preferred interval between births is 3-5 years in all regions of the world. If women were able to achieve the intervals they want between pregnancies, fewer babies would die in infancy. But many women who say they want to stop having children altogether or to delay their next pregnancy are not using the contraceptive methods that would help them achieve these goals. In the countries of Sub-Saharan Africa, 57-98% of women who want no more children are not using an effective family planning method. Nor are about half of women who want no more children in most countries of Asia and Latin America.

A CRUCIAL COMBINATION

Family planning services that help women avoid high-risk and unwanted pregnancies can contribute to improvements in infant and child health even in the poorest of countries. The impact of family planning is probably greatest when it helps women space births at healthy intervals, avoid having large numbers of children, and prevent unwanted pregnancies, especially in their later childbearing years. Programmes designed to encourage and enable women to avoid giving birth in their teenage years would also reduce infant mortality rates. However, this requires raising the average age at which most women marry or encouraging young women to postpone their first pregnancy-both difficult goals.

Nevertheless, the crucial contribution of social and economic development to better health should not be overlooked. The improved living conditions that contributed to a declining infant death rate in the United States have yet to reach many areas of the world. Millions of families in Africa, Asia and Latin America still lack clean water, decent housing, good medical services and sufficient food-basic elements needed to alleviate the causes from which most infants are dying: diarrhea, respiratory infections, malaria, measles and malnutrition. If Americans want their tax dollars to go toward programmes that would improve child health and survival in developing countries, such programmes should focus on improving broad health services and economic conditions, as well as on making family planning services available to women who want and need them.

Primary Health Care Programme

Although weighing has been used to monitor growth in children since 1910, the popularity of growth monitoring as a tool for child survival is recent. Growth monitoring differs from nutrition surveillance in that the objective of the latter is research and monitoring changes over time, while growth monitoring emphasizes promoting the growth of children through one or more of the following activities: counselling, education, treatment for growth-retarding illnesses, and feeding. With the initiation of the GOBI (growth-monitoring, oral-rehydration, breast-feeding, and immunization) strategy by UNICEF in the early 1980s, the role of growth monitoring in child survival was promoted and institutionalized. Unlike most other child-survival technologies, however, growth-monitoring programmes are difficult to implement, are controversial, and have not yet been accepted as a technology of choice in developing countries.

In 1987 growth monitoring was incorporated into a large primary health care intervention conducted by the Bangladesh Rural Advancement Committee (BRAC). A study of this component of the programme was undertaken in 1990 to help to clarify various factors contributing to the controversies surrounding the subject.

BRAC's Primary Health Care Programme

The health and nutrition status of the rural population of

Bangladesh, particularly mothers and children, is unacceptably low. A national nutrition survey of 1981 found that about 80% and 97% of children 0-11 and 12-23 months of age respectively were suffering from mild to severe malnutrition. The situation with respect to girls and women was even worse. Vitamin A intake was 808 IU per person per day, which meets only 40% of the requirement. Children 1-3 years old received only 25% of their vitamin C requirement. This has been attributed to numerous causes, including:

- Poverty-lack of employment, underemployment, insufficient food availability and consumption;
- Lack of knowledge-low family education; lack of awareness about child and maternal nutrition, feeding, and weaning practices, breast-feeding, hygiene, vitamin A, and low birth weight; lack of nutrition counselling;
- Underlying illnesses-tuberculosis, pneumonia, measles, anaemia, iodine deficiency, diarrhoea, worms, protein-energy malnutrition;
- Lack of or insufficient services-insufficient health facilities or coverage, irregular supplies, lack of follow-up, lack of a referral system;
- Socio-cultural factors-sex discrimination or preference, mal-distribution of intra-familial food, superstitions, food taboos.

In late 1986 BRAC, which is a non-government organization (NGO), launched a primary health care programme in six thanas (subdistricts), with a population of 1.2 million, with the major goal of devising a workable model of primary health care. It was hoped that such a model would ensure effective community participation and would be replicated by the government and other NGOs to improve the health and nutrition status of the population, particularly rural mothers and children. Eight components-promotion of oral rehydration therapy, immunization, vitamin A capsules, safe water, family planning, nutrition education, training of traditional birth attendants (TBAs), and basic curative services-were originally included in the programme. A year later, to address child malnutrition specifically, growth monitoring was added, with the objectives of educating mothers about child growth, health, and nutrition through a village forum; screening malnourished children as a channel to provide health and nutrition education to their mothers; and detecting severely malnourished children in order to refer them to nearby health facilities for appropriate care.

IMPLEMENTING GROWTH-MONITORING ACTIVITIES

All the BRAC field health workers and their supervisors underwent three days of training (two days in a classroom and one day of field practice) on the importance of growth monitoring, how to perform it, and the various equipment, materials, and techniques of nutrition education, in addition to the regular training they received from BRAC. The curriculum was designed in collaboration with UNICEF and Helen Keller International, an international NGO working in Bangladesh.

Prior to the formal launching of the activities, a two-stage pilot programme was undertaken to explore BRAC's management capacity to carry them out, to reinforce the training of health workers, and to assess people's response. The strategy was tried first in five villages of Manikganj Sadar thana and then in five villages of each of the other five thanas. Based on results from these initial experiments, the programme was gradually extended to all villages in the six thanas. Because of cost and management considerations, and because maximum growth faltering occurs between the ages of 6 and 12 months, BRAC decided to recruit children from among those under one year of age and maintain them in the programme until they were two.

Entry into a Village

As a first step, villagers, particularly prominent individuals such as teachers and social leaders, were contacted and briefed and their cooperation was sought in implementing the activities. Afterward a household survey was carried out to identify children 0-12 months old. Parents were then contacted and motivated about the importance of monitoring in promoting child growth and survival. Volunteers were selected and given on-the job orientation on how to assist in growth-monitoring sessions by bringing mothers with children, recording and plotting weights on growth charts (based on NCHS standards), demonstrating how to prepare a supplementary diet, and maintaining order in the sessions.

Growth-monitoring Sessions

A convenient place, preferably a house in the centre of the village, was chosen with the help of villagers as the site for sessions. The space was arranged in such a way that registration, weighing/charting, and nutrition education could be carried out sequentially. Resources such as scales, cards, and registers were provided by BRAC, and villagers provided the space and furniture. Health workers from BRAC conducted the sessions with active support from village volunteers, including TBAs. The mothers of the target children and volunteers were informed of the programme in advance. On weighing day, one BRAC worker prepared the centre with the help of volunteers while another worker and/or volunteer reminded the mothers to bring their babies for weighing and nutrition education.

When growth faltering was identified during the weighing and charting, the mother was advised to give the child more food. Children needing treatment for illnesses were referred to government health facilities. The volunteers demonstrated how to prepare a supplementary diet with locally available ingredients such as dark-green leafy vegetables, rice, lentils, and oil. The babies were fed as a part of the demonstration.

Health education covered supplementary diet, the diet of pregnant and lactating mothers, personal hygiene, vitamin A capsules, breast-feeding, colostrum feeding, immunization, and family planning. Before the mothers left the centre, they were told about the next weighing date.

Follow-up

Children who were identified during a session as being severely malnourished (< 60% of median weight for age) were visited in the homes by both health workers and medical officers of BRAC, who gave rehabilitative advice and, if necessary, referred them to nearby government health facilities. No feeding was provided.

Sustainability

Community participation played a significant role in the programme. In the early stages of introducing growth monitoring into a village, at least three BRAC workers were required to perform the entire gamut of activities. Gradually, volunteers such as village health committee members, TBAs, and mothers became involved in weighing, recording, and plotting weights, so that BRAC was able to reduce its staff involvement to 50% at the end of the programme. As noted, the villagers also contributed the space for holding sessions, as well as the demonstration food.

As a step towards sustainability, BRAC made a deliberate attempt to integrate growth monitoring with selected public-sector activities, namely the expanded programme of immunization (EPI) and the semi-mobile antenatal satellite clinics. Since the clinics were not made available in every village, however, this integration could not be carried out in all the villages. At the end of the programme, 10% of the villages had all three activities. In such villages, government workers carried out their own functions while BRAC workers and village volunteers conducted the growth monitoring.

The Study

Objectives: The objectives of the study were as follows:

- To determine the level of operational efficiency of the BRAC approach to growth monitoring;
- To evaluate the effectiveness of monitoring in increasing the use of other child-survival technologies such as oral rehydration therapy, immunization, and vitamin A capsules;
- To measure the changes in the nutrition status of the children due to the monitoring;
- To assess the perceptions of the villagers about the monitoring.

Methods: To address the above objectives, data from primary as well as secondary sources were used. For the first objective, data were collected from eight villages of Manikganj Sadar and Gheor thanas. In these villages the Research and Evaluation Division of BRAC had been carrying out a passive surveillance system through which, among other things, births and deaths had been recorded since 1987. Thus the precise ages of children born since 1987 were available. As the target population for the growth monitoring was children under two years of age, households with at least one child of this age were chosen for study.

Data covering different aspects of the operational efficiency of the monitoring were collected by a variety of methods. For example, the extent of the programme's coverage of target children was determined by asking households whether they had growth-monitoring cards or not; the accuracy of the records of the children's ages was determined using registration data; the accuracy of weighing scales was measured using a standard 5-kg weight on eight round (25-kg) and six cylindrical (15-kg) Salter scales; the consumption of supplementary diet was investigated through 24-hour recall; and the accuracy of recorded weights was checked by direct observation.

To determine mothers' knowledge and how they interpreted the growth card, the following questions were asked: (1) On which part of the card should your baby's weight be for you to know that he or she is growing well? (2) Which part is bad? (3) What happens if the weight mark falls below the green belt? (4) What happens if the weight mark is in the green belt? (5) What happens if the weight mark is above the green belt? (6) What does it mean if the present month's weight is more than the previous month's? (7) What if the present month's weight is less than the previous month? All these data for the eight villages were collected during November-December 1990.

To ascertain whether the growth monitoring increased the use of other child-survival strategies, data were used from a survey of 3,048 households in five of the six primary health care thanas in September 1989 to assess the midcourse effects of the BRAC programme on the knowledge and use of its components. The survey asked mothers with children under two years of age whether, at the time of the survey, they were participating in the programme or had ever done so. Since the survey also collected data from the same mothers on the use of other child-survival practices promoted by BRAC, this facilitated analysis of the data to see if participation in growth monitoring was related to their use of those components. No anthropometric data were collected during this survey.

To measure the impact of the monitoring on the children's nutrition status, data were used from a nutrition surveillance project in which BRAC had been participating since early 1990, together with several other NGOs, by providing data from two of its primary health care thanas (Saturia and Santhia). Through this project, the growth of a large number of children 6-59 months old was monitored quarterly using several anthropometric measures, under the supervision of Helen Keller International.

For the present study, all 496 children 623 months old from the two BRAC areas covered by the second and the third rounds of the surveillance were revisited. They were grouped according to whether or not they were participants in BRAC's growth monitoring, and the nutrition status (weight for age) of the children who participated was compared with that of those who did not participate.

To elicit villagers' perceptions of and attitudes toward the monitoring, qualitative data were collected through participant observations and 14 focus-group discussions.

Discussion

That growth monitoring can be an important tool in promoting child survival is beyond doubt, but its effectiveness in all developing countries has yet to be proved. A reason for this controversy is the confusion between monitoring and nutrition surveillance. Growth monitoring involves much more than just surveillance, such as nutrition education and community participation. The BRAC programme in Bangladesh included these activities and thus provided an opportunity to examine growth monitoring in the light of several questions that surround it. Is it difficult to implement? Does it really facilitate better use of other child-survival interventions and community participation? Does it improve children's nutrition? We attempted to throw some light on these Issues.

With respect to the operational aspects of the programme, the experience was mixed. Some of the activities, such as age determination, mothers' interpretation of growth cards, and reading and recording of weights, were done reasonably well. The ability of the Bangladeshi mothers to understand the meaning of the growth charts was remarkably good compared with what has been observed elsewhere, as in Zaire. Two major factors may have contributed to this result. First, the health workers explained to the mothers how to interpret the charts on the basis of the weights of their own children. Second, the mothers kept the cards, which gave them a chance to consult them at home. The health workers kept their own registers to follow severely malnourished children in their homes.

Not all of the results were encouraging, however. The coverage of target children was less than 50%. A large proportion of the weighing scales of a particular make were faulty, and this had escaped the notice of the programme managers.

The low coverage was a major failure. Our discussion with programme staff revealed a number of reasons for it. The principal effort to recruit children for monitoring was during their first six months of life. Many of the babies were born in their maternal grandparents' house and did not return to their own home before six months, and they tended to be missed. Since BRAC did not provide any other food or health service, weighing was not enough motivation for many mothers to bring their children. Superstitions and (in some areas) bad internal communication were other reasons. Incomplete registration of birth was yet another reason.

This was BRAC's (and the villagers') first experience with growth monitoring. Low coverage is not uncommon in other settings, however. In one large programme in India, coverage was 28% and 49% for children 0-6 and 7-12 months old respectively. Although the coverage was low, there was no sex bias in recruitment; both boys and girls participated equally. Also there was no socioeconomic difference between participants and non-participants, implying that children from all strata had equal access to the programme.

The participation of the community was commendable, given that this was their first exposure to growth monitoring and despite cultural taboos against weighing babies. Clearly, it was facilitated by the presence of BRAC. A pertinent question is what will happen when BRAC withdraws. For such a programme, complete withdrawal is not feasible; some staff must be left behind to support it. It was hoped that the village health committee would take over the programme after BRAC's withdrawal. Initial evaluations do not suggest that this will happen in the foreseeable future, however. If the programme is to continue, BRAC must maintain some presence in the villages.

Our data tend to support the suggestion that growth monitoring leads to better use of other child-survival interventions. Households whose children participated did better in most of the interventions that were investigated. It is not clear from the analysis, however, whether they represent a self-selected group who embrace all interventions, whether immunization or growth monitoring.

The data we analysed did not show any measurable impact of growth monitoring statistically. However, with a p value of. 051, the nutritional impact cannot be rejected outright. It should be remembered that only a few of the factors that cause malnutrition in Bangladesh were addressed through the monitoring. For a sustained impact, other causes such as poverty must be addressed.

Another aspect for which growth monitoring has been criticized is its cost. Unfortunately, we have not been able to examine this because of our inability to apportion costs for this component separately from those of the overall programme. Our impressions, however, suggest that the costs were quite high at the beginning of the programme, particularly with respect to staff involvement. Depending on how much community participation is obtained, they can be reduced over time.

One positive aspect of the programme was the partial success in having several activities undertaken under one umbrella (health post, as BRAC calls it). In several villages, growth monitoring was integrated with immunization and antenatal clinics, which helped the mothers to participate and encouraged health workers from BRAC and the government to interact with each other.

This occurred in only 10% of the villages, however; in the others, the BRAC workers were not as successful. Growth monitoring is also a designated activity for government family welfare clinics, but it is infrequently done. In other places where it has been more successful, such as in Tamil Nadu in India, it is part of an institutional activity involving several sectors such as agriculture, local government, and health and welfare.

This evaluation has been of value to BRAC. After careful review, it included growth monitoring in its new Women's Health and Development Programme but with several modifications suggested by the results of this study. To increase coverage, registration of births (and deaths) and of migration has been institutionalized and will be done quarterly in the programme areas (population, 2 million).

The cylinder scales, which were found to be defective, have all been replaced by round scales. A standard weight is being provided to each programme area for daily appraisal of the accuracy of the scales. Assistance to severely malnourished children in terms of food supplementation is also being considered.

The new programme is also different in that BRAC will never completely withdraw. After the three-year women's health and development phase, the institutional development and credit components of BRAC programmes will be introduced. Through this village-level effort, the poorer households will be identified and components such as children's education and credit will be introduced that will facilitate addressing other causes of malnutrition in a systematic and sustained manner.

7

Class Struggle and Caste Oppression

The political and ideological struggles of the left parties have reached a crossroads, as correctly emphasized by the political resolutions of the 17th Party Congress of the CPI (M). The communal fascism of the Sangh *parivar*, with its ideology of the *Hindu Rashtra*, now poses a grave and unprecedented threat to the secular fabric of Indian democracy. Gujarat-type genocides are likely to engulf the entitre country if the BJP and its perverted *parivar* are allowed to gain further strength. The so-called non-communal regional parties, which are supporting the Sangh *parivar* with a view to sharing the spoils of power, are too devoid of ideologies to be relied upon as anti-fascist political forces of the future.

The Congress is in a state of severe ideological atrophy and organizational decay. But it still retains a broadly and vaguely non-communal character and considerable following at the all-India level. It can conceivably become a tactical ally of the left forces in the struggle against communal fascism. But for at least two reasons the left parties and forces alone can spearhead the great coming struggle of the masses against the demonic communal and fascist forces. First, the left forces alone are committed to ideologies which not only aim to confront and combat the fascist forces without compromise, but also offer a clear alternative politicoeconomic programme to the people that is scientific and equalitarian. Secondly, for that very reason, fascists everywhere make leftists their primary political target in all countries, once they are in power. The rapid growth of the left forces in Indian politics is therefore an immediate ideological and strategic imperative.

Unfortunately, as the political resolution of the 17th Party Congress of the CPI(M) has forcefully pointed out, the left parties are weak as an all-India political force, their influence being limited to the three states of West Bengal, Tripura, and Kerala. The resolution has further correctly pointed that united front with non-left parties can only be a tactical necessity, and not the main path of progress for the left parties. The growth of the left movement in India would have to depend primarily on the independent growth of the left forces all over the country. In this context, the 17th Party Congress of the CPI(M) has emphasized the need, not only for sustained ideological work, but also mass struggles against caste oppression, communalism, and the oppression of women. Without minimizing the importance of protracted mass struggles on all other fronts, in this paper we wish to deal specifically with the question of integrating the struggle against caste oppression with the broader class struggle in the objective Indian context. For it appears to us that the adoption of a clear ideological and strategic position by the CPI(M) and other left parties on this question is the key to the accelerated development and proliferation of the ideology and organization of the left in the given objective conditions of society and politics in India.

MARXIST THINKING ON CASTE IN INDIA

Karl Marx was the first thinker to draw sharp attention to the highly deleterious impact of caste on Indian society and its causal link with the relations of production. In his famous essay on *The Future Results of British Rule in India* Karl Marx characterized the Indian castes as "the most decisive impediment to India's progress and power". Marx correctly argued that the caste system of India was based on the hereditary division of labour, which was inseparably linked with the unchanging technological base and subsistence economy of the Indian village community. At that time he believed that British rule would undermine the economic and technological foundations of these primitive, self-sufficient, stagnant, and isolated village communities, particularly through the spread of railways. The industrialization and commercialization of India under British rule, facilitated by the spread of railways, would lead to the breakdown of the traditional village communities, and with them also the caste system. But Marx wrote later on that he had exaggerated the possible impact of the spread of railways on the traditional relations of production characterized by the Indian village community. The important point, however, is that Marx clearly and causally connected the archaic social formation of caste in India with the relations of production. It followed logically that the abolition of the caste hierarchy and the oppression and exploitation of the 'lower' castes could not be separated from the Marxian form of class struggle.

Following this Marxian approach to the relationship between the class struggle and the struggle against caste oppression, the renowned Indian Marxist leader and thinker, E.M.S. Namboodiripad, placed the Marxian approach to the struggle against caste consciousness and caste oppression as a part of the class struggle in modern India when he observed in 1979:

One has to realize that the building of India on modern democratic and secular lines requires an uncompromising struggle against the caste-based Hindu society and its culture. There is no question of secular democracy, not to speak of socialism, unless the very citadel of India's 'age-old' civilization and culture – the division of society into a hierarchy of castes – is broken. In other words, the struggle for radical democracy and socialism cannot be separated from the struggle against caste society.

The same year another Indian Marxist stalwart, B.T.Ranadive, regretted the fact that "there has been a certain neglect in the ideological struggle against caste and communalism", and that "the common consciousness generated through the economic struggle cannot be pushed forward without such struggle and direct intervention of the movement on caste oppression." Three years later, in his book, *Class, Caste and Property Relations*, Ranadive strongly pleaded for the adoption of an anti-caste programme of struggle by all mass organizations. In his own words:

The decisive challenge of caste and untouchability has to be defeated by the leaders of the mass struggles by inculcating a strong anti-caste feeling among the fighting toilers – above all among the workers in the spirit of proletarian unity and solidarity. This can be achieved by strong ideological propaganda against the caste system and untouchability.

The mass organizations, besides, must devote special attention to the problem of the untouchables, tribals and oppressed castes as part of their work to unite the oppressed.

Then alone the mighty force of the united toilers will decisively strike for agrarian revolution, smashing the basis of caste distinctions and serfdom of the untouchables; then alone the democratic forces will open the way to political power and rapid industrialization on the basis of socialization of all means of production and usher in a casteless and classless society.

Both E.M.S. Namboodiripad and B.T. Ranadive thus felt the urgent need for integrating the class struggle with the struggle against the caste system in India, and considered this integration to be essential for the success of the proletarian revolution and the establishment of people's democracy in this country. This ideological position of the highest Marxist leaders and thinkers of India was reflected in a resolution of the Salkia Plennum of the CPI (M) in 1978, which stated that the ruling class took advantage of caste and communal divisions among the people, and emphasized the need for a mass struggle against casteism and communalism. The resolution further stated that the actual decision and strategy to be adopted in this respect was left to the Central Committee of the party.

But while the CPI (M) and other left parties have consistently organized mass protest and struggles against communalism, the exigencies and dynamics of the developing political situation in India in the 1980s and 1990s prevented them from organizing a simultaneous struggle against casteism and communalism. In particular, the acute caste conflict generated by the Mandal Commission Report and its aftermath made it extremely difficult to integrate the anti-caste ideology of the left with the class struggle against feudalism and capitalism in the 1980s. The rapid rise of communal fascism in Indian politics in the 1990s, leading to the capture of power at the Centre by the communal and fascist forces, impelled the left parties to mobilize all their organizational power against these forces, and to postpone the organization of a mass struggle against casteism and caste oppression to a later date. The issue was again taken up seriously at the 17th Party Congress of the CPI (M) at Hyderabad in 2002.

CASTE STRUCTURE AND RELATIONS OF PRODUCTION

The leading Indian Marxist thinkers and the Salkia Plenum and 17th Congress of the CPI (M) would not have pleaded for the organization of mass struggles against caste oppression in India if they had believed that there was any antagonistic contradiction between the class struggle and the struggle against caste oppression in the objective Indian context. It is therefore necessary, at a time when the major left parties have decided to integrate the class struggle with the struggle against caste oppression, to have a clear idea of the structural linkages of the caste structure in India with the relations of production in the perspective of Marxian historical sociology.

Caste formations, of course, are not identical with class divisions. There is a caste structure within each class, and a class structure within each caste. They generate different forms of sociopolitical belonging, loyalties, and consciousness. Both on the epistemological and the empirical planes, caste consciousness proves to be antithetical to class consciousness, and stymies the growth of proletarian class solidarity. As every leftist political worker knows, the unity of the working class in India is constantly vitiated by the caste consciousness and caste loyalties of the peasants and workers.

The poor 'upper' caste peasant or worker does not consider his poor 'lower' caste coworker or neighbour as his equal, tends to look down upon him, and generally refuses to build or accept any sociocultural linkages with him. While workers and peasants belonging to different castes do join trade unions and participate in common struggles on purely economic issues, they generally desist from developing life-sharing sociocultural linkages across caste barriers. In many cases, it is individual and collective economism rather than class consciousness that motivates participation in agitations for specific economic demands. This is also evident from the fact that support of workers for political parties does not always correspond with their trade union belonging.

The class consciousness of the workers and peasants can, of course, be best awakened by their continuous participation in the class struggle. But if the nature of the class struggle itself is often distorted by caste consciousness, we are in a vicious circle. On epistemological, sociological and organizational grounds, therefore, it is necessary to treat the caste structure as a semi-autonomous socioeconomic formation within the broader class structure of Indian society, and trace its historical and sociological roots in the evolving relations of production in India from the ancient times to the modern period. This, for course, cannot be done exhaustively within the short span of this paper. We shall confine ourselves to portraying, in a few bold strokes, the outlines of the relationship between caste formations and the relations of production in India. This will then enable us to appreciate the strategy of integrating the struggle against caste oppression into the broader class struggle, as recommended by Marxist stalwarts like E.M.S. Namboodiripad and B.T.Ranadive, as well as the Salkia Plenum and 17th Congress of the CPI (M), and formulate appropriate tactics for an integral form of class struggle with Indian characteristics.

There is a widespread belief among orthodox Hindus that *chaturvarnya,* or the hierarchical four-tier social structure of ancient India, had a religious origin. This belief is engendered by the apparently religious justification of *chaturvarnya* in the *Rig Veda*, the *Manusmriti*, and the interpolated forms of the *Ramayana* and the *Mahabharata*, where it has been declared to be of divine origin. In reality, however, the support to *chaturvarnya* given by the religious texts on the pretext of its allegedly divine origin served merely to sanctify and perpetuate an ancient form of unjust division of labour that was based on the oppression and exploitation of the entire working class, which constituted the overwhelming majority of the population in ancient India, by a small and parasitic ruling class. The 'other-worldly' religious injunctions were in the nature of a deliberately contrived functional ideology that served to camouflage a this-worldly socioeconomic structure of exploitation. In other words, the social roots of the metaphysics of *chaturvarnya* were embedded in the relations of production in ancient India.

As is well known, the religious texts assigned the parasitic functions of teaching, preaching, and the performance of religious rituals to the Brahmins, ruling and fighting to the Kshatriyas, and trade and business to the Vaishyas. The sociopolitical status of the Vaishyas was, however, somewhat ambivalent and fluctuating. In the age of the *dharmasutras*, all peasants, except rural artisans, craftsmen, and landless labourers, were reckoned as Vaishyas. By the middle of the period of the *dharmasastras*, however, most of the peasants, including those who tilled their own land, were demoted to the status of Sudras. Only that small section of peasants who were big landowners and produced a marketable agricultural surplus, were now counted as Vaishyas. From that time onwards, the Brahmins and Kshatriyas effectively constituted the ruling class of ancient India, with the Vaishyas playing a somewhat auxiliary role.

Thus by about the 1st or 2nd century A.D. the entire working class, including all small and marginal farmers, landless labourers, artisans and craftsmen, and all manual labourers, was relegated to the status of Sudras. The Brahmins and Kshatriyas naturally constituted only a small proportion of the population. Since industry and trade were undeveloped in that ancient period, the Vaishyas also constituted an insignificant proportion of the population. The Sudras therefore constituted the overwhelming majority of the people of the country. It was this vast class of Sudras that was relegated to the bottom of the socioeconomic pyramid and ruthlessly exploited by the composite ruling class of the Brahmins and Kashatriyas, using both the power of religion and the power of the state as its instruments of control.

The concept of *swadharma* was central to the injunctions of the religious texts regarding the division of labour consummated by *chaturvarnya*. Manu defined *swadharma* as *swakarma*, or the occupational duty as prescribed by the *dharmasastras*. All major religious texts, including the *Manusmriti*, the *Bhagavadgita*, and the interpolated versions of the *Ramayana* and the *Mahabharata*, prescribed the unquestioning service of the three 'higher' *varnas* as the *swadharma* of the Sudras. The vast working class of Sudras was thus denied all social, economic and political rights, which were, of course, monopolized by the Brahmins and Kshatriyas. The *Manusmriti* also denied the Sudras the right to education, the right to property, the right to carry arms, and even access to religious observances. The *Manusmriti* declared that if a Sudra acquired any property, any Brahmin or Kshatriya had the right to take it away from him forcibly. As regards the carrying of arms, even the Brahmins were empowered to carry and use arms in times of trouble, although it was alien to their *swadharma*. But the Sudras were totally forbidden to carry or use arms. The denial of the right to property in a social structure based on private property perpetuated the proletarianization of the Sudras, while the denial of the right to carry arms rendered them incapable of overthrowing the structure of exploitation. Thus the whole purpose of the ostensibly religious injunctions regarding *chaturvarnya* was to reduce the entire working class to the status of subsistence labour, close to that of slaves, and generate a huge surplus value through its productive labour for the enjoyment of a parasitic ruling class.

The religious texts have also forbidden the change of occupations prescribed by them for the four *varnas* respectively on pain of dire consequences in this world as well as the next, because this would destabilize and destroy the prevailing social order. The *Manusmriti* makes the change of occupations a serious and heavily punishable offence. The *Bhagavadgita* says that it is better to die in the performance of one's own *swadharma*, even if it be without merit, than to practise the *swadharma* of another *varna*, even if the latter be easier to perform. But not being sure of the effectiveness of religious injunctions by themselves, the wise writers of religious texts also provided for political safeguards against any potential challenge to *chaturvarnya*. The *Manusmriti* enjoins upon the king the duty of preserving the four-tier social hierarchy, and to inflict severe punishment on those who attempt to change their occupations. The *Bhagavadgita* cautions the Kshatriyas against the non-performance of their *swadharma* of fighting, lest such an example inspired the 'lower' *varnas* to change their occupations. The *Manusmriti* also advises the Brahmins and Kshatriyas to form a class alliance in their common class interest. Such an alliance, it says, would ensure tremendous gains for themselves in this world and the next, whereas in the absence of such an alliance both the *varnas* would perish. For the same reason, the *dharmasastras*, including the *Manusmriti*, made it a major political duty of the king to suppress all forms of atheism and to inflict severe punishment on atheists. Any atheist challenge to the *dharmasastras* would have seriously undermined the foundations of the exploitative structure of *chaturvarnya*. Thus the opium of religion as well as the power of the state, both of which were mere instruments of exploitation in the hands of the ruling class, were used to perpetuate the oppressive and exploitative socioeconomic structure of ancient India.

CLASS STRUCTURE, DALITS AND ADIVASIS

One special characteristic of this exploitative socioeconomic structure was the marginalization, alienation, economic exploitation, and geographical separation of the *atisudras*, also called *asprishyas* or *panchamas* or *antyajas* in the *dharmasastras*. Originally stigmatized on account of the 'unclean' jobs assigned to them, they were subjected to numerous inhuman disabilities, in addition to those suffered by the rest of the Sudras. Perhaps the most disabling injunction against them proclaimed by Manu and other law-givers was the one that denied them the right to live in the main village inhabited by the exalted 'upper' *varnas*, and were compelled to live in separate hamlets on the outskirts of the village. It was from this geographical and social exile that they acquired their status as *antyajas*, meaning "born on the margin". According to the injunctions of the *dharmasastras*, they were obliged to wear the mark of untouchability on their bodies, and eat only the foulest kind of food, including the leftovers thrown away by the 'higher' *varnas*, from iron or broken earthen pots. They were allowed to wear only iron 'jewelry' on their bodies. They were not to draw water from the wells used by the 'upper' *varnas*, not to enter temples, not to enter areas inhabited by the 'higher' *varnas* except to perform menial jobs for the latter, and not to tread the roads used by the latter. They had to wear a bell in their necks in order to warn the 'higher' *varnas* of their approach, so that the latter could move out of sight in time. They were permitted to move around only in the darkness of the night, avoiding the areas inhabited by the exalted ones.

The *adivasis* or indigenous people of ancient India suffered more or less the same socioeconomic disabilities as the *atisudras*, and were virtually indistinguishable from the latter with regard to their status in relation to the socioeconomic structure of *chaturvarnya*. They were also both geographically isolated and socially marginalized, and relegated to the bottom of the socioeconomic pyramid. They represented that section of the pre-Aryan population of India, which had retreated into the jungles and hills in the face of the Aryan advance, and remained by and large inaccessible to the conquering Aryan 'civilization' and its *chaturvarnya*. Those who lived in the forests were generally called *nishadas* or *shabaras*, depending on their tribal belonging as well as occupation, while those who dwelt on the mountains were generally called *kiratas*. There is abundant evidence in the *dharmasastras* and Sanskrit literature to show that these indigenous people were also treated as untouchables.

This forest and mountain-dwelling section of the people of India differed from the rest of Aryan-dominated ancient Indian society in at least three important respects. In the first place, they practised a form of primitive communism of property that was diametrically opposed to the system of private property on which the Aryan 'civilization' was based. Hence, unlike the exploitative class structure of the Aryan-dominated society, the relations of production of *adivasi* society did not generate a class structure. Secondly, they had refused to come under Aryan domination, and hence, were outside the purview of *chaturvarnya*. There never was any *varna* or caste system in *adivasi* society. Thirdly, They had refused to be a part of the Vedic and *dharmasastra*-based Brahminical religion of the Aryas, and never practised the rituals and ceremonies of the latter. Because of their refusal to be integrated into mainstream Aryan society, the *adivasis* remained even more isolated, geographically as well as socially, than the *asprishyas* within the fold of *chaturvarnya*. As regards their socioeconomic status vis-à-vis Brahminical society, they were also treated in practice like *atisudras* and untouchables. Like their counterpart within Brahminical society, they also belonged to the most exploited section of the proleatariat of ancient India, and were assigned to the bottom of the socioeconomic pyramid. They were not a part of *chaturvarnya* in terms of religious doctrine. But along with the *panchamas* or *atisudras*, they were the worst victims of the exploitative class structure of ancient India.

The grossly exploitative class structure of ancient India, which was cleverly camouflaged and sanctified by the *dharmasastras*, particularly by *chaturvarnya*, has remained virtually unchanged to this day. Unchanged feudal relations of production, poverty, illiteracy, and crystallized superstition among the masses, and the oppressive and exploitative strategies of the ruling classes over many centuries have contributed to the perpetuation of the ancient relations of production and their sociocultural superstructure. The original four *varnas* have proliferated into over three thousand castes and subcastes due to numerous socioreligious and economic factors. These include false ideas regarding hereditary transmission of purity and impurity, differences of rituals and ceremonies, endogamous marriage and other forms of sociocultural intercourse, geographical location, and above all, economic status, particularly land ownership. Some cases of Sanskritization, or the vertical movement of the 'lower' castes, have also taken place over the centuries, mainly due to their rise in economic status. The myriad castes and subcastes of contemporary India cannot in all cases be classified under the original *chaturvarnya* of the *dharmasastras*, although they have all risen on the matrix of the four-tier hierarchical socioeconomic structure of ancient India. Perhaps the most important retrograde development is that the entire caste system has become hereditary and transformed itself into a crystallized prejudice structure. Although it is still a superstructure of the relations of production, it has over the centuries acquired a measure of autonomy, and in some ways behaves independently of the relations of production. This is the most distinctive characteristic of class relations in India today. This is also the single most important social reality that the left forces spearheading the class struggle in India must weave into their strategy.

The proliferation of castes, and the relative improvement of the socioeconomic status of some of the 'middle' castes, have to some extent diluted the structure of the four-tier hierarchy of ancient Indian society. But so far as the relations of production are concerned, the slave-like condition of the *dalits* – descendants of the *panchamas* and *asprishyas* – has remained unchanged at the bottom of the socioeconomic pyramid. Similarly, the *adivasis* – descendants of the *shavaras, nishadas* and *kiratas* – have remained the victims of the grossest and most acute form of socioeconomic exploitation. This is mainly because neither the basic class structure of India nor the crystallized prejudice structure of caste has changed significantly for many centuries, including the fiftyfive years since India's independence, except to some extent in the left-dominated states. The existential characteristics of the collective historical condition of these two socioeconomic classes make them the 'wretched of the earth' who truly belong to the fourth world of nearly total alienation and exploitation. Apart from being the victims of gross economic exploitation, they also suffer from the stigma of low social status imposed on them by the prejudice structure of caste. It follows logically that those leftist forces in India which are engaged in class struggle for the collective emancipation of the proletariat must accord the highest priority to the emancipation of the *dalits* and the *adivasis.* For there are no worse sufferers from class exploitation, and no proletariat more impoverished than them anywhere in the world.

Numerous studies, including the Mandal Commission Report, have established beyond any doubt that that there is a high correlation between poverty and social 'backwardness' in India. This is particularly true of the *dalits* and the *adivasis.* It was estimated by the Commissioner for Scheduled Castes and Scheduled Tribes in 1981 that 85 % of the Scheduled Castes and Scheduled Tribes belonged to the poorest 35% of the population. Another indication of the absolute poverty of the SCs and STs is that 84% of the SCs and 94% of the STs live in the rural sector Moreover, 90% of all bonded labourers and 80% of all child labourers come from the SCs and STs. Several investigations, including those by the Planning Commission, have revealed that landlessness and illiteracy are much greater among the SCs and STs than in the rest of the population.

The fact that the SCs and STs, which belong to the bottom of the caste hierarchy, are also in the lowest economic class was highlighted by the Eighth FiveYear Plan when it said: Thus, while there has been a reduction in the percentage of population below the poverty line in the case of both Scheduled Castes and Scheduled Tribes, the incidence of poverty is still very high. Most of the Scheduled Caste and Scheduled Tribe families do not own land and other productive assets. They constitute the bulk of agricultural landless workers, construction workers and women in the unorganized sector. They suffer from long periods of unemployment and underemployment. They are also handicapped due to non-enforcement of protective laws such as the Minimum Wages Act and Prevention of Land Alienation Act. Inequality and exploitation of the Scheduled Castes and Scheduled Tribes, particularly in the rural areas ... still continue.

Even the Mandal Commission, while emphasizing the role of traditional sociocultural prejudices in perpetuating the economic exploitation of the 'lower' castes, fully recognized the fundamental significance of the relations of production in the shaping of the class-caste structure. Hence it called for the radical restructuring of production relations in order to liberate of the oppressed castes from economic as well as social exploitation.. In the Commission's own words:

> Under the existing scheme of production relations, Backward Classes, comprising mainly small landholders, tenants, agricultural labour, village artisans, etc. are heavily dependent on the rich peasantry for their sustenance. In view of this, OBCs continue to remain in mental and material bondage of the dominant castes and classes. Unless these production relations are radically altered through structural changes and progressive land reforms implemented vigorously all over the country, OBCs will never become truly independent. In view of this, highest priority should be given to radical land reforms by all the states.

For several reasons, however, it would be misleading to assume that caste oppression can be eliminated through the class struggle on the economic plane alone. In the first place, the crystallized prejudice structure of caste tends to rationalize and perpetuate the economic exploitation of the oppressed castes. By confining the 'low' castes to the lowest paid occupations on a hereditary basis through religious dogma and cultural prejudice, they are kept perpetually in a state of absolute poverty. Their poverty, in turn, reinforces the sociocultural prejudices against them, and tends to perpetuate the stigma of inferiority with which they have been branded from ancient times. Secondly, unlike the poorer sections of the 'upper' castes, the *dalits* and *adivasis* have been compelled to live in separate hamlets in the rural areas, and in separate slums in the urban areas.

This geographical isolation of the oppressed castes is more due to social stigma than to economic status. Thirdly, although feudalism prevails in many parts of the world, particularly the Third World, the caste system does not exist in any other country. Hence caste oppression must be attributed at least partly to the peculiar religious and sociocultural tradition of India. Finally, even with the advent of capitalism, caste prejudices do not seem to have lost their vigour in the capitalist sector of the Indian economy. Hence in determining their strategy of class struggle with Indian characteristics, the left forces have to take into account the dialectical relationship between class and caste.

CLASS STRUGGLE WITH INDIAN CHARACTERISTICS

Thus the integration of the fight against caste oppression with the class struggle in India, as prescribed by EMS Namboodiripad, B.T. Ranadive, the Salkia Plenum and the 17th Congress of the CPI (M), implies that a three-pronged class struggle has to be organized in India with certain specifically Indian characteristics.

The 17th Congress of the CPI (M) has correctly highlighted the importance of the independent growth of the left parties, as distinguished from the united front tactics. For while united front tactics become necessary for electoral purposes and for organizing mass struggles, steady and sustained growth in the strength of the left parties can alone be the ultimate guarantee for a successful struggle against the forces of communal fascism and for the emancipation of the Indian proletariat.

Moreover, a sustained and long-term cultural revolution, through which the proletariat will capture the commanding heights of a scientific and socialist culture, is also a necessary component of the class struggle for destroying the sociocultural foundations of the archaic social formation of caste. In the objective socioeconomic conditions of India, the Marxian strategy of class struggle must incorporate these specifically Indian characteristics.

Independent Growth of Left Parties

Since the SCs and STs are the most oppressed and exploited sections of the Indian proletariat, they qualify to be the natural allies of the CPI (M) and other left parties. The left parties must therefore unequivocally align themselves with the SCs and STs, and fight for their economic as well as social rights. This struggle must include the uncompromising implementation of the policy of reservation, which is correctly based on the principle of positive discrimination in favour of the traditionally disadvantaged sections of the population. There appears to be a general suspicion among the SCs and STs that although the CPI(M) and other left parties have accepted the policy of reservation, they are not always sincere in implementing this policy on account of their apparent ideological position that caste is a false socioeconomic category.

It is necessary to dispel this misperception, and to draw increasing numbers of SCs and STs within the ideological and organizational fold of the left parties by building sympathetic linkages with their life experiences and aspirations. It should be remembered that some otherwise misguided ultra-left forces in Bihar, Andhra Pradesh and West Bengal have succeeded in increasing their strength to some extent in recent years mainly by taking up the cause of the SCs and STs. It is necessary for the major left parties with a mass base to seize the initiative from these misguided ultra-leftist elements in order to carry forward the class struggle along correct lines.

The Tamil Nadu branch of the CPI (M) has already taken up ideological and organizational work among the SCs and STs in right earnest, and obtained visible results. Small as it is in terms of its total numerical strength, about one-third of its membership comes from the SCs and STs.

Harkishan Singh Surjeet, General Secretary of the CPI (M), has rightly commended this achievement of the CPI (M) in Tamil Nadu. If the Tamil Nadu CPI (M) does not deviate from this correct strategy of class struggle with Indian characteristics, it will certainly be able to increase its organizational and political strength significantly in the near future. There can also be little doubt that if the CPI (M) as a whole and other left parties persist with this strategy, and treat the SCs and STs as their natural allies in the class struggle, they will grow from strength to strength in the not too distant future.

United Front Tactics

Needless to say, the tactic of united front is only an element of the class struggle at a time when the left forces are not strong enough to capture power in the whole country on their own strength. Hence it is necessary for every left party to choose even its temporary allies in the united front, whether for electoral purposes or for the purpose of organizing mass struggles, very carefully in terms of a correct class analysis. Since the SCs and STs represent the most oppressed, exploited, and impoverished section of the Indian proletariat, their parties and organizations should be accorded the highest priority by the left parties in forming a united front. The left will have to strive to draw the dalit organisations into joint struggles against social oppression, land, wages and other issues affecting the SCs and STs. Even when some of these organisations are imbued with casteist ideologies, it must be seen in the historical and existential experience of caste oppression, endured for centuries. It is the task of the left parties to engage them in dialogue and persuade them, through both ideology and practice, that their true destiny lies with the left.

It should not be forgotten that the grievances of the dalit-adivasi groups against Manuvada and their deep-seated sense of socioeconomic injustice is quite legitimate and not inconsistent with the class struggle. Their only fear seems to be that the left parties, in their apparently exclusive preoccupation with the economic dimension of the class struggle, would fail to pay special attention to the issue of caste oppression, and hence not serve the true socioeconomic interests of the SCs and STs. But in the context of the clear espousal of the cause of caste oppression by the CPI (M), which is the largest leftist party in the country, there is no valid reason for this misperception. Once they are persuaded to realize, by word and deed, that the left parties regard them as natural allies and assign the highest priority to their emancipation, the parties and organizations of the SCs and STs may not be slow to form permanent alliances with the left. The formation of a united front with other democratic parties need not be ruled out in a given situation, but in no case should the most oppressed and exploited section of the Indian proletariat be left out of a united front led by the left parties. There can be little doubt that the left parties will make rapid headway in Indian politics, outside the states of West Bengal, Kerala and Tripura, if united fronts are formed in this manner, keeping in view the long-term strategy of the class struggle with Indian characteristics.

Cultural Revolution

As we have tried to show above, the crystallized prejudice structure of caste has acquired a certain autonomous character over the centuries, and often stymies the growth of class consciousness and thwarts the growth of the class struggle for the radical restructuring of the relations of production in India.. It has grown out of ancient religious dogmas and cultural prejudices, and is unique to India's long and unbroken sociocultural tradition. Feudal social formations elsewhere, such as the estate system of Europe, were not sustained and perpetuated by any archaic social hierarchies based on socioreligious strictures and taboos enforced by the state. The socioeconomic structure of medieval Europe represented a simple division of the population in terms of economic status that was functionally and almost exclusively derived from the relations of production. The transition from feudalism to capitalism, accompanied by an intellectual renaissance and religious reformation, led to a simple division of society into classes. Even in China, which was a feudal country at the time of the communist revolution, there were no archaic and rigid sociocultural formations intervening in class relations. The class struggle there was carried out by the peasants and workers against the landlords and capitalists, as well as against the state controlled by the latter. But the existence of the crystallized prejudice structure of caste as a palpable objective element of India's socioeconomic structure makes it imperative to add a specifically cultural dimension to the class struggle.

A direct assault on the economic structures of feudalism and capitalism, and the transformation of these structures into socialist relations of production should, of course, remain the central thrust of the class struggle in India. But on account of the complex class-caste relationship outlined above, the class struggle on the economic front will have to be supplemented by a great intellectual and cultural movement among the masses against the religious and cultural prejudices that sustain the caste hierarchy and perpetuate caste oppression. Here the struggle against caste oppression and the struggle against communal fascism are likely to converge in one gigantic cultural revolution. The struggle for the replacement of the unscientific and bourgeois religious culture that sustains both caste oppression and communal fascism by a scientific, proletarian, and socialist culture will have to be an integral element of the class struggle in India. Moreover, this will have to be a protracted cultural revolution that will continue for a long time after the socialist revolution, as and when it takes place.

A proletarian socialist revolution does not seem to be an immediate possibility in India, although this must remain the inalienable long-term goal of the class struggle. But this is not sufficient reason for arguing that the class struggle must therefore confine itself to something close to economism in the immediate future. Even within the constraints imposed by the objective politicoeconomic conditions of India it is possible, in fact imperative, to carry on a massive intellectual struggle against religious and obscurantist belief structures and values. Even partial success of such a cultural revolution would in fact lead to an awakening of class consciousness among the masses, reinforce the class struggle on the economic and political fronts, and pave the way for the rapid growth of the left forces all over India.

8

Structure of Indian Society

THE CASTE SYSTEM

The first literary traces of the caste system are to be found in the *Rig-Veda,* where three groups are mentioned: *Brahma* (Priests), *Ksatra* (Kings or Rulers), and *Vis'* (common people). The *Purusasukta* hymn, however, speaks of four classes originating from four parts of the body of the Creator. These classes, *Brahmana, Rajanya, Vais'ya and Sudra,* are referred to in later literature as *Caturvarna.* The term *varna* does not seem to have been applied to these classes in the earliest literature, except to contrast the fair *Arya* with the dark *Dasa.* The initial distinction of people into two *varnas* later developed into three *(Brahma, Ksatra* and *Vis)* and finally into four. The occupations of the first two *varnas* are clearly stated to be priesthood and administrative and military duties, respectively. But the duties of the Vaishya and Sudra are not very clear. The village headman was usually a Vaishya, and Sudras were servants. The *varna* categories do not, however, exhaust the various occupations practised in Vedic India. The *Rig-Veda,* for instance, mentions several occupations by name—chariot-builder, goldsmith, barber, physician, leather-worker, potter, merchant and others. The question arises whether these occupations referred to endogamous *jatis* as we know them today. It is not known how they noted into the *varna* framework.

The post-Vedic period saw the growth and consolidation of the power of the Brahmins. Brahmin writers continually discussed and defined the duties and rights of each caste and its place in the hierarchy. (The relation which these writings bore to the empirical reality is not clear). Justifications and rationalisations of the hierarchy were also produced during this period. In the *Bhagavad-Gita,* for instance, the caste system is sought to be justified on the basis of the ideas of *guna; karma* and *dharma.*

The 6th century B.C. saw the rise of Buddhism, which is believed to have questioned the basis of the caste system itself. Some scholars, however, have said that Buddhism on its social and political side was chiefly a Ksatriya movement against Brahminical supremacy.

Post-Vedic Brahminical writers continued their attempts to systematise and codify inter-caste relations. The idea of pollution was elaborated to define the distance separating the castes. Violations of caste rules were punished either by the village Panchayat or panchayat of the locally dominant caste or by the king.

The Bhakti movement with its long history contained elements which ran counter to caste ideology. The Bhakti saints came from all castes, including the Harijans. It appears as though the path of *Bhakti* offered a way out of the tyrannies of the caste system, and as the Bhakti saints commanded respect from every one, the movement itself served to stress the worth of an individual irrespective of his caste affiliations. The origins of the Bhakti movement are traced to the Krsna-Vasudeva cult in the first century B.C. The Saiva (Nayanar) and Vaisnava (Abarlvar) saints of the Tamil country, the Haridasas and Lin'gayat saints of Karnataka, Vallabhacarya and his followers in Gujarat, Caitanya in Bengal, and Tulasidas, Surdas, Kabir and Ramanand in the North, were all representatives of the Bhakti movement. The movement was more or less continuous in Indian history, and it spread right across the subcontinent. It may not be too fanciful to regard it as a protest, in the realm of religion, against the division of human beings into high and low caste.

The Lingayat movement, which came into existence in Karnataka in the 12th century A.D., rejected many ideas of traditional Hinduism, including *karma,* ritualism and caste. It also emphasised the necessity as well as the dignity of labour. The movement attracted converts from all castes including

Harijans, but over the centuries it became a congeries of small, endogamous *jatis.* The followers of Kabir (Kabirpanthi) also became a caste. Caste even survived conversion to Christianity and Islam. During the last century there came into existence the Arya Samaj in the Punjab and the Brahmo Samaj in Bengal. These movements, as well as the Ramakrishna Mission, represented a shift towards the liberalisation of caste.

MAIN FEATURES

We shall now consider the main features of caste before it was deeply affected by recent changes. Those changes, which present a quite different picture of the Indian social structure today are discussed in the last pages of this chapter.

The features of caste prevailing through the past centuries may be described under nine heads: hierarchy; endogamy and hypergamy; occupational association; restriction on food, drink and smoking; distinction in custom, dress and speech; pollution; ritual and other privileges and disabilities; caste organisation and caste mobility.

The essence of caste is the arrangement of hereditary groups in a hierarchy. The popular impression of the hierarchy is a clear-cut one, derived from the idea of *varna,* with Brahmins at the top and Harijans at the bottom. But, as a matter of fact, only the two opposite ends of the hierarchy are relatively fixed; in between, and especially in the middle regions, there is considerable room for debate regarding mutual position. In a dispute over rank each caste would cite as evidence of its superiority the items of its dietary, the other caste groups from which it accepted or refused to accept cooked food and water, the ritual it performed and the customs it observed, its traditional privi-leges and disabilities, and the myth of its origin. The fact that mutual position is arguable, if not vague, over great areas of the hierarchy permits social mobility. Mobility, it may be noted, is not a recent phenomenon. Even in the traditional system it was possible for a caste to move up. The Raj Gonds of Central India, for instance, successfully claimed for themselves the rank of Ksatriyas on the basis of their acquisition of political power. At the coronation of Sivaji, Brahmin priests declared him a Ksatriya. Not infrequently the claim of a caste to a higher ranks is not conceded. Thus, the Smith group of castes in South

India have claimed to be a twice-born caste and call themselves Visvakarma Brahmin. The other castes resent this and even the Harijans do not accept drinking water from a Smith. The Lingayats consider themselves superior to the Brahmins but other do not accept their claim.

Disputes regarding mutual position occur even at either extremes of the hierarchy. In Kerala, Nambutris consider themselves superior to Tamil Brahmins, and among the Nambutris those who have a hereditary right to study the Vedas claim superiority over the others. Again, there are very low groups among the Brahmins. No caste, including the Harijan, will accept cooked food or water from the Marka Brahmins of Mysore. Likewise, the Vatima Brahmins in the Tamil country and the Tapodhan Brahmins in Gujarat are considered as inferior.

All Caste Hindus regard Harijans as being at the bottom rung of the ladder. But the category of Harijans is not homogeneous. In each linguistic area there are a few Harijan castes which form a hierarchy. The leather-working Camar in Uttar Pradesh considers himself superior to the Bhangi, a sweeper. The Kannada Holeya places himself above the Madiga; he proudly stresses the fact that he does not accept even water or betel leaf from either the Smith or the Marka Brahmin.

Islam proclaims the idea of equality of all those who profess the faith, but in India it has been characterised by caste. Muslim caste differs in some respects from the Hindu caste system; there are no ethico-religious ideas justifying the hierarchy or regulating inter-caste relations through ideas of purity and pollution; there are no *varna* categories. What we have is a hierarchy formed by several *jatis.*

In Uttar Pradesh, Muslims who have a tradition of foreign ancestry (Iran, Arabia) are called Shurafa or Ashraf and are considered to be the highest. After the come converts from high-caste Hindus, such as Rajputs. Next come occupational castes such as the Weaver (Julaha), Barber (Nai), Cotton Carder (Dhuniya), Potter (Kumhar) and Oilman (Teli). Last come the Sweepers. Among the Ashraf, the Syeds rank as the highest.

The Moplah (Mappilla) Muslims of Kerala are also divided into castes. The Thangals, claiming descent from the Prophet's daughter, Fatima, are at the top; next to them are the Arabs, descendants of immigrants from Arabia. The Pusalars, said to be recent converts from the Fisherman caste, occupy the third position while the Ossans, who are barbers, are at the bottom.

Equality is a tenet of Sikhism also, but that has not prevented me existence of castes, including Brahmins, among Sikhs. Sikhs are broadly divided into Sardars and Mazhabis, the former consisting of high castes and the latter of Sweepers. The Sardars include Jat and Kamboh (landowners). Tarkhan (Carpenter), Kumhar (Potter), Mehra (Water-carrier), and Cimba (Washerman). The first two castes regard themselves as superior to the others. The Mazhabis, not only came from a low caste but were converted to Sikhism later than the higher caste groups. In some parts of Punjab there exist the Sansi (Shepherd) who were formerly included among the "Criminal Tribes"; Sansi converts to Sikhism rank even lower than Mazhabis.

There are three divisions among Indian jews: Beni-Israel, Chochin Jews and Baghdadi Jews. The Beni-Israel are to be found principally in Bombay. They are divided into groups, *Gora.* (White) and *Kala* (Black), the former being considered higher in rank. The Cochin Jews are divided into similar White and Black groups, and there is a third division called Meshurarim comprising the descendants of Cochin Jews andtheir slave concubines; the Meshurarim, who are decended from a White Cochin Jew, claim superiority over those descended from a Black Cochin Jew. The third Jewish group, the Baghdadi, are later immigrants, and are found in Bombay and Calcutta.

Caste divisions occur among Indian Christians, Catholics as well as Protestants. The Syrian Christians of Kerala, the earliest converts to Christianity in India, claim to have been recruited originally from Nambutri Brahmins and Nayars, and caste distinctions are conspicuous among them. Caste restrictions are rigidly observed among the Christians of the West Coast. A Catholic Brahmin from Maharashtra would marry none other than a Catholic Brahmin. Some West Coast Christians have migrated to East Africa and their descendants try to marry within their particular subcaste.

Conversion does, however, weaken pollution ideas, and social life among Christian converts is more free than among Hindus. Again, all over India, caste restrictions are far less meticulously observed today than they were a few decades ago. Social institutions are changing, and this affects all social groups, though in varying degrees.

OCCUPATIONAL ASSOCIATION

The hereditary association of a caste with an occupation has been so striking that it has occasionally been argued that caste is nothing more than the systematisarion of occupational differentiation. Even though a caste is not only associated with an occupation but has a limited kind of monopoly over it, it is not true to say that every member of the caste practises that occupation exclusively. This kind of association is suggested when, for instance, the term Kumhar is translated as Potter, and Dhobi as Washerman. But, generally speaking, most castes also practise agriculture in addition to their traditional occupation. A Kumhar may be an agriculturist in the monsoon months, and a trader in grain for a brief period after the harvest Often, the artisan and servicing castes do not have an adequate income from their traditional occupations and they therefore work on land, either as tenants or as casual labourers. It could be argued that, in the context of a growing population, the occupational aspect of the caste system would have broken down com pletely if the surplus in the artisan, trading and servicing castes had not been either absorbed in agriculture or able to migrate to other areas.

To associate a caste invariably with a single occupation is an oversimplification. Even "agriculture" can mean a variety of things: landownership, tenancy and labour. Each may be practised exclusively or in combination with the others. Sometimes cultivation includes processing the grown crop into a saleable commodity. Thus the cultivation of sugarcane, except when grown for a factory, includes the processing of cane into jaggery and its sale to a middleman. Again, different members of a family may have different occupations. All women cook and they may also take some part in agriculture. Women of the artisan castes may in addition participate in the caste craft.

Occupations are also classified into high and low, those practised by the high castes being regarded as high. Manual labour is looked upon as low, and certain occupation like swineherding and butchery are considered to be polluting.

Among Muslims, only artisan castes such as the Teli, Darzi, and Julaha are associated with traditional occupations. Priests tend to come more from the Syed and Shaikh castes than from the others. Among the Sikhs, the traditional occupation is often practised along with agriculture. Jats are generally landowners, while the Mazhabis are agricultural labourers. Sikh Tarkhans are carpenters. An occupation which is indispensable everywhere except among the Sikhs is hair-cutting. But the Sikh Nat renders other services: he clips the nails of his patrons; he carries news of birth, marriage and death. He is also a *masseur*.

An individual in a caste society lives in a hierarchical world. It is not only the people who are divided into higher and lower groups, but also the food they eat, the dress and ornaments they wear, and the customs and manners they practise. In India's dietetic hierarchy the highest castes are usually vegetarians and teetotallers. Even in meat there is a hierarchy. The highest nonvegetarian castes eschew chicken, pork and beef. Wild pork is superior to domestic pork, since the village pig is a scavenger. Eating beef in rural India means eating carrion and it comes accordingly under a double ban. Liquor is prohibited to the high castes.

Elaborate rules govern the acceptance of cooked food and water from another caste. Food cooked with ghee, milk or butter is called *pakka* food and may be accepted from inferior castes. (Higher castes buy sweets from the *Halwai* because he is supposed to be cooking them with ghee.) *Kacca* food, on the other hand, is food cooked with water and it may be accepted normally only from one's own or equivalent or superior castes. When two castes are contending for superiority, they stop accepting cooked food and water from each other. Sometimes, a very low caste refuses cooked food or water from a high caste. We have already mentioned the instance of the, Kannada Holeya. The explanation of these usages lies in the history of inter-caste relations in the area in question, and in particular, in the attempts of individual castes to raise themselves up.

There are exceptions to the general restrictions on the acceptance of food and water. Food or drink which has been sanctified by being offered to deity in a temple may not be refused, even though the cook is from a low caste. (The cooks in the famous Jagannath temple at Puri are Barbers by castes.)

Significant regional variations also occur. Further, women tend to observe restrictions more strictly than men, and the old more strictly than the young. Among the highly Westernised sections in the big cities, such restrictions are minimal.

In North India, *hukka* smoking offers an index of caste-status. Castes which may share, on occasions, a single *hukka* are equals. Thus Jats and Ahirs may smoke from the same *hukka*. Sometimes the Lohar (Blacksmith) and Khati (Carpenter) are allowed to smoke from the same *hukka* as the Jat and Ahir. The Nais (Barber), like many other castes, have their own *hukka*.

Muslim castes freely accept cooked food and water from one another. Such restrictions regarding food and drink as obtained among Muslims are common to them all. As for the Sikhs, Sardars have reservations about *kacca* food cooked by Mazhabis, but accept liquor brewed by them.

Each caste has a culture which is to some extent autonomous: there are differences in dress, speech, manners, ritual and ways of life. The higher castes wear fine, clothes and gold ornaments while the lower castes wear coarse material and silver ornaments. The speech of the higher castes is refined while that of the lower castes is rugged. Traditionally, the lower castes were prohibited from taking on the dress, ornaments and customs of the higher, and the offenders were punished by the village panchayat.

The concept of pollution plays a crucial part in maintaining the required distance between different castes. A high caste man may not touch a low caste man let alone accept cooked food and water from him. Where the two castes involved belong to extreme of the hierarchy, the lower caste man may be required to keep a minimum distance between himself and the high caste man. In Kerala a Nayadi had to keep 22m. away from a Nambutri and 13 m. from a Tiyan, who himself had to keep 10 m. away from a Nambutri. A few decades ago in most areas of South Indian there were rules which laid down what parts of a high caste man's house the others could enter. The rules of pollution, at least so far as inter-caste relations were concerned, were more clearly elaborated in South than in North India.

There is board line between Caste Hindus and Harijans in the matter of pollution. The village barber and washerman will not serve Harijans, and the latter have to provide for these services from among themselves. Harijans have to take water from a lower end of a river or canal than the high castes and they may not use the Caste Hindu well.

The breaking of pollution rules results in the higher castes becoming "impure", and the latter have to perform certain purificatory rites to regain their normal status. Where the breach of the rule is serious, as when a high caste person eats food cooked by a Harijan or a high caste woman has sex relations with a Harijan, the offender may be thrown out of caste irrevocably.

The idea of pollution is present among the Sikhs. The Mazhabis have a well of their own everywhere, and in rural areas they may not be allowed to enter the houses of Sikh high castes beyond the cattle-yard.

The culture of each caste is to some extent peculiar to itself, and this is related to the fact that the lower castes are barred, at least in theory, from taking over the customs and rituals of the higher castes. Only the "twice-born" castes are entitled to study the Vedas and perform rituals in which Vedic mantras are chanted. Traditionally, the Brahmin was exempt from capital punishment and his land was assessed at a lower rate. These restrictions and disabilities operate fully against the Harijans—they may not use Caste Hindu wells or enter temples and teashops. In some parts of the country they were prohibited from entering the high caste streets. The high castes also kept away from the Harijan ward of the village.

Among the Sikhs, Mazhabi wedding parties are not accommodated in gurdwaras as they are regarded as impure. Among Muslims, however, lower caste groups are not subjected to disabilities. The Christians on the west coast of India observe caste restriction: there are separate pews for the Brahmins and the Harijans in some churches, and very rarely, even a separate church for the Harijans.

Villagers are subject to the two-fold control of caste and village panchayts, (Caste panchayats, however, are not will developed among Brahmins.) When the disputes concern law and order in the village—for example, setting fire to someone's hayrick, grazing cattle on another's land, stealing fuel or vegetable—it is reported to village elders who may levy a fine on the offender or subject him to corporal punishment or declare a boycott against him. In a marital dispute the council of the concerned caste is the proper body to adjudicate. But the village council may take a hand in the dispute. Where a man is accused of having sex or commensal relations with a member of a lower castes his own caste or the council of the locally dominant caste, the village council might be called upon the adjudicate. Punishment may include a fine, temporary outcasting and fine, of permanent outcasting. Re- admission to caste requires that the offender undergo purificatory ritual, express his regret to the caste assembly, and give a dinner to the caste. Occasionally an offender may be re-admitted to caste after having been outcasted for a decade or two.

Many Muslirn castes, excepting the *Ashraf* and *Shaikh,* have councils like Hindu castes: Generally, a caste council deals with all questions concerning trade, morals and religion. Sometimes a caste may not permit its members to take up an occupation considered less honourable than its traditional one.

CASTE AND VILLAGE COMMUNITY

We have given a brief description of the general features of the caste system and we shall now show how it actually functions in the context of the village community. Inter-caste relations at the village level constitute "vertical" ties. They may be classified into economic, ritual, political and civic ties. The castes living in a village, or a group of neighbouring villages, are bound together by economic ties. Generally, peasant castes are numerically preponderant in villages and they need the Carpenter, Blacksmith and Leather-worker castes to perform agricultural work. Servicing castes such as Priest (Brahmin as well as non-Brahmin), Barber, Washerman and Water-carrier cater to the needs of everyone except Harijans.

Artisan castes produce goods which are wanted by everyone. Most Indian villages do not have more than a few of the essential castes and depend on neighbouring village for certain services, skills and goods. In rural India, with its largely subsistence and not fully monetised economy, the relationship between the different caste groups in a village takes a particular form. The essential artisan and servicing castes are paid annually in grain at harvest. In some parts of India, the artisan and servicing castes are also provided with free food, clothing, fodder and a residential site. On such occasions as birth, marriage and death these castes perform extra duties for which they are paid a customary sum of money and some gifts in kind. This type of relationship is found all over India and is called by different names: *jajmani* in the North, *bara balute* in Maharashtra, *mirasi* in Madras and *adade* in Mysore. The relationship between a *jajman* and his *kamin* is unequal, since the latter is regarded as inferior. Though primarily an economic or ritual tie, it has a tendency to spread to other fields and become a patron- client relationship. The relationship is generally stable, and usually inherited. The right to serve is hereditary, transferable, saleable, mortgageable and partible. Thus, for instance, the right to officiate as priest to high castes living in some sixty villages in the Mysore District is shared among the different branches of a single Brahmin lineage in Bannur.

The *jajmani* system bound together the different castes living in a village or a group of neighbouring villages. The caste-wise division of labour and the consequent linking up of different castes in enduring and pervasive relationships provided a pattern of alliances which cut across the ties of caste. The modern "caste problem" is to some extent the result of the weakening, in the last fifty years or more, of these vertical and local ties and the consequent strengthening of horizontal ties over wide areas.

Caste was related to the exercise of differential rights in land. At the top were the caste who were either absentee or non-cultivating owners. Next came the cultivating tenants (not infrequently owning a little land as well), and at the bottom of the hierarchy came the landless labourers. There was regional variation in this matter. Kerala, for instance, had a chain of intermediaries between the owner and the actual cultivator. There was more or less perfect congruence between caste hierarchy and differential rights in land in Kerala. At the top of the hierarchy were the Nambutri Brahmins who were non-culti-vating owners *(jenmi)*. The "high" Nayar castes were the non-cultivating lessees of Nambutri land on twelve-year leases *(kanam)*. The agricultural labourers, both tied and free, came from the castes like Ceruman and Pulayan and from the Parian tribes. In Punjab, however, there was a lack of coherence between the agricultural and caste hierarchies, Brahmins being the cultivating tenants of Jat landowners. But, in both areas, agricultural labourers came from the Harijan castes. In some parts of Punjab and Uttar Pradesh, only a few castes showed a direct concern with land and agriculture, the owner-cultivators being either Jats, Ahars and Rajputs (Thakurs) or Gujars, while the agricultural labourers were mostly Camars.

The existence of a high degree of congruence between caste and agricultural hierarchy meant that the stratification ran deep; economic stratification strengthened ritual stratification and *vice versa*. This enabled the landowners to exploit the tenants as much as they could—rack-renting, eviction and forced labour were usual features on rural life. But where the tenants' caste was higher than that of the landowner, and particularly when a tenant was also the landowner's priest (as was sometimes the case with the Brahmin tenant of a Rajput landowner), exploitation had to be much less extreme.

In pre-British India, in many parts of the country, the lower castes were serfs or slaves, either attached to the land and liable to be transferred along with it, or attached to the landowner and liable to be sold by him. The economic forces released under British rule (e.g., the starting of tea and coffee plantations, and of factories and railways) enabled the law abolishing slavery to be translated into reality. But even now the agricultural hierarchy is mixed up in different ways and degrees with the caste hierarchy in several parts of India.

The relationship between master and servant is another type of bond which often cuts across caste, and more rarely, even religion. The terms and conditions of this bond vary from region to region. A common form is the advance by the master of a loan which is worked off by the servant in the course of two or three years in the master's house. Frequently, before the expiry of the period, the servant takes another loan which results in prolonging his servitude. It is not unusual to come across families linked with each other for generations by ties of master and servant. In some parts of the country, like Mysore, there was until recently a traditional bond as of master and servant between the landowning castes and the local Harijans. The obligations involved were only a few duties on occasions such as marriage and death. The payments were also traditionally fixed.

The relationship between landowner and tenant, master and servant, creditor and debtor, may all be subsumed under a single category—patron and client. This relationship is widespread and crucial to the understanding of rural India. Voting at elections, local and general, is influenced by the patron-client tie.

Ritual occasions, e.g., life-cycle ceremonies, festivals and fairs, require the co-operation of several castes. Life-cycle ceremonies are somewhat more elaborate for the "twice-born", especially the Brahmin castes. Certain rituals which are common for all the castes occur at birth, a girl's puberty, marriage and death. Thus when a son is born to an Ahir or Thakur, a Bhaksorin (Harijan) woman helps in the delivery and a Bhangi beats a drum before the house in which the birth occurred. A Brahmin casts a horoscope, while the village barber acts as a messenger and also serves food at the feast. These services are paid for by gifts in cash as well as kind. In Kerala, the Washerwoman gives freshly- washed clothes to her high caste patrons after the termination of birth, menstrual and death pollution. In rural Mysore, there is a saying that eighteen castes have to come together at a wedding: the Harijan servants cut the wood, whitewash the house and dean the grain; the Barber not only shaves the groom but provides the wedding band; the Washerman supplies the washed cloth for the bridal pair to walk on; the Potter provides the utensils and ritual pots, the Carpenter puts up the wedding *pandal;* the Goldsmith makes the ornaments; the Oilman supplies the oil; the Brahmin acts as priest; the dancing girl threads the *tali;* the Trader supplies several articles; the Shepherd provides a woollen which is tied as *Kankan* round the wrists of the bridal pair, and so on.

Several castes are also required to co-operate in the performance of calendrical festivals, and festivals of village deities. In the case of the latter, the castes may come from more than one village. Thus, Bannas from Malabar dance at the festivals of some Coorg village deities. The festival of a village deity always involves the co-operation of several castes, and frequently few of these castes come from neighbouring villages.

The temple organisation itself needs the coming together of several castes. In Kerala, for instance, the head priest of a Sanskritic, vegetarian and teetotal deity is a Nambutri Brahmin. A few Nayar castes have the task of washing the vessels and cleaning the temple. The Ambalavasis perform a variety of tasks and they make garlands, assist the chief priest, provide music. There is a caste of story-tellers attached to the temple. In temples to non-vegetarian deities, a member of the *Piddown*100aarar caste is the priest. Low caste dancers get possessed by the deities, and sing and dance in that state. It may be taken as axiomatic that all the local castes are involved in the festival of a village deity. Even the Harijans have important duties, such as beating the drum, carrying messages, and removing the leaves on which the villagers have dined.

In many parts of India, villagers believe (or at least believed until recently) that the goddesses Mari Kali and Sitala presided over epidemic diseases such as smallpox, plague and cholera. An outbreak of one of these diseases was attributed to the wrath of the village goddesses and their propitiation followed. The priest was usually a member of a non-Brahmin caste and occasionally even a Harijan. Members of all castes including the Brahmin sent their contributions in cash as well as in kind to the ritual propitiation. The fact that occasionally a Harijan or other low caste priest catered to the religious needs of all, including the highest castes, affected the quality of inter-caste relations.

Sometimes the ties of ritual stretch even across religious cleavages. A Sikh farmer may go to a Brahmin priest to find out an auspicious hour for starting ploughing operations. Until forty years ago, Brahmin priests officiated a life-cycle ritual in Sikh homes. In recent years the Akali Movement has enjoined religious self-sufficiency on the Sikhs, and the Sikh Granthi is increasingly acting as priest at Sikh weddings. The Sikh priest may come from any caste except Mazhabai. Sikhs and Hindus attend festivals in honour of Purs (Muslims saints). In Mysore a Muslim peasant may vow to Mades vara that he will give a money-offering if his cow calves, or if it is cured of a disease. However, the tendency to religious and even sectarian self sufficiency has gained strength in recent years. The functioning of the village as a political and social entity rought together members from different castes. First, there was the traditional village panchayat which, though run by the locally dominant caste, usually included a few representatives from the other castes. The available historical evidence points to the existence of vigorous communities in South India in the Panchayats of which members of every caste took part.

Every village had a headman usually belonging to the dominant caste. The accountant was always a Brahmin in South India. Every village had a watchman and messengers and towncriers. In irrigated areas, there was always a man to look after and regulate the flow of water in the canals feeding the fields. The headman and accountant collected the land taxes withtheaidof the Harijan village servants.

The village council performed a variety of tasks, including the maintenance of law and order, settling of disputes, celebration of festivals and construction of roads, bridges and tanks.

In many parts of rural India there exist castes which are locally numerically preponderant, own the bulk of the arable land, occupy a fairly high position in the ritual hierarchy and wield power over the other castes. Examples of such castes are Jats. Ahirs and Rajputs in the North. Patidars in Central Gujarat, Marathas in Maharashtra, Kanata and Reddi in Andhra Pradesh, Lingayat and Okkaliga (Vakkaliga) in Mysore, Vellala and Gounder in Madras and Nayar in Kerala. Sometimes the dominance of a caste is decisive, all types of power being concentrated in it.

At other times, however, the different elements of dominance may be distributed among several castes. In the first instance, the dominant caste wields great power over the others, while in the second there is likely to be a balance of power among the powerful castes. It should be noted in this connection that the maintenance of law and order in areas even now depends to some extent upon the leaders of the dominant caste. They are the people who can punish errant individuals and ensure the maintenance of the caste codes. When a caste is politically or economically dominant its religious position tends to fall in line with its secular position.

The Sikhs as a whole are dominant in many parts of Punjab and Sikh Jat*down* 100s are dominant among the Sikhs. Similarly, in parts of Kerala, the Syrian Christians and Moplahs are dominant. In Malihabad Tahsil in the Lucknow District there are village in which Pathans are dominant.

The village community consisted of hierarchical groups, each with its own rights, duties and privileges. The castes at the top had power and privileges which were denied to the lower castes. The lower castes were tenants, servants, landless labourers, debtors and clients of the higher castes. There was competition among the former to be clients of the rich and powerful patrons while the latter wanted to have as many clients as possible. The patrons had duties towards clients and *vice versa.* The caste system together with the inequalities of landownership produced a deeply stratified society, but that did not prevent the village from functioning as a community. Conflict and co-operation went together. There was economic conflict between masters and servants, landowners and tenants, and competition between members of the same caste. The struggle for higher status between structurally neighbouring castes also produced conflict. And in recent years the lower castes have shown an increasing desire to free themselves from the control of the locally dominant caste. This has been assisted by political forces operating from higher levels.

RELIGIOUS GROUPS

The 1931 Census classifies Indian population under ten religious groups. They are Hindus, Sikhs, Jains, Buddhists, Zoro-astrians, Muslims, Christians, Jews and Other Religions (Tribal), and Other Religions (Non-Tribal). The designation of tribal religion as separate from Hinduism (except where a tribe had been converted to Christianity or Islam) was unsatisfactory. A study of the religion of the different castes and tribes will show the presence of elements from different layers of Hinduism, from the Sanskritic to the tribal, mixed in different proportions; and it is arbitrary to draw a sharp line between Hinduism and tribal religion. It is difficult to separate the religion of castes at the bottom rung of the hierarchy from the religion of the tribes. The former contains many tribal elements just as the latter contains many "Hindu" elements. Thus the Santals observe several high caste festivals; Bhagwan is the supreme deity of the Bhils; the Solagas of Mysore worship Ranganatha in the Biligiri hills; and the Todas and Badagas of the Nilgiris worship S'iva in Nanjangud. Different tribes are Sanskritised in different degrees, and different sections of the same tribe may not be uniformly Sanskritised. Thus, the Khonds of Khondmals are less Sanskritised than Khonds in Puri who resemble an Oriya caste in their religious life. These remarks should be borne in mind while reading the census.

The highest increases have been experienced by the Hindus, Christians and Sikhs. The decline in the number of the followers of tribal religions may be attributed to their inclusion in one or the other of the advanced religions. The decline in the number of Muslims and the increase in the number of Sikhs are both due to the partition of the sub-continent into India and Pakistan and the immigration of Sikhs into India.

A proper explanation of the differential rates of growth of various religious groups can only be made after a religion-wise study of the birth and death rates, and of migration and other factors. But a detailed discussion of the demography of religious groups is outside our scope. One factor which has been significant in the growth of some of the largest religious groups in this country is conversion. According to the Census Report of 1931, "The increase under the head of Christian is of course largely due to conversion which causes a steady transfer to Christianity from the depressed classes and still more except in Madras, from the hill and forest tribes. If the natural increase be 12%, then over 20% of the total increase of 32.5% must be due to conversion." There are similar remarks about the sizeable (33.9%) increase in the number of Sikhs. The Census Report of 1931 also states that some Muslims and Christians, but not a large number, have been reconverted to Hinduism. The increase in the number of Christians and Sikhs is complementary to the decrease in the number of people under Tribal Religions. The Census Report again comments that the decrease in the percentage of tribal people is primarily due to losses by conversion to Hinduism or Christianity. A similar remark is made in the 1951 Census Report. (It is more likely that nowadays many tribals declare themselves as Hindus.) In the last few years, thousands of Harijans in Maharashtra became converted to Buddhism. Before describing the role of religious groups in Indian social structure, we shall consider the relation between religion and rural-urban residence, and literacy and occupational affiliation. According to the 1931 and 1941 censuses, the tribal people were predominantly rural. The relative urban percentage of Muslims, Christians and Jains was higher than their rural percentage. Parsis and Jews were mainly urban while Jains, Sikhs and tribals were minimally urban.

Again, religious groups were least urbanised in the provinces where they were numerically preponderant. Even Parsis were less urbanised in Bombay than in other places. Conversely, religious groups were most urbanised in provinces where they were least represented. Another point worthy of note is that migration was generally to urban areas and not from one village to another. This may, however, be due to the fact that intervillage migration is more difficult to trace than migration to towns.

Kingsley Davis has said that on the basis of census figures for the period 1891-1931 for persons aged ten and above, Parsis show the highest percentage of literacy. Jains, Jews and Christians follow in order. It is pointed out in the Census of India, 1931, that the high literacy rate for Parsis and Jews is due to their activity in trade, which requires literacy. This explanation is perhaps too simple. It does not explain why Christians, who as a body are not active in trade, show a high literacy rate.

In his book *Hinduism and Economic Growth* (Bombay), (1962), Dr. Vikas Mishra has made a study of the occupational pattern of the different religious groups in India. He concludes that the occupational distribution of the Parsis, Jews and Jains is "advanced" though not diversified. Hindus and Muslims have a diversified occupational pattern while the tribals' pattern is neither advanced nor diversified.

Dr. Mishra's analysis points to the conclusion that minority religions are advantageously situated as far as occupational distribution is concerned. It is likely, however, that there are differences between one region of India and another. Syrian Christians, for instance, show a more "advanced" pattern in Travancore than in North Kerala. Similarly, Moplahs in North Kerala are more advanced than their co-religionists in South and Central Kerala. This is perhaps related to the fact that in North Kerala the Moplahs formerly wielded political power.

On the whole, minority religions have fared better in the economic field, and especially commerce. Caste seems to be of crucial significance in this connection. Where there was no local trading caste, a minority religious group seems to have stepped in to fill the breach. The Moplahs have, for instance, played an important role in Kerala commerce.

In the case of Christians, especially recent converts, conversion has been followed by intensive efforts to educate the converts and to find employment for them. The money and political influence commanded by the foreign missions enabled them to provide employment for the converts in a variety of occupations.

ROLE IN SOCIAL STRUCTURE

We shall now consider the role of religious groups in the social structure, the latter term being used broadly to include also the economic and political structure. This topic may be discussed under the three following heads: (i) The relations between different castes and religious groups at the village and other local levels; (ii) the general role of religion in the economic development of the country; and (iii) religion and socio-economic privileges.

Though villages embrfacing multi-religious groups are not as common as multi-caste villages, they are not infrequent. Such villages are not confined to any one part of India, but are found everywhere. There are villages with Hindu tenants and Muslim landlords (Uttar Pradesh), and Hindu landlords and Muslim tenants. Rampura village in Mysore, for instance, was dominated by Kannada-speaking Okkaligas (Hindu peasant caste) who owned the bulk of the land. There were also many landowners from other Hindu castes (from the Brahmin to the Harijan), and a few Muslim landowners as well. A few big Hindu landowners had Muslim tenants and servants, while Muslim landowners had Hindu servants. The bulk of the Muslims were engaged in a variety of activities—trading in several articles including paddy and mangoes hiring out carts, cycles and gas lanterns; tailoring; carpentry; smithy; and butchery. Ownership of land, except in the case of a few big landowners, seemed to prevent a majority of the Hindus from becoming traders. Thus, though the mango trees were by Hindus, the entire mango trade was in the hands of Muslims. This phenomenon (as was the trade in hides) is regional and not confined to Rampura. There are prosperous Muslim traders and landowners in the neighbouring villages of Kalguni, Bannur and Gargheshwari. There exist in this area Hindu and Muslim families linked together by friendship and patron- client ties. Apart from this, Muslim perform certain tasks which the dominant Hindus cannot undertake. For instance, Hindu reluctance to kill cattle gave rise to a form of exchange trade called *cati* by which itinerant Muslims exchanged their superior animals for the inferior ones of Hindus for a consideration. These animals ultimately reached the butcher's yard. Muslims often provide the goods needed in Hindu festivals. Muslims are invited to Hindu weddings, and sheep and goats are slaughtered ritually by a Muslim butcher so that Muslims may eat the wedding dinner. Occasionally, an old Muslim client may be sent by his Hindu patron to find out the correct sub-caste and sectarian affiliation of a Hindu peasant with whose family matrimony is contemplated.

When the members of a religion or sect dominate trade or commerce, the customers are drawn from several religions. Thus the basis of the specilisation itself creates ties between several religious groups. This is true of all parts of India. Parsis controlled the liquor trade not only in the former Bombay Presidency, but outside as well. Moplah traders are to be found not only in Kerala but also in Mysore, Madras and Bombay. Jain traders are prominent in Bombay, Ahmedabad, Rajasthan and Mysore.

In brief, economic, social and other ties obtain between members of different religious groups at the local level. It is, however, true thai the pro-Pakistan movement of the forties disturbed the integration of Hindus and Muslims into local communities.

It is well known that some religious groups have played an important role in the, economic development of the country. The small community of Parsis in Bombay is an example. (The Bombay or urban Parsis offer, however, a contrast to the poor and backward Parsis in the rural areas of the Surat District.)

The Jains have also played an important part in economic development, especially Jains from Bombay, Gujarat and Rajasthan. Some Muslim groups in Gujarat, the Daudi Bohoras, Khojas and Kutchi Memons, have shown a marked predilection for trade and commerce. The Syrian Christians of Kerala have played a pioneering role in banking and in growing plantation crops such as tea, coffee and rubber.

It is necessary here to enter a caution against a conclusion likely to be drawn from the above remarks. While minority religions have undoubtedly played an important part in economic development, a closer look will show that in India commercial activity has always been confined to small groups. Among Hindus, a few groups such as the Gujarati Baniyas, Telugu Komatis, Tamil Cettiars and the trading castes in Uttar Pradesh have shown a greater sensitivity to commercial opportunities than non-trading castes. It is hardly necessary to add that an effect of the caste system is to confine a skill to a hereditary group. In some areas there are Muslim trading groups—Moplahs in Kerala, Labbe in Madras and the Gujarati Muslim groups mentioned earlier. Nowadays, however, with growing population and the weakening hold of caste, new groups have entered the commercial and industrial field. The Patidars of Charotar, originally a peasant caste, have shown ability in commerce and industry and not only in Gujarat and the rest of India but also in East Africa. In South India the anti-Brahmin movement forced the Brahmins out of Government jobs and made them enter trade, commerce and industry, fields in which some, of them are doing remarkably well.

So, too much should not be read into the fact that minority religions are found to be active in trade and commerce. Even among Hindus, trade is confined to a few caste groups. Again, in a changing socio-economic situation, new groups have entered the field and shown their competence. Finally, it is beyond dispute that Western India, especially the area including modern Gujarat, Rajasthan, Punjab, and the Pakistan areas of Sind and West Punjab, have produced commercial groups which have dominated trade and industry in India and even beyond. On the East Coast, only the Cettiars have shown similar ability.

Religious and sectarian organisations are frequently found running schools and colleges in which members of the religion of sect running the school or college enjoy some preference. Christian missions have been responsible for starting many a school and college in various parts of the country Khalsa colleges in Punjab and Western Uttar Pradesh are run by the Siromani Gurdwara Prabandhak Committee which is in charge of gurdwaras. The Arya Samaj and the Sanatan Dharam Sabha likewise run several schools and colleges in Punjab and Uttar Pradesh. Sectarian and religious organisations try to find employment for their members. Caste may be said to be an effective employment in all parts of India.

RELIGION AND POLITICS

The role played by religion in the political life of the country is similar to that of caste. In the thirties the Muslim League first began to press its demand for an independent Muslim state to be called Pakistan. Before the formulation of this demand, Muslims and Hindus together formed fairly integrated local communities in many parts of the country and we have already given an idea of the kind of ties binding them. The intimacy and closeness of these ties did not prevent an occasional outburst of rioting over religious matters. But that was not very different from intercaste or inter-village fighting which also occurred in spite of normally friendly and intimate bonds prevalent between neighbouring castes or villages.

It may be noted in this context that Muslims lagged behind the Parsis and Hindus in taking to Western education, and in attempting to reform their traditional institutions. That meant exclusion from Government service and the professions. It was with a view to remedying this situation that Sir Syed Ahmad founded the Muhammadan Anglo-Oriental College at Aligarh in 1875, and this developed into the Aligarh Muslim University in 1920. The Muslim League was founded in 1906 and it became the spokesman for the protection and furthering of Muslim interests conceived in a narrow sense. It did not emulate the Indian National Congress and try to speak for the country as a whole. Mahatma Gandhi's espousal of the cause of the displaced Turkish Caliphate in 1919 resulted in the League and the Congress coming together but only for a brief while. In the thirties, the Muslim League found an astute leader in M.A. Jinnah, an ex-Congress member and he succeeded in founding

Pakistan. The creation of Pakistan did not, however, mean the dissolution of the Muslim League in India. It is still active in the South, and in the 1959 elections in Kerala it formed an alliance with the Praja Socialist Party, the Congress, the Catholics and the Nayar Service Society against the Communists.

The Akhil Bharat Hindu Mahasabha is another religious party, which has as its aim the promotion of Hindu culture and Hindu Rastra. It aims at re-establishing the integrity of India through constitutional means. Its membership in 1960, was 4.5 lakhs and in the General Elections of 1957, it secured seats in the Lok Sabha and won 7 out of 40 seats it contested in Madhya Pradesh. In the General Elections of 1962, it secured 1 seat in the Lok Sabha and 6 seats in Madhya Pradesh Legislature. The Bharatiya Jan Sangh is yet another party with membership of 6 lakhs. In the General Elections of 1962, it won 14 seats in the Lok Sabha and 116 in the various State Legislature.

In this connection, reference must made to the Rastriya Swayam Sevak Sangh. While claiming to be an organisation interested only in reviving Hindu religion and cultures it exhibited a para-military character, with uniforms, drill and training in the art of self-defence. The movement grew as a reaction to the Muslim Leagues activities in the forties. After the assassination of Mahatma Gandhi in 1948, the Sangh came under a cloud.

Sikh politics is closely connected with the control of the gurdwaras, which are in charge of the Siromani Gurdwara Prabandhak Committee (S.G.P.C.). The Akali Dal, led by Master Tara Singh, was long in control of the S.G.P.C., but it has recently come under the control of another Akali group. The Akali Dal has been agitating for a Sikh-dominated "Panjabi Suba.

The Christians have not formed a separate political party anywhere in India. The Syrian Christians, however, have had a part in Kerala politics similar to that played by dominant castes elsewhere in the country. The politics of the former Travancore State was marked by keen rivalry between the Syrian Chris-tians and the Hindus. For a year before the general elections in 1951, the Democratic Congress, a Hindu-dominated party, carried on propaganda against the Indian National

Congress on the ground that the latter was dominated in Travancore by the Syrian Christians. The attempt of the Congress Government in Travancore-Cochin to obtain financial control of the schools in 1951 resulted in its alienating the Christian mission which can many schools. The clergy and the Catholic Congress supported Independent Catholic candidates against the National Congress nominees in the General Elections of 1957. In the 1959 elections, however, the attempts of the Communist Government of Kerala to exercise control over the appointment of teachers in schools and to extend their authority in other matters relating to education evoked systematic opposition from the Christians, especially the Catholics. An alliance of the Catholics, the Muslim League, the Nayar Service Society, the Praja Socialist Party and the National Congress resulted in the defeat of the Communist Government and in the establishment of a Coalition Government.

According to the 1951 Census (adjusted to 1961 boundaries), the Hindus represent 85% of the total population, Muslims 9.9%, Christians 2.3%, Sikhs 1.7%, Jains & Buddhists 0.05%, Zoroastrians 0.03%, Other Tribal Religions 0.47% and Non-tribal Religions 0.03%. Systematic information is lacking on the place and role of religious minorities in Indian social life, and on the relations between majority and minority religious groups. It may be noted in this connection that, even after the creation of Pakistan, India has a large Muslim population of more than 40 millions. The Republic of India is a secular state and there is no discrimination between one citizen and another on religious grounds.

During British rule the Sikhs, Punjabi Muslims, Rajputs, Gurkhas and Marathas were classified as "martial races" and enjoyed preference in recruitment to the armed forces of the country. The distinction between martial and non-martial races was ignored in World War II, when there was a large demand for fighting men at all levels. In Independent India only the Scheduled Castes and Schedule Tribes enjoy some concessions and privileges, including reservation of seats in the legislatures and the local self-governing bodies. The Anglo-Indians (numbering 111,637 in 1951) also enjoy some concessions including reservation of seats in the Central legislature and a few State legislatures. Every State in the Indian Union has made rules giving preference to "Backward Castes" in the matter of appointment to Government posts, admission to schools and colleges, and the award of scholarships and free studentships.

With the achievement of Independence, Sikhs, and Punjabi and Sindhi Hindus poured into India from West Pakistan, while the bulk of the Bengali-speaking Hindus evacuated East Bengal and moved into West Bengal. The problem of the resettlement of refugees from West Pakistan is no longer there, but that cannot be said about refugees from East Pakistan.

The sociologist looking at the problem of minorities in a segmented, stratified and multireligious society finds that really speaking, everyone is in a minority. The numerically small Hindu castes feel that they are not getting their due share of power and Government jobs. The tribes are in a minority vis-a-vis the total Hindu population. The sense of being in a minority is widespread; but even so, the problem of religious minorities is a special one.

In Independent India legislation has been passed modifying some institutions of the Hindus. (The term "Hindu" includes also Buddhists, Sikhs and Jains.) Monogamy is binding on Hindus and bigamy (including polygyny and polyandry) is an offence. Certain female relatives such as widow, daughter and mother are now entitled along with the sons to a share in the estate. The payment of dowry has been banned. But there is reluctance on the part of the Government to undertake legislation to change any institution of Muslims and Christians. Only social legislation (e.g. factory laws), which does not touch religious susceptibilities, has been made applicable to all.

TOWNS AND VILLAGES

A population of 100,000 or more entitles a place to be classified as a "city."* Census Superintendents have the power to classify places with less than 100,000 people as cities when they have special reasons (unspecified) to do so. It may be noted here that whereas in the previous censuses all places with a population of 5,000 and more, and in some special cases, even places with less than 5,000 were classified as towns, in the 1961 Census, certain uniform criteria have been laid down for determining whether a place is a village or a town.

SOCIAL STRUCTURE AND THE IDEAL SOCIETY

Societies pass through periods of relative stability and change, relative calmness and turmoil. It was during one such period of rapid change and upheaval in the European society in the Eighteenth century that the foundations of the social science disciplines were laid with the major objective of finding solutions to the social problems of the time. Reacting to the social malaise of their age, the Enlightenment thinkers of the seventeenth and eighteenth centuries in Europe, proclaimed that liberty, equality and fraternity, as the cardinal principles of the ideal social order that was in the making. Therefore all attention was focussed on ushering in such an ideal society.

The social thinkers, however, were not in agreement as to the manner of the emergence of the ideal society. Between the two opposing viewpoints prevailing then, one maintained that the ideal society would unfold itself from the existing social order through peaceful evolution; whereas the other viewpoint asserted that the ideal society would be born only when the existing unjust social order was destroyed through a revolution, even though it might be a violent one. These viewpoints have deeply coloured the different theoretical perspectives about society, which have been formulated in social sciences and which in their turn, have influenced the paths of development adopted in different countries.

However, both the evolutionists and the revolutionists have given primacy to economic and technological factors in bringing about the desired social order. But the outcome of economic development in the liberal democracies which adhere to the evolutionary doctrine, and in the socialist countries which have adopted the revolutionary model of reconstruction, during the last half a century or so, lays bare the shortcomings of both of the models of development. Whereas both the liberal-democratic societies and the socialist societies have pursued the goals of the ideal society through economic development, the former category has achieved a greater measure of individual freedom but at the expense of equality, whereas the latter category of societies has succeeded in securing for their citizens a greater degree of equality but at the expense of individual freedom; and in neither case the ideal of universal brotherhood if either assiduously pursued or established.

It is true that in both the systems, because of their success in economic development, more and more individuals have been freed from economic wants, but in the process, rather than broadening their sympathies for their fellow human-beings, the successful persons are becoming more and more selfish and are being alienated from their societies. Societies in both the systems are now facing a series of similar problems of personality and social disorganisation, and their members are becoming increasingly dependent upon what is termed the 'mechanical way of life.' Puzzled by the persistence of nagging problems in the midst of plenty, perceptive observers have redesignated the advancement in the economically developed countries as 'maldevelopment'.

The unsatisfactory state of affairs in the economically developed countries, irrespective of their ideological hues, might prompt one to ask whether the principles of the ideal society enunciated by the Enlightenment thinkers have led us into a blind alley. Such a question, however, seems to be a little too premature, knowing full well that so far these societies have been preoccupied only with the ideals of freedom and equality and have rarely paid attention to the third ideal of fraternity. Therefore, speaking from hindsight one may say that the three principles of the ideal society are indivisible and for their successful realisation, all three should be pursued in their togetherness, simultaneously. The error lies in assuming that economic development automatically leads to the attainment of the ideal society although such an assumption is not without its own logic.

In the final analysis, liberty, equality and fraternity are as much the attributes of the developed individual as those of the developed society, as the individual and the society are interrelated. A developed individual is defined as one who is self-reliant, creative and sociable and a developed societal is one which provides its members with freedom of choice and action equality of opportunity and the scope to mix freely with one another. For the true development of the individual and the society, the development of the economy is necessary insofar as it sustains the above attributes of the individual and the society but by itself it is insufficient, since it does not automatically lead to such attributes.

Since the 1950s a large number of the former colonial countries, having won their independence, have undertaken ambitious development planning. All these societies, including India, badly need a transformation. The Indian society, for example, especially in its traditional setting, rectifies the negation of the principles of the ideal society, and the caste system with its lack of freedom for the individual for choosing his occupation, lack of equal opportunities and with its social exclusivism, is the epitome of such a situation. Therefore, one of the major avowed objectives of these Third World countries in undertaking development planning, is to bring about a transformation in their societies so as to embody the principles of freedom, equality and fraternity. The instrument employed for this transformation is economic development which is the sheet anchor of development planning undertaken by these societies. But the results achieved so far in most of these societies are far from satisfactory, which belie the hope placed on economic development as an instrument of social transformation.

That economic development would bring about a desirable transformation in society is an illusion given rise to by the commonplace assumptions about the market mechanism and the social structure. According to the classical economists, the impersonal market mechanism exerts a wholesome influence on society, which is beneficial to all concerned. Therefore, economic development, through the market mechanism benefits everyone in the society.

Similarly, an analysis of the social structure in terms of its basic elements of position, role and status, shows the interrelationship between the economy and the social structure. Such a relationship can be easily deduced from the recognition that the social structure and the economy intersect in the variable of occupational prestige. The occupations are generated by the division of labour in the economy. On the other hand, for the most part, the position, role and status of units in the social structure are derived from the occupations which members follow. Therefore, when there is change in the occupational structure, say through economic development, it is bound to have repercussions which would affect the social structure.

To give an example, it has been generally observed that when a traditional agricultural economy with its informal organisation and with the household as the unit of production, change into the industrial economy with its formal organisation depriving the household of its production function, fundamental changes take place in the relationship between men and women, between senior and junior members, in the structure of the family, in the system of social stratification and in a host of other factors. From such changes, one gains the impression that in that process the traditional society is transformed into a modern one with the marks of the ideal society. But in fact, while it leads to change, economic development does not automatically bring about social transformation in the desired direction.

A closer look at the commonplace concepts of the market mechanism as well as of the analytical framework of social structure would show that the assumptions underlying these concepts are rather naive. Economists nowadays increasingly question the validity of the classical view of the market mechanism, pointing out the growing control of the government and the invisible influence exerted by various social forces on the market (Kurien, 1986). So also the usual understanding about the relationship between economy and the social structure would make it appear that economy is the independent variable and social structure a dependent one. It does not account for the possible or potential influence of the social structure upon the economy.

For the time being, it is proposed to reconceptualise the framework of social structure so as to bring out its implications for development. For present purposes, I should like to take as my point of departure, the distinction made by Raymond Firth (1964:57-58) between social structure and social organisation. Speaking about the simpler societies, Firth defined social elements of society, representing the expected pattern of behaviour which is relatively long persisting and more pervasive; whereas social organisation is the process of ordering of actions and of relations in reference to given social ends, and in terms of adjustment resulting from exercise of choices by members of society. Social organisation also has its particular behaviour pattern which is formed out of the basic elements of society derived from the social structure. But these and modifications in the social organisation, which in turn may affect the social structure. There is thus a constant interplay between social structure and social organisation, each influencing the other.

Both social structure and social organisation are patterns of social relationships and have aspects of groups. Speaking of complex societies, social structure can be distinguished as the more pervasive kind of groupings in the society, which are relatively loosely organised with diffused goals and which are products of the historical past; whereas social organisation can be identified with the relatively more tightly organised groups, aimed at pursuing definite goals. The various economic enterprises, administrative and voluntary bodies, in which the means-ends relationships are clearly specified, can be regarded as examples of social organisations.

The groupings in the social structure may be identified in terms of their peculiar relational dimensions on which they are based. For present purposes, three basic kinds of relational dimensions may be identified— hierarchical, affiliational and territorial—which give rise to their characteristic form of groupings. The hierarchical dimensions is derived from a differential distribution of political and economic power. A good example of the hierarchical order is the system of social classes based on economic and occupational differences. Such groupings are marked by superior-subordinate relationships. The hierarchical dimensions is actually the dimension of power.

Social relationships in general have two major dimensions woven together. One of them is the hierarchical dimension or the dimension of power noted above. The other is the dimension of affiliation or the affective tie of liking and dislike or the love-hate dimension. This dimension can also be identified with the relationship of mutual concern or lack of it. In the hierarchical groupings the dimension of affiliation is underplayed; on the other hand, there are groupings in which this dimension is predominant. By and large, the groupings based on cultural bonds, such as ethnic, religious, and racial groups which are characterised by a strong sense of solidarity among members as well as indifference or antagonism between groups, can be included in the category of affiliational groupings.

The third principle of group formation in social structure considered here may be formed the "territorial imperative" which is an impulse shared by human beings with some of the species of the animal and bird kingdoms, because of which a social group inhabiting a given geographical area tends to claim sovereignty over that area. There is thus a tendency in every region among people to distinguish between original inhabitants and the immigrants. Groupings based on such a distinction may be termed territorial groups.

Although, in an ideal-typical sense, grouping based on any of the three dimensions can be regarded as constituting a pure type, in reality two or three dimensions often interesect in a given grouping but with different degrees of intensity. When all the three dimensions interpenetrate with a high degree of intensity in the same grouping, such a grouping becomes a potent factor in the social structure. For example, the concept of dominant caste embraces all the three dimension of hierarchical, affiliational and territorial varieties.

The religious grouping is a very good example of a predominantly affiliational group. Religion, for the most part, develops as well as sacralises the self-identity of its followers and hence fosters a high degree of solidarity among them. Sometimes economic interests and political power are differentially distributed among religious groupings, in which case they also require a hierarchical dimension. If in addition, a religious grouping is concentrated within a geographical territory, it acquires a high potency in the social structure.

A territorial group migrating to a different region, while losing its territorial prerogative, acquires a greater depth in its affiliational dimension. Usually it is a relatively more homogeneous section from a region, which migrates to another region and in the host region tends to occupy a distinct economic position and therefore, it also tends to acquire a sharper hierarchical dimension in its host region.

Thus the social structure would constitute a wide variety of groupings based on the hierarchical, affiliational and territorial ties which may interpenetrate among themselves in the same grouping in different degrees. Just as the different dimensions of relationships may interpenetrate themselves in the same grouping different groupings may also intersect among themselves as when the members of the religious grouping may belong to different linguistic, regional and class groupings. So also some categories of groupings, such as the castes, may be subsumed under large categories such as the religious or linguistic groupings.

An individual, however, may belong to several groupings in the social structure at the same time. But not all the groupings to which an individual belongs are equally important to him at a given point of time. The importance of a grouping to an individual will be determined by several contextual circumstances.

The social structure based on the three relational dimensions mentioned above relates to relatively complex societies with multi-ethnic groupings and with fairly crystallised market mechanisms and political systems. In a purely simple society, such as an ideal typical tribal society, there is no need for the market mechanism based on exchange values, as the elementary needs of its members are met by the use value economic activities. Market mechanism becomes necessary when the economy of a simpler society is integrated with that of strangers and outsiders. The complex societies with multi-ethnic groups are in a way societies of strangers living together. Usually, some groups become economically and politically more dominant then others and inequalities along group lines become established.

Most of the developing societies, and particularly the Indian society, are complex ones, with social structures characterised by all the three relational dimensions. But all these societies have some common features. Although they are integrated in local, national and international markets, much of their economy is made up of subsistence production and use-value activities. There is also a greater degree of congruence among the three relational dimensions inasmuch as economic and political power is, by and large, channelled through affiliational and territorial groupings. These societies, therefore, are characterised by rigid inequalities.

We may now try to visualise the likely impact of economic development on the social structure. Economic development brings in its train a series of changes, apart from growth of income. Some of the noteworthy changes for purposes of this discussion are: The transformation of subsistence and use-value economic activities into exchange-value activities thereby strengthening the market mechanism; the sectoral and occupational transformation of the economy resulting in new economic opportunities and a large scale spatial and social mobility. If the social structure were to passively respond to these changes, one would expect that they would provide a greater degree of equality of opportunity to the various individuals and hence lead to a greater degree of homogenisation of the various affiliational and territorial groupings. But in reality the social structure has a dynamism of its own, derived mainly from the affective ties among members of the various groupings and so, to a large extent, it is able to adjust the changes towards the maintenance of its own form such, the fruits of development accrue to different individuals according to their positions in the social structure, the dominant groupings benefiting more than the others.

The aggrandizement of the dominant groups in the economic hierarchy is made possible by the network, of affective ties among these people who are all socio-economically powerful. By the same token, the disadvantaged groups in the economic hierarchy are left behind because they have no affective ties with powerful persons and the members of their own affiliational groupings are placed in similar disadvantaged circumstances. As a rule, all over the world, the poorer sections belong to ethnic or affiliational groupings different from those of the more powerful members of their society. For the same reason, the same groups of people remain poor for generations and even for centuries together, as witness by the Scheduled Castes and the Scheduled Tribes in India.

However, economic development is influenced by social structure in different degrees depending upon the nature of the interrelationships among the social-structural groupings. Under certain circumstances, the social structure may yield to the economic changes. Thus, economic development may lead to both change and continuity in the social structure. The social structure of the Indian society is closer to the structure of the traditional society in which there is a greater degree of congruence among the different relational dimensions as manifested in the caste system. Even the religious groupings in a given region tend to have different economic interests and elite sections among them are vying with one another for economic dominance. The immigrant groups in a given region also tend to be different from the native ones in terms of the distribution of economic and political power. The introduction of democratic polity in India has added political strength to numbers, which, in some regions, has tended to upset the congruence between the political and the economic hierarchies. We, therefore, have the politics of 'nativism' wherever the immigrant groups have stolen a march over the indigenous territorial groupings in the economic field.

Economic development therefore does not automatically transform the Indian society into the model of the ideal society because of the social structural constraints. The social structure, as it is constituted at present, channels economic changes so as to reproduce its own image.

There have been, no doubt, some changes in the relative positions of some of the groupings in the hierarchical order on account of economic development. Changes of this nature are due to special reasons such as the traditional occupations of some groupings giving them a head-start in the new economy.

Such changes also upset the existing balance of relations between groups, thereby giving rise to tension and conflict. There has also been some relative improvement in the socio-economic conditions of some of the disadvantaged sections such as the Scheduled Castes. But whenever the advancement of the lower sections has infringed upon the privileges of the higher sections, there has been resistence and retribution on the part of the latter. Instead of becoming a matter of satisfaction and joy, the improvement of the underprivileged, is provoking the resentment among the better-off sections.

Economic development, as it is promoted today, draws the economy more and more into the vortex of the market forces which favour the strong and deprive the weak. For example, when a subsistence economy is rendered market-oriented, new occupations are introduced which displace the older ones. The new occupations, however, go to people different from the workers in the old economy, who are marginalised; the latter very often become unemployed and underemployed. The new occupations usually require skills at higher levels, for which the disadvantaged sections are illequipped. Therefore, very often, people at the bottom of the hierarchy are unable to avail themselves of the developmental opportunities even when they are presented to them.

It has often been found that the developmental resources intended for poorer sections are underutilised in areas where most people are poor. On the other hand, the better-off sections manage to snatch away much of the resources meant for the poor.

The primary components of legal systems and the paradigms of modernisation of the industrially advanced countries are based on the ideology of rational utilitarianism. Their *Gesellschaft* mode of society implies movement from the status to contract; from community to individual, from participation to administration, from guild to state, and from empathy to selectivity. It was the product of the *laissez faire* ethos of a market-oriented, no-personalised legal system.

Bentham, Weber and Schumpeter, the mentors of this "rational legal order" created bridges between the legal system and the social structure. The crisis of the late 1960's early 1970's in the industrial societies gave impetus to the awakening of interest in the Frankfurt School of Sociology, of neo-Marxism and phenomenological existentialism. These new interests tended to shift the pendulum, in ideological if not structural terms, towards the search for alternative models of both modernisation and the legal system.

This development is largely a product of the structural contradictions of the post-industrial society; it surpasses the ideological confines of the capitalist and socialist states. Kamenko and Tay have written: In the communist world, the tension is between revolutionary transformation and the desire for social stability, between mass campaigns and the provision of social and psychological security for individuals, social spheres and activities, between Utopian spontaneity and technical-administrative realism. In the west, the crisis is a crisis in the individualistic view of society, in a legal model attuned to the need of the individual house or property holder, the entrepreneur, the settled citizen living on terms of equality With those around him, secure and confident as an individual in his bearing vis-a-vis the state and the rest of society. Against this, the new demands elevate the interests of "requirements" of the comparatively poor or underprivileged as contrasted with those who are "at home" with law: they pit the interest of "society" or of "humanity" against "excessive" respect for individual rights and powers, especially proprietarial rights and powers; they tend to see men as social products and not as free moral agents, as people to be cured or helped rather than judged. The new demands are suspicious of lawyers as a profession in the common law world because they see them as a privileged caste with guild traditions and powers; in Continental Europe they see them as characterless servants of state.

This new perception of the legal system and its paradigm obviously inheres the contradictions of an industrial society: its increasing unidimensionality, its failure in the liberation of human personality, and its de-humanising abstractness resulting in the alienation of man. This process represents a legal order which, in the course of the structural and normative changes that it brought about, also introduced seeds of disenchantment and mystification.

This challenge necessarily brings sociological jurisprudence into full play as the social dialectic tends to deeply influence the legal system. It spurs the shift from Private law, concerned with the security of the individual, to public law, concerned with welfare and the social utility. Even in the heart of he private law, in the law of tort or torts, and in contract, they have discerned similar developments. In torts there is the movement from the legal-individualistic principle of fault liability to the social, actuarial cost- benefit analysis that leads to the principle of loss distribution; in contract, the concept of a bargain struck between ideally equal and freely contracting parties is increasingly infringed upon by the courts' recognition of social and economic inequalities and of the one-sided restriction of the power to bargain by the existence of standard contract.

In addition to the above, new areas of law in the fields of industry, environment, consumer protection and social services have come into being. These fields, are beyond the nineteenth century conception of the common law and its judicial processes. The deeper implications of the changes in the industrial society are responsible for these legal innovations as the response to the demand for basic alterations of the paradigm of industrial society. Thus, the crisis of the legal system is also simultaneously a crisis of the industrial society. The transition from an industrial to a post-industrial stage of development ushers in social demands on the one hand, and structural changes in the society on the other. These structural changes especially in the society's modes of production and patterns of leisure time, necessitate redefinition of the legal order of society at the inter-personal, inter-group, and inter-societal or international levels. New meanings of "responsibility," "freedom," "civic culture," and "rationality" emerge. The structural changes which occur at the post-industrial stage of development tend to contribute to not only formal "differentiation," in roles and relationships, but also their "de-differentiation," "personalisation," and possible revitalisation of the principle of "status" in "contract." These changes may be made possible by the giant leaps in both technology and culture; they are already evident in the current electronic and computer revolutions.

We have thus far discussed the challenges faced by the industrial societies at a higher stage of development. The dialectic of law and social change in the industrially developed nations has a historically endogenous character. The new challenges and contradictions that legal systems face in these societies are generally different from the ones faced by the developing societies. In the nations such as India, where a colonial interlude fundamentally transformed the indigenous evolution of the legal system, the early legal structures were characterised by the dualism of the indigenous hierarchical and colonial utilitarian traditions. The universalistic element in the contradictions of the Indian legal system is confined to the utilitarian-Benthamite legal administration and philosophy which the British imposed on India. The British system is itself faced with contradictions in the light of the waning impact of utilitarian liberalism and the increasing demands of welfarism and socialism.

The dialectic of the legal system in India, with its entrenched "multiplex of social structures" on the one hand, and its multiplicity of indigenous, colonial, and developmental traditions on the other, is tremendously complex. The significant elements in the interaction between law and society in India rests on the heavy burden of these multiple traditions and the social concerns and orientations of each. The convergence between the dialectic of legal systems in the industrialised nations and the legal system in India points to the developmental phase of legal system in India following independence. The contradic-tions inherent in the administration of justice, exemplified by the conflict between abstract individual property rights, the pursuit of profit, and he protection of the weaker and more vulnerable groups, represents a crisis in the paradigms of both society in general and the legal system in particular in India. The situation in the West is similar, but probably less complex.

Bibliography

Abbasayulu, Y. B.: *Scheduled Caste Elite*, Hyderabad, Osmania University, 1978.

Ainapur, L. S.: *Dynamics of Caste Relations in Rural India*, Jaipur, Rawat Publications, 1986.

Anant, S. S.: *Changing Caste Hindu Attitudes Towards Harijans: A Follow Up After Four Years*, New Delhi, Vikas, 1979.

Atal, Yogesh: *The Changing Frontiers of Caste*, Delhi, National Publishing House, 1968.

Bailey, F. G. : *Caste and the Economic Frontier: A Village in Highland Orissa*, Manchester, University of Manchester, 1957.

Benjamin, Joseph: *Scheduled Castes in Indian Politics and Society*, New Delhi, Ess Ess Publications, 1989.

Beteille, Andre.: *The Backward Classes and the New Social Order*, Oxford University Press, Delhi, 1981.

Bhatt, Anil: *Caste, Class and Politics: An Emperical Profile of Social Stratification in Modern India*, Delhi, Manhohar Book Service, 1975.

Blunt, E. A. H. *Caste System of Northern India*, London, Oxford University Press, 1931.

Bose, Pradip Kumar: *Social Mobility and Caste Violence: A Study of the Gujarat Riots*, Delhi, Adjanta Publications, 1985.

Chatterjee, Partha: *Caste and Subaltern Consciousness*, Delhi, Oxford Unviersity Press, 1994.

Dumont, Louis: *The Caste System and Its Implications*, London, Granada Pub. Ltd., 1970.

Freeman, James M.: *Untouchable : An Indian Life History*, CA, Stanford University Press, 1979.

Ghurye, G. S. : *Caste and Class in India*, Bombay, Popular Books, 1950.

Hutton, J. H.: *Caste in India: Its Nature, Function and Origins*, London, Cambridge University Press, 1946.

Jaiswal, S.: *Caste: Origin, Function and Dimensions of Change*, New Delhi, Manohar, 1998.

Kakade, S. R.: *Scheduled Castes and National Integration: A Study of Marathwada*, New Delhi, Radiant Pub., 1990.

Kananaikil, Jose: *Constitutional Provisions for the Scheduled Castes*, New Delhi, Indian Social Institute, 1984.

Lakshmanna, C.: *Caste Dynamics in Village India*, Nachiketa Publications, Bombay, 1973.

Majumdar, D. N.: *Caste and Communication in an Indian Village*, Asia Publishing House, Bombay, 1958.

Mayer, A.: *Caste in an Indian Village: Change and Continuity 1954-1992*, Delhi, OUP, 1996.

Mohan, P.E.: *Scheduled Castes: History of Elevation, Tamil Nadu, 1900-1955*, Madras, New Era Pub., 1993.

Nath, Trilok: *Politics of the Depressed Classes*, Delhi, Deputy Publications, 1987.

O'Malley, L. S. S.: *Indian Caste Customs*, Delhi, Vikas Publishing House, 1974.

Omvedt, Gail: *Land, Caste and Politics in Indian States*, Authors Guild Publications, Delhi, 1982.

Parvathamma, C.: *Scheduled Castes and Scheduled Tribes: A Socio-Economic Survey*, New Delhi, Ashish Publishing House, 1984.

Ram, Jagivan: *Caste Challenge in India*, New Delhi, Vision Books, 1980.

Roy Burman, B.K.: *Beyond Mandal and After Backward Classes in Perspective*, New Delhi, Mittal, 1992.

Sharma, K. L.: *Caste, Class and Social Movements*, Rawat Publications, Jaipur, 1986.

Silverberg, James: *Social Mobility in the Caste System in India*, Mouton Publishers, The Hague, 1968.

Index

□□□